THE 'TINKERS' IN IRISH LITERATURE

THE 'TINKERS' IN IRISH LITERATURE

Unsettled Subjects and the Construction of Difference

JOSÉ LANTERS

University of Wisconsin-Milwaukee

IRISH ACADEMIC PRESS

DUBLIN • PORTLAND, OR

First published in Paperback in 2011 by Irish Academic Press

44 Northumberland Road,
Ballsbridge,
Dublin 4, Ireland

920 NE 58th Avenue, Suite 300
Portland, Oregon,
97213-3786

First published in cloth in 2008

www.iap.ie

British Library Cataloguing in Publication Data
An entry can be found on request

ISBN 978 0 7165 2959 0 (cloth)
ISBN 978 0 7165 2960 6 (paper)

Library of Congress Cataloging-in-Publication Data
An entry can be found on request

Printed by Good News Digital Books, Ongar, Essex

FOR KEITH

Contents

Acknowledgements

In writing this book I received assistance from a number of people and institutions. The research for this project was supported in part by funds provided by the University of Wisconsin-Milwaukee, specifically by the Center for International Education, the College of Letters and Science, and the Graduate School. The Institute for Research in the Humanities of the University of Wisconsin-Madison awarded me a semester-long fellowship that gave me the opportunity to focus on my scholarship and share my findings with the other Institute Fellows. The librarians at the Gypsy Lore Society Collections of the University of Liverpool, the staff at Pavee Point Travellers Centre in Dublin, and Sunniva O'Flynn at the Irish Film Archive gave me help and information that is hereby gratefully acknowledged. I also appreciate the support of editors Tom Redshaw and James Rogers, and Munira Mutran and Laura Izarra, who accepted articles for their respective journals based on aspects of my research: a version of Chapter 7 of this book appeared under the title '"We Are a Different People": Life Writing, Representation, and the Travellers', in *New Hibernia Review*, 9, 2 (2005), pp.25–41, while part of the research for Chapter 3 was included in an article entitled 'The "Tinker" Figure in the Children's Fiction of Patricia Lynch', published in the *ABEI Journal: The Brazilian Journal of Irish Studies*, 7 (2005), pp.151–62.

For a number of years, as I was working on this book, my friends and colleagues in the American Conference for Irish Studies and the International Association for the Study of Irish Literatures encouraged me by listening with apparent interest to my conference presentations about parts of the work in progress, and providing helpful feedback. Ideas for material to be included in the book came from some of these scholars, but also from more unexpected sources; I thank everyone who contributed suggestions and actual materials for their invaluable assistance, particularly Colleen Booker, Mary Burke, Ann Butler, Zella Christensen, Joan Dean, James Doan, Mika Funahashi, John Gleeson, Michael Hayes, Maureen Murphy, Mark

Netzloff and Mary Ann Ryan. Dawn and Dennis Duncan were, as ever, supportive friends and good companions on the road. Jack Niles was encouraging about the project from the very beginning and generous with his extensive knowledge about the Travelling people of Scotland. Emmet Larkin showed great interest throughout and kept me intellectually honest. In addition to alerting me to relevant publications, Andrew Kincaid read part of the manuscript, provided helpful comments, and motivated me with his enthusiasm. I was also cheered on by Peter van de Kamp, who took time from his busy schedule to read the entire text with a critical eye; for his enduring friendship I am truly grateful. Lisa Hyde was a most efficient and supportive editor. The responsibility for any errors and infelicities in the text is, of course, mine alone. The book's dedication is for my husband, scholar and brewer extraordinaire, with love.

Introduction

There is a moment in Honor Tracy's novel *The Quiet End of Evening* when the book's protagonist, Sabina Boxham, enjoys the spectacle of a group of tinkers passing by:

> For a stirring sight they were, the tinkers, with their gay wagons, the skewbald ponies running free alongside, the shawled women, bright-eyed and hard-faced with stolid babies on their lap, the lurchers nosing hungrily here and there as they followed in the train. Sabina hated to think of the authorities' efforts to end their wild poetic existence and mew them up in settlements and schools.[1]

When one of the tinkers comes to Sabina's door to ask for 'any old lamps, pots or scrap metal', his rough manner and matter-of-fact language therefore take her by surprise: 'It was hardly what she expected, her ideas of tinker speech being drawn from romantic writers of the Celtic Movement.'[2] While herself creating an imaginary 'tinker' figure in this scene, Tracy at the same time reveals the gap that exists between the 'wild poetic tinker' as a construct in Irish literature, and the Traveller as a real person with a function in Irish society. The present study concerns itself with the development of that 'tinker' figure as a fictional character, and with 'tinkerishness' as a trope, in literature written or set in Ireland since the first half of the nineteenth century.

The prevalence of 'tinker' characters in Irish literature should be considered within the broader context of discourse about Gypsies in European literature in general and British literature in particular. In Europe, Heinrich Grellmann's 1783 *Historischer Versuch über die Zigeuner* (Dissertation on Gypsies) was largely responsible for inventing 'the category of "Gypsy" as [it] has been understood since then'.[3] The Gypsies' exoticism placed them

> outside of historical record and historical time, outside of Western law, the Western nation state, and Western economic orders, outside of writing and discursivity itself ... Anchored themselves in an eter-

> nal present, a self-continuity that transcends context and time, they seem able to remove and replace the memory of others at will. Those who join them – whether as stolen children, 'scholar-gypsies', or willing or resistant fellow travellers – seem not only to forget who they are but to lose all sense of time.[4]

There are many similarities between the way Gypsies have for centuries been portrayed by British writers, and the way in which Irish writers have depicted 'tinkers' since the early nineteenth century. In *Gypsies and the British Imagination, 1807–1930*, Deborah Epstein Nord discusses the pervasiveness of images and tropes of Gypsy life in British literature and culture, and the extent to which the nomadic Gypsy 'was associated with a rhetoric of primitive desires, lawlessness, mystery, cunning, sexual excess, godlessness, and savagery – with freedom from the repressions, both constraining and culture building, of Western civilization'.[5] Gypsies were alternately constructed as pastoral figures who were living remnants of an ancient and authentic Britishness, and forces of anarchy and transgression that threatened the very fabric of the family and society.

Nord suggests that the literary representation of the Gypsies 'was intimately connected to an obsession with origins of all kinds – linguistic, personal, and national. A people "without" origins came to stand, paradoxically, for the question of origins itself and to be used as a trope to signify beginnings, primal ancestry, and the ultimate secret of individual identity.'[6] Not surprisingly, the question of the 'origins' of the Irish Travellers has also played an important role in the discussion (dominated by voices from the hegemonic 'settled' world) about the place of Travellers within Irish society, since '[c]ultural legitimacy has often been predicated on historical origins'.[7] Such debates take little account of the fact that origin myths are, by and large, of little interest to Travellers themselves: 'that they regard such as "baggage": that questions of ancientness/roots do not fit into the meaning systems of many commercial nomads such as Travellers, who find their sense of validity in a vital network of relationships rather than in a sense of an ancient historicity'.[8]

Within the context of Britain's status as an empire, Gypsies figured as 'domestic' Others, as opposed to the 'foreign' subjects in the vast colonial domain that stretched from India to Ireland. Given Ireland's position as a colony and, subsequently, a post-colonial nation, the question of Irish 'identity' within Ireland itself was different from that of 'Britishness' in Britain, and always a pressing one in literary discourse, especially from the Irish Literary Revival onwards. Within that (post-)colonial discourse, the Travellers, as an indigenous Irish group that was perceived as markedly 'different' from the norm in cultural and ethnic terms, took up a problematic position. Newly independent nationalist states (read: Ireland after 1922) typically find themselves considering two questions: who are we, and where do we fit in?[9] In Ireland, the 'tinkers' frequently became the medium through which those questions were explored, and the entity against which 'Irishness' was defined. While the Travellers, as a cultural and ethnic minority, arguably faced similar questions about their own identity, the only answers considered valid were those emanating from sedentary society, whose print media had the power and influence to shape the discourse about Travellers. Such discourse, as Fintan O'Toole has remarked, 'is not really about Travellers at all but about the rest of us, the "settled" people'.[10] Máirín Kenny speaks in this regard of a form of 'internal colonialism', in that the terms of the debate about Travellers are set by non-Travellers, and the cultural space of Travellers is interpreted only in the light of an assumed sedentary 'norm'.[11]

The chapters in this book consider how Traveller 'difference' has been constructed in Irish literature over time and in various ways according to that sedentary perspective. A broadly chronological approach is combined with a thematic one: three chapters, on the pre-Famine period, the Revival period, and the mid-twentieth century respectively, discuss the creation of the 'tinker' figure within a specific historical context. Three other chapters focus on thematic contexts that are particularly prevalent in, or have particular relevance for, the literary construction of the 'tinker' figure: Irish children's literature; literature based in mythology and fantasy (or 'otherworldliness'); and Irish crime and detective fiction. A final chapter considers self-representations by Travelling people – often framed in terms of a dialogic response to the sedentary construction of the stereotypical 'tinker' figure – as presented in autobiographical narratives by individual members of the Travelling community.[12]

Chapter 1 begins by considering the textual and historical evidence for, and speculation about, the 'origin' of the Travellers, and the emergence of the 'tinker' (as opposed to the Gypsy) as a historical and literary type in Britain in the early modern period. It goes on to discuss the earliest appearance of tinker characters in Irish literature in the first half of the nineteenth century. From these portrayals it is clear that the 'tinker' stereotype was already well established in Irish society by the time the tinker made his appearance as a character in Irish fiction. These depictions also serve as evidence – if such were needed – that the tinkers were recognized in Ireland as a minority group with distinctive characteristics well before the Famine, which was therefore not responsible for 'creating' the Travellers through evictions and deprivation, as some have argued.

Chapter 2 discusses the popularity of 'tinker' characters in the literature of the Irish Literary Revival of the early twentieth century by focusing on the sudden proliferation in 1902 of texts thematically preoccupied with the idea of the 'tinker's wedding'. Between the creation of the Irish Literary Theatre in 1899, with its nationalist aim of depicting Ireland as the home of an ancient and heroic idealism, and the formation of the Free State in 1922, when that idealism was put severely to the test, the 'tinker' trope underwent a remarkable transformation, from being the abstraction on which Anglo-Irish nationalists projected all their desires and anxieties about the independent nation that was yet to be created, to becoming the embodiment of everything that was objectionable about the Irish past and worrisome about its future.

Children's literature from and about Ireland, which is the focus of Chapter 3, functions as a particularly sensitive barometer for gauging the prevailing ideological climate of the Irish nation, from its emergence in 1922, via the repressive environment of the mid-twentieth century, to the years of the Celtic Tiger economy at century's end. In the didactic context of children's fiction, the fleetingly attractive but eventually always undesirable life of the tinkers, who in such narratives are frequently depicted as being without homes, without occupations, and even without families, is contrasted sharply with the desirable and necessary attributes of a structured environment and the routine and discipline of sedentary domesticity. In contemporary fiction aimed at older teenagers (so-called young adult literature), the Traveller figure is usually a teaching tool for addressing questions of individual development and personal responsibility; whether used as positive or negative examples, Traveller characters are merely conduits through which a sedentary author speaks to a sedentary teenage audience.

In Chapter 4, which discusses texts from the middle part of the twentieth century, 'tinkers' are at the heart of the discourse of and about modernity, which contrasts the itinerant's perceived lack of discipline and self-control with the ordering and regulatory impulses generated by the modern bureaucratic nation-state. Increasingly within the modern context, 'tinkers' come to stand for a manifestation of an atavistic, primitive inner self that has been repressed but not eradicated. For the modern Irish character in mid-twentieth-century literature, the 'tinker' represents both the lure and the danger of a potential regression into primitivism. The literature of this period displays a particular fascination with the tinker's perceived association with moral and physical dirt, a manifestation of the modern preoccupation with issues of contamination and hygiene that reflects a repressed awareness of modernity as the producer of the very waste its sanitation mechanisms so obsessively keep at bay.

Since the perceived alterity of Travellers is easily translated into otherworldliness, the use of mythology and fantasy has played a large part in the way sedentary authors have used tinker figures to explore questions about their own social and cultural identity. Chapter 5 analyses the place of the tinker in fiction based in myth and fantasy. Often depicted as a utopian alternative to the excesses of contemporary society, the transient lifestyle of Travellers in fantasy fiction features as a possible escape from a fallen world and a way back to a simpler and more peaceful past. Mythic plots, often borrowed from Celtic sources, not only relegate Traveller characters to an 'older' way of life, but also confine them within a preconceived scenario not of their own making (frequently starkly concerned with issues of good and evil, or power and victimhood) – an apt if usually unintentional metaphor for the way Travellers are often not in complete control of discourse about their own community in the actual world.

In the popular crime literature discussed in Chapter 6, the 'tinker' figure is cast in the role of the victim or the perpetrator of a murder, or sometimes both, but never in that of the investigator. Within the formulaic genre of detective fiction, in which a mystery is solved and the disruption to the social fabric is healed and order restored, tinkers often take on the role of trickster figures: themselves beyond the pale of what society finds acceptable, and impervious to its rules and regulations, they can be used to expose, sometimes mischievously, sometimes more violently, the lawlessness and bigotry of characters who belong more centrally to the sedentary realm. Like Loki in the Norse myths, the tinker in crime fiction is an annoyance, an irritant, sometimes dangerous and at other times a source of entertainment, but not usually or intentionally the creator of the evil he helps to expose and, at times, in unorthodox fashion, eradicate. This is not to say that the tinker figure is perceived as innocent: being a tinker is itself an infringement of what passes for acceptable behaviour in respectable society, but it also situates the character in a parallel universe largely beyond the reach of the official justice system.

The final chapter of this study deals with the ways in which a number of individual Travellers have represented themselves in narratives based on their own lives. As a relatively recent phenomenon, Traveller life writing, while autobiographical in nature, is a dialogic response to the way in which Travellers have been represented in sedentary writing, and is aimed at a settled audience with the purpose of countering some of the stereotypes about Travellers prevalent among the settled population. In their eagerness to explain Traveller culture and create greater understanding, these narratives may end up sounding defensive, but they also reveal how strongly members of the community feel about being recognized as both Irish citizens and Travelling people. The gap between those two identities (Travellers are seen, and see themselves as, a 'different' people) can only begin to close when the definition of Irishness, which was shaped by the nationalist movement and culminated in de Valera's ideal of a Catholic rural nation of small farmers, becomes more inclusive of cultural, ethnic, and racial diversity.

In the following consideration of the 'tinker' figure in Irish literature, the term 'tinker' is not used to refer to actual members of the Traveller community, for whom it is a derogatory term, except when the context is historical or in instances when it refers to the specific trade of tinsmithing. About another term for Travellers, which was often used by Irish authorities in the 1960s and 1970s, one Travelling woman remarked, 'I'd drink my blood before I'd answer to the word, "itinerant"'.[13] The term 'tinker' is used in the overwhelming majority of fictional texts discussed in this study, even by contemporary writers who ought to be aware of its offensive quality. In the same way that there exists a dissociation between rhetoric and referent in British literary texts dealing with Gypsies, in that 'Gypsy' is used by writers as 'a sign or symbol that is completely emptied of reference to reality, history, or experience',[14] in Irish literature the 'tinker' is a largely self-perpetuating phenomenon, in the sense that one fictional tinker begets another without the need on the author's part for recourse to the touchstone of reality. It is therefore unsurprising that many settled Irish people are still more familiar with the stereotypes surrounding that literary construct than with the real circumstances of the lives of their fellow citizens in the Traveller community.

NOTES

1. Honor Tracy, *The Quiet End of Evening* (New York: Random House, 1972), p.38.
2. Ibid., p.44.
3. Mary Burke, 'Eighteenth-Century European Scholarship and Nineteenth-Century Irish Literature: Synge's *Tinker's Wedding* and the Orientalizing of "Irish Gypsies"', in Betsey Taylor FitzSimon and James H. Murphy (eds), *The Irish Revival Reappraised* (Dublin: Four Courts Press, 2004), p.206.
4. Katie Trumpener, 'The Time of the Gypsies: A "People without History" in the Narratives of the West', *Critical Inquiry*, 18, 4 (1992), pp.860–1.
5. Deborah Epstein Nord, *Gypsies and the British Imagination, 1807–1930* (New York: Columbia University Press, 2006), p.3.
6. Ibid., p.8.
7. Michael Hayes, *Irish Travellers: Representations and Realities* (Dublin: Liffey Press, 2006), p.11.
8. Máirín Kenny, 'Final Thoughts: A Case for Celebration?', in May McCann, Séamas Ó Síocháin and Joseph Ruane (eds), *Irish Travellers: Culture and Ethnicity* (Belfast: Institute of Irish Studies/Queen's University Belfast, 1994), p.181.
9. Ibid., p.182.
10. Fintan O'Toole, *Irish Times*, 16 June 1995. Qtd. in Hayes, *Irish Travellers*, p.109.
11. Kenny, 'Final Thoughts', p.180.
12. The term 'community' is used here and throughout as a way of indicating that Travellers share a common culture and ethnicity. It does not suggest that all Travellers know each other or relate to each other in the same way and on the same level. Economic circumstances and living conditions vary, and families are related to each other in complex ways. Research into Traveller family relations and naming practices indicates that families with particular surnames 'do not intermarry indiscriminately, but within finite clusters, and have done so for generations'. This means that 'each intermarrying cluster effectively comprises a microethnicity which sees itself as distinct, particularly from those with which no intermarriage takes place'. See Sinéad Ní Shuinéar, 'History as Dialogue: An Anthropological Perspective', in Ciara Breathnach and Aoife Bhreatnach (eds), *Portraying Irish Travellers: Histories and Representations* (Newcastle: Cambridge Scholars Press, 2006), pp. 75; 82.
13. An Anonymous Traveller, 'Who We Really Are: Language and Identity', in John M. Kirk and Dónall P. Ó Baoill (eds), *Travellers and their Language* (Belfast: Queen's University Press, 2002), p.170.
14. Nord, *Gypsies and the British Imagination*, p.16.

CHAPTER 1

Before the Famine: Historical Origins and Literary Beginnings

For I take in old iron
I take in old bones and rags
And all other different kinds of stuff
And I put them in separate bags
For I have travelled this country o'er and o'er
And I'm known by everyone
My name is Pat O'Flanagan
I'm a travelling candyman.
'The Travelling Candyman', folk song

It seems likely that a variety of circumstances contributed to the formation of what is today a distinctive ethnic minority of about 30,000 Irish Travellers with its own culture and traditions. There is abundant documented evidence that Travellers or 'tinkers', as they used to be called until the middle of the twentieth century, existed as a distinctly recognizable group in Ireland before the Famine, although references before 1800 are scarce. Prior to that date, the evidence points less specifically to 'shuilers' (*fir siúil, mná siúil*) or 'Travelling people' – tinsmiths, musicians, beggars – at least some of whom 'were the antecedents of the group known until recently in Ireland as "tinkers"'.[1]

In recent years, the debate about the 'origin' of the Travellers has been intense, not least among sedentary researchers. Travellers themselves have not maintained a cohesive oral or written account of their history as a group, perhaps because there is no such collective ancient past, or because they do not validate themselves in terms of ancient roots. Jane Helleiner considers the origins debate to be part of a broader post-colonial nationalist discourse 'in which Irish citizenship, identity, and culture are opposed to the colonial past', and the focus on a single 'origin' 'excludes the possibility of a more dynamic historical process'.[2] Certainly there were periods of upheaval in Europe in past centuries, particularly in the early modern period, when droves of people, including large numbers of Irish, took to the roads (semi-) permanently in search of a living, and the occupational and migratory practices of many of these itinerant workers in several ways resembled those of the Travellers of more recent times. Michael Flynn has likened the originating process of the Travellers to a conveyor belt: 'There would have been a steady trickle of families dropping off and settling in houses while other persons or families would "hop onto the conveyor belt", or drop out from society, or take on some of the former crafts or occupations of the travellers.'[3]

In an article published in 2004, Sinéad Ní Shuinéar points out that it is now commonly believed among the general Irish population that Travellers 'are descended from Irish peasants forced onto the roads, most significantly as a result of the Great Famine of the 1840s'. Ní Shuinéar objects to this persistent 'drop-out' theory, not because it is 'unpalatable', but because 'it is demonstrably untrue and blatantly motivated by a political agenda' that seeks to justify the Travellers' 're'-assimilation into mainstream Irish society.[4] In an article published a decade earlier, in which she made a case for considering the Travellers as a distinct ethnic group, Ní Shuinéar presented three hypotheses for the emergence of Travellers in Ireland, all of which suggested they were descended from ancient Celtic or pre-Celtic population groups.[5] In a response to this article, Dymphna McLoughlin argued against a separate Traveller ethnicity, claiming that contemporary differences between the Travellers and the settled population did not originate in the distant past, but that mobility and economic adaptability were general characteristics of the survival strategies of the Irish labouring classes. She therefore concluded that 'Travellers do not figure as a distinctive group amongst the wretched and subsistence-based in nineteenth century Ireland'.[6]

The objection often raised to what is negatively dubbed the 'drop-out theory' is that Travellers are born Travellers, or have 'always' been Travellers. Contemporary accounts suggest that settled individuals who marry into the Traveller community remain 'buffers' (the Cant word used by Travelling people to refer to non-Travellers), but that their children are considered Travellers, so that such distinctions disappear over time. Some Travellers, both in the past and the present, readily acknowledge that their families were once part of sedentary society. Dorothy Wordsworth, for example, recorded in her diary entry for 10 June 1800 that a tall Scottish woman came begging at her door whose face 'was excessively brown, but it had plainly once been fair'. She said her husband was a tinker, and 'that they could not keep a house and so they travelled'. Dorothy later saw the husband sitting by the roadside with two donkeys and two young children, but 'he did not beg'. The tinker's older boys, however, addressed her 'with the Beggar's cant and the whining voice of sorrow'.[7] Contemporary Traveller musician Pádraig 'Pecker' Dunne acknowledges that his mother was a 'townie',[8] and that his family 'took to the road because they had to. They were evicted by the local landlord.'[9] Sharon Gmelch notes that Nan Donohoe's paternal grandmother was the daughter of a settled labourer.[10] At the same time, there are some Traveller families whose status is legendary, such as the Wards, who, according to Gmelch in *Nan*, 'are acknowledged by other Travellers to be one of the "oldest families on the road"' and who may originally have been travelling 'bards' or entertainers (p.235 n.11), although Gmelch also refers to them as 'one of the oldest tinsmithing families on the road' (pp.29–30).

While Irish Travellers have their own set of unique circumstances and customs, it should be realized that many aspects of Traveller culture, including settled responses to it, are not unique to Ireland. In The Netherlands, to use but one example, the members of the community of 30,000 people known as *Reizigers* or *Woonwagenbewoners* (caravan-dwellers) originate from within the country, but consider themselves culturally distinct from the sedentary population. Though they were forced into permanent halting sites by the government's assimilation policy of the 1960s, the *Reizigers* fiercely resist being integrated into mainstream Dutch society, citing their independence, distinctive life/work practices, family-oriented mentality and group solidarity as their defining cultural characteristics. While the practice of living in caravans dates from the late nineteenth century, Travelling people such as tinkers, knife-grinders, hawkers and agricultural workers were a common feature of the Dutch landscape for centuries.

Research into the histories of Dutch Travelling families living in, respectively, the north-eastern province of Overijssel and the city of The Hague between the two world wars, revealed that the provincial families had strong ties to the area and had lived and worked there for generations, while the *Reiziger* (Traveller) families in The Hague had only moved there a generation earlier from the south or the northeast of the country. Before moving into caravans, their ancestors had mostly led a sedentary existence as farmers and farm labourers, while the parents and grandparents of the other families travelled around as knife-grinders or chair-menders. In the twentieth century, these older families of *Reizigers* did not differ in their way of life from those who had started to travel for the first time between 1900 and 1940.[11]

While Irish Traveller history does not suggest the recent addition of entire families, and Irish Travellers may have been more resistant to newcomers, the research from The Netherlands does indicate that the transition from being settled to being a 'true' Traveller (from the perspective of Travellers themselves) can happen in the space of a few generations, and should serve as a caution against making absolute statements about the Irish Travellers. The Irish examples cited above also indicate an awareness among Travellers themselves that some families have been on the road longer than others. That in itself indicates that it must have been possible to 'become' a Traveller, at a time when distinctions between settled and itinerant people were perhaps not as fixed as they are today. Anecdotal evidence also indicates that some Travellers have merged into sedentary society, but that they are often unwilling to acknowledge their heritage openly, for fear of being treated differently by their neighbours.

GENETIC AND LINGUISTIC EVIDENCE

Genetic research first carried out by Michael Crawford in the mid-1970s, and confirmed by a study conducted in the late 1990s, shows that the Travellers are 'undoubtedly of Irish ancestry'[12] and form 'a heterogeneous group that has been relatively isolated through time', whose genetic markers in the later study were found to cluster 'with several heterogeneous counties in Ireland, including Wexford and Westmeath'. The data show that 'the origin of the Travellers was not a sudden event; rather a gradual formation of populations'.[13] The later study follows the earlier one in speculating that the origin of the Travellers may lie with craftsmen and artisans forced to leave the monasteries where they were employed after these were closed in the twelfth century, whose numbers were subsequently increased by people forced to leave their homes during periods of upheaval. However, the authors concede that 'the timing of the Traveller origin is not certain'.[14] There is no corroborating evidence to support the monastic origin theory.

The theory of monastic origins depends heavily on an association of Irish Travellers ('tinkers') with tinsmithing. From what is known of Traveller occupations over the centuries it is evident that this may be too limited a view, for while metal-work was important, Travellers in Ireland and elsewhere made a living in a wide variety of ways, which included hawking, making horn spoons, baskets and brooms, carrying out various types of repair work, collecting and selling rags, feathers, horse hair, metal, bottles, etc., providing seasonal farm labour, and sweeping chimneys.[15] Versatility best characterizes how Travellers survived on the road, as confirmed by William Cameron's description of a Scottish Travelling woman from the first half of the nineteenth century: 'the woman with me was a bred tinker, and could turn her hand to anything in travelling'.[16] Scottish Traveller musician Davie Stewart told Alan Lomax that his father 'did everything': he made tin, played the pipes for a living, but mostly he hawked around the country with a horse and cart, as did his mother, whose father 'was come of the Irish'.[17] An Irish Traveller cited by Sharon Gmelch in *Nan* defined a 'real tinker' as 'a man who thought of a hundred ways of surviving. If he was selling delph [crockery] and the delph failed him, he'd switch to somethin' else. Maybe he'd buy somethin' else or resell it. There were always a hundred ways out' (p.15). It seems safe to say that the Travellers' preference for self-employment and independence and their adaptability and versatility are more characteristic of their culture than any specific occupation.

While the genetic evidence is scant and has yielded limited results, linguistic research into the language spoken by the Irish Travellers may help throw light on their history. In the late nineteenth century, academics coined the term 'Shelta' for the language spoken by the Irish Travellers. It is not a term used by Travellers themselves, who call their language 'Cant' or 'Gammon', which are two variants of the same vernacular. Generally speaking, 'cant' is a form of communication within minority groups that are considered outsiders by the dominant population, and that also regard themselves as being outside the mainstream in terms of their lifestyle. Members of the gay community in Britain, for example, at one time used a form of cant known as 'Polari' ('parlare'). Traveller artist William Cauley acknowledges that Travellers sometimes used Cant or Gammon 'for privacy', but contends that 'one of the main reasons Travellers used gammon was because it was their own language that they had learnt from childhood'.[18] Pecker Dunne, a Traveller musician from the west of Ireland, also notes that 'Travellers spoke it because it was their own language and it kept them close together'.[19] Cant, then, has both a negative and a positive function: it shuts out those who do not belong to the minority group, and it reinforces a sense of belonging and togetherness among those who do.

Sinéad Ní Shuinéar rightly claims that Gammon or Cant is spoken by all Irish Travellers, both in Ireland and Britain, and by their descendants in the United States,[20] but Pecker Dunne suggests an even greater number of varieties and gradations within the Traveller vernacular, claiming that there were at least six types of Cant when he was growing up in Ireland in the 1950s: Romani (actually a language); the Cant or Gammon of the 'tinkers'; the Cant of travelling tailors; buskers' Cant or 'parley', used by carnival workers and entertainers such as himself; and the Cant of travelling stonemasons. He also refers to two types of Scottish Travellers' Cant, one more heavily influenced by Gaelic than the other. According to Dunne, the Travellers 'could speak some of them fluently or bits of all of them'.[21] Moreover, he distinguishes between 'many types of parley depending on the families who use it', and also claims that Irish parley includes a good deal of Gammon 'because a lot of Travellers worked as tinkers and as showpeople'.[22] Different types of affiliations determine the Cant one speaks: 'The different Travelling families in Ireland all have their own ways of *parlian*' or *whiddin*' (speaking) in the Cant, depending on their own dialect of Cant and what trade their families specialized in.'[23] Dutch *Reizigers* sometimes speak Bargoens, a form of Cant, but it is an overstatement to say that they 'have their own language', as Ní Shuinéar contends,[24] because its use is not confined to the Travellers.[25]

The grammatical structure of Shelta (used here as a collective term for the variants of Traveller language) is Hiberno-English, while much of its vocabulary is derived from Irish, although many of the words have been altered in a variety of systematic ways (reversal, metathesis, replacement of initial consonants by others, and so on). Dónall Ó Baoill argues that, if a variety of Shelta had ever existed that did not use English words or grammar, it would have survived intact; that it was therefore formed outside of the structure of Irish, and that Irish words were 'borrowed' to replace the English content words. If so, Shelta must have been formed when its original speakers were bilingual, or at least had a good working knowledge of English. In Ireland, the presence of such conditions restrict its formation to the last 350 years or so, when the general population made the transition from speaking Irish to using English as their primary language, although among the poor, Irish was widely spoken until the Famine.[26] Alice Binchy suggests that constantly switching from one language to another can erode grammatical differences, and that this may have happened in the case of Shelta as it did with Anglo-Romani.[27]

If Shelta developed during the seventeenth century, and if Travellers originated in Ireland long before that period, one might wonder why Travellers started using Shelta when they did. It is conceivable that the number of 'traditional' travelling tinkers (who may have been predominantly metalsmiths) was small before 1650, whereas the number of travelling families increased after that time, which made the tinkers more visible, as a result of which they were perceived with greater suspicion by the settled population, and hence were more likely to feel the need to develop a private form of communication. The earliest mentions of 'tinkers' in Irish texts suggest that their occupation was tinsmithing; but if these were the descendants of medieval metalsmiths, one may still wonder why the Shelta word for tinker (disguised as 'minker' and Gaelicized as 'mincéir'), as well as terms for objects associated with the tinker's trade ('borer' for gimlet, 'grader' for solder, 'ruket' for bucket, 'srittle' for kettle, etc.) are derived from English, even though Shelta has a largely Irish-based vocabulary.[28] Language is a living entity, of course, in which meanings shift and new words are borrowed. Michael Hayes reports from his research among Rathkeale Travellers that some 'consider *rodas* (or its variants *rudus* and *rodus*) from Irish *doras* to be a more authentic Shelta word for door than *jigger*, a word from English Cant'.[29]

The fact that a group of words (including 'jigger') is found both in Irish Traveller's Cant and in the Cant of sixteenth-century English 'pedlars' suggests that the history of the Travellers as a group goes back at least as far as the early modern period, when there may have been significant contact between the English and Irish Travelling people. Both R.A. Stewart Macalister's Shelta lexicon, and the list of contemporary Cant words in Sean Maher's semi-autobiographical account *The Road to God Knows Where*, contain a number of words that are also found in the vocabulary of 'pedlars' French' provided by Thomas Harman in *A Caveat for Common Cursitors*, which was first published in 1566. The words in Harman's list that coincide with Travellers' Cant include 'cant' itself, meaning 'to speak', as well as 'cheat' (thing), 'jigger' (door), 'cean' or 'ken' (house), 'glimmer' (fire), 'lour' (money), 'whid' (word), and 'strummel' (straw). John Sampson pointed out a century ago that Scottish Travellers' Cant also includes words from Harman's list, including 'fammels' (hands), 'bing' (go), and 'mort' (woman). The common word among Irish Travellers for a settled person, 'buffer', may derive from 'bluffer' or 'buffer', which, according to Nathan Bailey's mid-eighteenth-century *Dictionary of Cant Words*, means 'an inn-keeper or victualler'.

Sampson saw the presence of 'the cant of the Elizabethan rogue or vagabond' as evidence of 'the class of people with whom the Scottish Tinklers interbred',[30] but regarded the Irish tinkers as 'an ancient and widespread caste' unrelated to the 'tinklers' of Scotland, and their language, Shelta, as evidence of their Celtic roots. Although Macalister later found that 'Shelta contains next to nothing ancient and exclusively Celtic',[31] he nevertheless went along with Sampson's purist theory and attempted to compile an 'Ur' Shelta lexicon from which Romani and Elizabethan Cant words had been removed as much as possible, even when such words had been collected from Irish Travellers. Binchy suggests that it was the Irish Travellers who 'shared some parts of their language with the other non-Gypsy wanderers with whom they were associated by the majority population',[32] but the linguistic traffic may also have moved in the opposite direction. The notion that Irish and Scottish Travellers were to some greater or lesser degree related to English rogues and vagabonds should be re-examined in the light of recent historical research into the population that constituted the 'rogues and vagabonds' of the Elizabethan period, since 'vagabond' was a derogatory term used to describe all Travelling people at the time, whose numbers included individuals and families from Scotland and Ireland as well as England.

The presence of Irish and Scottish pedlars and other Travelling people in England during the early modern period is well documented and will be discussed hereafter. Sources about Travelling families in Ireland before 1800 are harder to find. This is not the same as saying, of course, that there were no Travellers in Ireland, but perhaps rather that, unlike in England, their presence was not perceived as remarkable or problematic within Irish society. The stigmatization of itinerant workers in England and elsewhere in Europe from the fourteenth century onward is often associated with anxieties created by 'the transition from a feudal to a market-oriented capitalist system, which entailed a change from bound to free labour'.[33] Changes in the poor laws, which increasingly focused on local residents and excluded 'vagrants', contributed to the negative image of Travelling people. The unusual status of Ireland as a British colony, whose population was impoverished and frequently negatively stereotyped as a whole, may have kept the Travellers within Ireland mostly 'invisible' until the nineteenth century. While itinerant labour should not in itself be regarded as a sign of crisis, since Travellers provided services for which there was a demand, at the same time there were periods of upheaval in early modern Europe, including Ireland, as a result of which more people moved around in search of work and income. The adverse conditions in Ireland that caused whole families to leave the country for England in the sixteenth century (some of whom may, of course, have been Travellers before they crossed the water, as were the Irish Travellers who moved to the United States in the mid-nineteenth century) may also have increased the number of Travelling people at home. Sharon Gmelch cites the fact that the majority of the most common Traveller surnames in Ireland today originate in the west of Ireland, where the greatest number of evictions occurred, as evidence of possible origins in dispossession.[34] What we learn about Irish Travelling people in England in the early modern period can help us understand how aspects of the culture of the Irish Travellers may have developed, whether in Ireland, in England, or as family groups travelled between the two countries, voluntarily or driven by some form of need or coercion.

ENGLISH HISTORICAL AND LITERARY EVIDENCE

Historical and literary sources of the early modern period suggest that many Irish and Scottish people, along with even greater numbers of English, began travelling the roads of England in the sixteenth century, as a result of various crises. In *A Caveat for Common Cursitors*, Thomas Harman writes disapprovingly about 'vagabonds' in the counties around London, and mentions 'above an hundred of Irishmen and women that wander about to beg for their living, that hath come over within these two years. They say they have been burned and spoiled by the Earl of Desmond.'[35] The reference is to the feud between the Earls of Desmond and Ormonde in Munster, which culminated in the battle of Affane in 1565. Crises in subsequent decades increased the number of entire families among the itinerant population: famine, civil wars and conquest tended 'to throw victims on to the roads, which for many led to England'.[36] The Irish travelled in large groups, often including families:

> In a group of seventeen seized in Wiltshire in 1629 the three families had different surnames, and these companies were probably drawn together by common origins or embarkation points. Two families apprehended together in the county in 1637 came from the same area in County Cork. The Irish also moved in large bands because of their extended family structures at home.[37]

In more recent times, Irish commentators also noted that Travellers moved around in this way. Seán MacGrath observed in 1955: 'Seldom will you see a solitary caravan or cart load of tinkers. They travel in groups, and possibly they too believe about there being security in numbers.'[38]

In the early modern period, the Irish and the Gypsies were singled out by the English legislators as being particularly worrisome. Among itinerant people in England, these groups formed a minority (the majority being English), but because they were 'foreign' and because the Irish were associated with 'popery' and rebellion, they stood out and aroused suspicion. Acts against Irish 'vagrants' and 'beggars' were passed in 1572 and 1629. The terminology used in many such historical documents is a significant obstacle to determining the exact status of these people, since all sorts of 'masterless men', including tinkers and hawkers, tended to be lumped together as 'vagabonds', 'rogues' or 'beggars'. Robert Jütte cautions that vagrants should not be confused with 'travelling people',[39] and points out that most of the latter group 'lived by a variety of occupations. Some of them were tinkers, repairing and manufacturing tinware. Others were pedlars trading with all kinds of goods. But as occasion demanded and opportunity permitted they accepted also other menial and temporary jobs. When this ... failed, they had ... also an accomplished hand at begging, small-time swindling and petty theft.'[40] This may be a fair point, but the indiscriminate terminology in legal documents of the period often made no distinction between these different groups, or if it did, it was often only in order to specify which particular groups in society should be treated as undesirables.

The vagrancy Acts of 1572 and 1597 made pedlars and tinkers illegal, and hence 'officially' relegated them to the population of 'vagabonds'. In 1604 the same occupations were omitted from the new vagrancy Act, which meant that tinkers and pedlars were still 'despised, ridiculed, stigmatized and marginalized, but not prosecuted for their deviant way of life'.[41] Treatises from this period show an acute awareness among the educated public of the contested status of tinkers and hawkers, and of the legislation concerning them. In *A Caveat for Common Cursitors*, Harman describes 'drunken tinkers' as 'beastly people' who pass the time 'with picking and stealing, mingled with a little work for a colour',[42] and while he grudgingly admits that pedlars 'be not all evil', he cites some instances of pedlars who were arrested 'for bribering and stealing', and warns that many thieving vagrants disguise their booty as 'a packful of wares' to avoid arrest.[43] In the first decade of the seventeenth century, Samuel Rid wrote that anti-vagrant legislation meant that itinerants 'dare no more be known by the name of Egiptians [Gypsies], nor take any other name upon them then poore people', but that 'still they wandered, as before up and downe',[44] although increasingly not as beggars: 'these fellowes ... doe daily decrease and breake off their wonted society, and betake themselves many of them, some to be Pedlers, some Tinkers, some Juglers, and some to one kinde of life or other'.[45] Around the same time, Sir Thomas Overbury included among his 'witty descriptions' the character of 'a tinker' who travels the roads with his wife, speaks Cant, delivers shoddy workmanship, and abides by the laws against vagrancy in creative ways: 'He observes truly the statutes, and therefore he can rather steal than beg.'[46]

Pedlars and tinkers operated at the lowest end of the migrant labour force in England. The record of a couple arrested in 1607 describes the husband as a saddler and the wife as a pedlar 'of thread and other small wares', while documents from 1630 indicate that some families of hawkers collected and sold feathers and old metal.[47] This division of labour, where the husband had a trade, and the wife peddled small wares around the farms, also existed among Irish and Dutch travellers as late as the twentieth century.[48] In early modern England, the Irish appear to have been among the poorest of the pedlars, at least outside London. The lowest pedlar was known as 'an Irish toyle', described by John Awdeley in *The Fraternity of Vagabonds* (1561) as

> he that carrieth his ware in his wallet, as laces, pins, points and suchlike. He useth to show no wares until he have his alms; and if the goodman and wife be not in the way, he procureth of the children or servants a fleece of wool, or the worth of twelve pence of some other thing, for a pennyworth of his wares.[49]

The definition is more negative in Bailey's eighteenth-century dictionary, which describes Irish toyles as 'rogues, &c. carrying pins, points, laces, and such like wares about, and, under pretence of selling them, commit thefts and robberies'. In London, street hawking of fruit and vegetables seems to have been a notably Irish occupation as early as 1607, when Thomas Dekker wrote that the Irish 'love ... to be costermongers'.[50] In 1602, an order of the London Court of Common Council objected to street hawkers because they hurt the trade of regular shopkeepers.[51] The Irish still dominated the London costermongering scene in Victorian times, according to Henry Mayhew, who also observed that they kept mostly to themselves and did not mingle with other traders. Costermongers lived in the city, but some would make occasional forays into the surrounding countryside.[52]

In early modern England, tinkers (travelling tinsmiths) were less numerous than pedlars, and generally poorer, even if they had sometimes served apprenticeships. Like pedlars, they were disliked by the authorities because they showed occupational solidarity, had extended family ties, and a reputation for disruptive behaviour, including drinking and cursing. Tinkers' wives often supplemented their meagre income by peddling or begging. In Thomas Overbury's 'witty description', the tinker is accompanied by 'some foul sun-burnt quean, that, since the terrible statute, recanted gipseyism and is turned pedlaress'.[53] It is not clear whether any of the small and elusive group of tinkers in England at this time were Irish, but it seems unlikely. In his list of seventy-four 'vagabonds' known to him in the counties around London, Thomas Harman includes five Irishmen: two 'rogues' and three 'palliards', one of whom has 'a counterfeit licence'[54] – that is, a licence allowing the man to beg for alms on the grounds of ill health. Harman writes: 'There be many Irishmen that go about with counterfeit licences. And if they perceive you will straitly examine them, they will immediately say they can speak no English.'[55] Harman, of course, is biased against all Travelling people, but his remark serves as an indicator that the Irish on the roads of Elizabethan England, around the time of the origination of Travellers' Cant, spoke both Irish and some degree of English.

Harman argues that palliards 'have their morts with them, which they call wives. And if he go to one house to ask his alms, his wife shall go to another; for what they get, as bread, cheese, malt and wool, they sell the same for ready money; for so they get more [than] if they went together.'[56] The author appears to suggest that selling donated goods, especially food, is a form of cheating rather than trading. Overbury, too, proposes that peddling is a front for begging, while Awdeley claims that '[a] tinkard leaveth his bag a-sweating at the ale-house ..., and in the mean season goeth abroad a-begging'.[57] Patricia Fumerton regards such depictions of nomadic traders as vagrants in disguise as evidence of anxiety among the middling and lower orders of the settled population about the prevalence of unsettled labour: 'the itinerant laborer becomes thinly disguised as a deceitful rogue. Instead of changing jobs or holding multiple jobs, the diversified worker is imaged as donning various disguises.'[58] Indeed, deceitfulness becomes almost synonymous with itinerancy and nomadism in the discourse of this time period.

In early modern England, Travellers and Gypsies were defined by their mobile way of life rather than in terms of their occupation or ethnicity. Bona fide itinerancy was essentially a contradiction in terms, and laws were constructed or interpreted in such a way that to be on the road was always potentially a punishable offence. An Act passed in England in 1562 'confirmed the status of native-born gypsies as English subjects' and instead 'singled out for punishment "counterfeit Egyptians", masterless men who disguised themselves as gypsies'.[59] Over time, '"Egyptian" exclusively came to refer to counterfeit gypsies, displaced laborers who disguised themselves as gypsies in order to evade antivagrant statutes'.[60] As the quotations from Harman and Overbury cited above make clear, pedlars and hawkers were also routinely suspected of being 'Egyptians' pretending to be something else. While vagrants were suspected of disguising themselves as 'bona fide' gypsies to evade the law against vagrancy, gypsies were themselves often 'classified as "counterfeit Egyptians" because they lacked origin and occupation'.[61]

It was nomadism, then, that caused anxiety in early modern England, and led to legislation that increasingly distinguished between criminally inclined 'vagrants' and the law-abiding sedentary population. In the nineteenth century some scientists attempted to employ the principles of phrenology (a pseudoscience concerned with detecting evidence of underlying mind patterns in the shape of the skull) to explain the difference between nomadic and sedentary peoples, and to relate variations in physiognomy to relative levels of 'civilization'. Henry Mayhew sums up the researchers' findings as follows in his mid-nineteenth-century study *London Labour and the London Poor*:

> (1) There are two distinct races of men, viz.: – the wandering and the civilized tribes; (2) to each of these tribes a different form of head is peculiar, the wandering races being remarkable for the development of

> the bones of the face, as the jaws, cheek-bones, &c., and the civilized for the development of those of the head; (3) to each civilized tribe there is generally a wandering horde attached; (4) such wandering hordes have frequently a different language from the more civilized portion of the community, and that adopted with the intent of concealing their designs and exploits from them.[62]

Mayhew himself concludes that similar mental and physiological characteristics also apply to the 'nomadic races of England', among whom he numbers 'habitual vagrants', as well as 'pedlars, showmen, harvest-men, and all that large class who live by either selling, showing, or doing something through the country':

> Whether it be that in the mere act of wandering, there is a greater determination of blood to the surface of the body, and consequently a less quantity sent to the brain, the muscles being thus nourished at the expense of the mind, I leave physiologists to say. But certainly be the physical cause what it may, we must all allow that in each of the classes above-mentioned, there is a greater development of the animal than of the intellectual or moral nature of man, and that they are all more or less distinguished for their high cheek-bones and protruding jaws – for their use of a slang language – for their lax ideas of property – for their general improvidence – their repugnance to continuous labour – their disregard of female honour – their love of cruelty – their pugnacity – and their utter want of religion.[63]

TINKERS IN ENGLISH AND IRISH LITERATURE

Fully-fledged tinker characters appear in English literature long before they are found in Irish literary texts. In Thomas Dekker's 'The Wonderfull Yeare. 1603', characteristics such as adaptability and cunning that become stereotypical 'tinker' traits are already well established. In the story, a Londoner has died while staying in a country inn. As everyone else is afraid of catching the plague, a tinker is prevailed upon to remove the body, at a fee of ten shillings. He takes the corpse to a field, appropriates the dead man's clothes, finds seven pounds in his pocket, buries him, and walks back through the town, crying, 'Haue yee any more Londoners to bury, hey downe a downe dery'.[64] The tinker in this tale is braver and hardier (or, depending on one's point of view, less cautious and foolhardier) than the more refined country folk, but the distinction, in this case, is to their mutual benefit.

A more fanciful tale from eighteenth-century Britain is William Thomson's *Mammuth; or, Human Nature Displayed on a Grand Scale in a Tour with the Tinkers, into the Inland Parts of Africa* (1789), a Gulliverian journey in which the author refers to the 'vagrant mode of life' adopted by his Scottish protagonist in the company of a group he alternately calls 'tinkers' and 'gypsies'.[65] Their primary occupations are fortune-telling and begging, although they sometimes make cups and spoons out of horn, and their 'wandering life on the face of the earth' makes them to some degree 'enemies to the mass of men'.[66] According to *Mammuth*, the tinkers of the British Isles meet every year at a gathering (something also suggested by Samuel Rid in *The Art of Jugling*), while the Travelling people from all over the world, who all resemble each other to some degree, get together for a meeting every fifty years – hence the journey with the tinkers to Africa. Fantastic though it may be, Thomson's tale suggests that by the end of the eighteenth century a recognition had developed that identifiable groups of Travellers or nomadic people, with distinctive characteristics and customs, existed in different parts of the world, including the British Isles – a notion that would, in the next century, lead to the theories of racial pathology advocated by the likes of Henry Mayhew.

The search for representations of tinkers in pre-Famine Irish literary texts is complicated by the nature of the Irish literature of the period. Maria Edgeworth's *Castle Rackrent*, published in 1800 but written about a decade earlier, is often referred to as the first Irish novel – that is, the first to focus entirely on Irish subject matter. Earlier Irish writers in the English language like Jonathan Swift and Laurence Sterne wrote for English publishers and English or Anglo-Irish readers, and mostly about non-Irish topics. Indeed, according to the historian J.C. Beckett, during the eighteenth century 'no Irish novelist published a novel of Irish life'.[67] It was not until the arrival of Edgeworth and Lady Morgan that Irish writers began to include Irish characters in their works who belonged to the 'lower orders', although the novels of neither of these ladies include tinker characters.

Maria Edgeworth's story 'The Limerick Gloves', however, does provide some insight into her attitude towards nomadic people such as Gypsies. Set in Hereford, and written in the wake of the Act of Union, one of the story's intentions is to convince its English readers that a United Kingdom can only flourish if the English are prepared to accept the Irish in a partnership of (near) equals. The English tanner in the story, Mr Hill, is greatly prejudiced against Mr O'Neill, the

Irish glover who has set up shop in his town, suspecting without any reason that the Irishman has stolen his dog, and is harbouring a plan to blow up Hereford Cathedral. He is confirmed in his suspicions by a fraudulent fortune-teller, whom Edgeworth describes as 'the successor to Bampfylde Moore Carew, king of the gipsies, whose life and adventures are probably in many, too many of our readers' hands'.[68] Soon, however, it is revealed that the hole underneath the cathedral had been caused by a rat rather than Mr Hill's subversive activities, and that the dog had been stolen by Bampfylde himself, since it 'used to bark at him at night so furiously that he could not commit certain petty depredations, by which, as much as by telling fortunes, he made his livelihood'.[69] The Gypsy is reprimanded by the magistrate for accusing an innocent man and causing bad feelings between two families, thereby becoming the scapegoat for Mr Hill's sins. He is put in gaol, and '[t]he whole set of gipsies decamped, upon the news of the apprehension of their monarch'.[70] The tanner and the glover of Hereford 'became, from bitter enemies, useful friends to each other; and they were convinced, by experience, that nothing could be more for their mutual advantage than to live in union'.[71] Edgeworth's tale ties the political success of the Union to its economic well-being, a contract from which the Gypsy, as a thief and a vagabond, on a par with rats, is emphatically excluded.

Mention of tinkers in works by Irish writers of the pre-nineteenth-century period, including Maria Edgeworth, takes the form of brief, metaphorical references, which also tend to be negative. Given the focus of these writers on the English market, and their reliance on English literary models, the presence of such tropes in their work need not be evidence of the presence of actual tinkers in Ireland, but might simply be the use of a rhetorical device long established in English literature. Swift's 1724 lampoon 'Prometheus', for example, subtitled 'On Wood the Patentee's Irish Half-Pence', refers to the maker of this coinage as 'the 'Squire and Tinker *Wood*'. The allusion is not merely to the tinker's metal-working skills, but also to his dishonesty: 'This Thief and Blacksmith was so bold, / He strove to steal that Chain of Gold, / Which links the Subject to the King, / And change it for a *Brazen* String.'[72] In Maria Edgeworth's 'English' novel *Belinda* (1810), the metaphor has similar overtones: to Mrs Freke's remark that she is 'not tinker-general to the world', Mr Percival responds that he is glad of it, 'for I've heard that tinkers often spoil more than they mend'.[73] Such statements suggest that the stereotypical reputation of tinkers as dishonest and unreliable purveyors of substandard metal-work was already well established in both England and Ireland long before the Famine, although they say little about the actual presence and circumstances of tinkers in Ireland at the time of writing. However, Mary Burke argues that the 'foreign' (non-Dublin) beggars Swift complains of in *A Proposal for Giving Badges to the Beggars in all the Parishes of Dublin* are in fact Travellers, because they travel *en famille* and marry young.[74] This suggests that the term 'tinker' had not yet become a generic word for Travelling people when Swift was writing, although that shift was taking place (at least in Scotland) by the time William Thompson wrote *Mammuth* some sixty years later.

If, in the early modern period, Travelling people were often covered by the umbrella term 'vagabond', the word 'tinker', conversely, was loosely applied to any metal-worker, settled or travelling. As Ní Shuinéar points out, the occupational marker 'tinker' should not be considered synonymous with the ethnic marker 'tinker', since not all those referred to as tinkers were Travelling people, and not all Travelling people (even those referred to as 'tinkers', at least after 1800) were tinsmiths.[75] Early textual references to tinkers in Ireland are rare, and two instances from the seventeenth century present very different pictures. In a description of Ireland and its people published in 1619, Thomas Gainsford wrote:

> The people are generally haters of bondage, and beyond measure proud: so that the yonger brothers, and bastards, who are as deare as the other, scorne all endeavours, but liberty and warre. The Gentlewomen stomach [resent], and in truth vilipend [despise] others, who get their living by trade, merchandice, or mechanically: yet are divers Gravers in gold and silver, called plaine tinkers, who make their challices, harpes, buttons for their sleeves, crucifixes, and such like, in estimation amongst them.[76]

Ní Shuinéar claims that the account books kept from 1672 to 1680 by a vicar in County Antrim frequently mention 'tinklars' or 'tinkers' and describe 'the annual visits of a family group to the rectory, begging food and clothing',[77] but from her citation it is unclear whether the document makes reference to any kind of occupation or trade. Gainsford's tinkers were skilled craftsmen who made objects from precious metals for the nobility and may not have travelled, whereas the Antrim tinkers appear to have followed a set route, and eked out a much more precarious living. Whether these 'tinkers' had much in common besides their designation is debatable.

'Tinker' or 'tinkler' appears to have become a generic term for Traveller in the course of the eighteenth century, and by the mid-nineteenth century the word seems to have been in general use in Ireland and Scotland for all indigenous Travellers, regardless of their occupation, although that usually included metal-work. William Chambers's account of *Exploits, Curious Anecdotes, and Sketches of the Most Remarkable Scottish Gypsies or Tinklers* (1823) nostalgically recalls a time, '[a]bout sixty years ago, when the gypsies began to be called Tinklers', when they 'asked nothing but house-room and grass for their horses' and the farmer who gave them hospitality 'could have left every chest and press about the house open, with the certainty that nothing would be missing'.[78] In the first half of the nineteenth century, the term 'tinkler' is still used in the same breath as the equally generic 'Gypsy'. A letter published as a broadside in Scotland in 1821 refers to an Irish family named Dougherty living in Glasgow as 'a wild and unruly sett of people, and I suppose a kind of travelling Gypsies, as they profess to be boiler-makers, or, as we call them, tinklers', who arrived in Lauder 'on purpose to be hired ... for the Harvest'.[79] Several Scottish historical documents of the early nineteenth century refer to all Travelling people as 'Gipsies' and list their occupations as 'muggers' or 'potters' (dealers in earthenware), 'tinkers', and 'horners' (makers of horn spoons),[80] although other sources qualify the terminology by arguing that Scottish Gypsies are 'not pure Gipsies' but have intermarried with 'other idle wandering people'.[81]

Irish texts of the same period suggest that tinkering was the primary occupation of Travellers in Ireland, although the novels by George Brittaine and William Carleton discussed hereafter also make mention of other trades and refer to the Travellers' occupational versatility. In 1835, a resident of County Longford told the Commissioners on the Condition of the Poorer Classes in Ireland that, while 'ordinary' beggars do not form a separate class of the community, 'wandering tinkers, families who always beg, do', and an informant from County Mayo stated that '[t]he wives and families accompany the tinker while he strolls about in search of work, and always beg'.[82] In the course of his work for the Ordnance Survey in Donegal in 1835, John O'Donovan encountered a tinker named MacSweeny, who claimed to be the descendant of a local nobleman, but to have been obliged 'to exchange the sword and battle-axe for the budget and the soldering (saudering) iron'.[83] MacSweeny travelled his route accompanied by his extended family. His sons were also accomplished musicians, and at the time of the encounter were temporarily employed in the house of a local sea captain. O'Donovan was less interested in documenting the tinker's current occupation than in his alleged noble heritage, but a stray remark elsewhere in his letters suggests that tinkers were a common presence in Ireland in his day, and that they also routinely traded in donkeys. Nursing a sprained ankle while waiting for the mail to arrive in Glenties, O'Donovan told his correspondent: 'I have not received the Books of Iniskeel as yet, but when I do, you will find that the sore foot will not detain me, for I will purchase an ass and sell him to a tinker at Ballyshannon.'[84] It is around the time of this letter, written in October 1835, that the tinker makes his appearance as a character in Irish literature.

TINKERS IN GEORGE BRITTAINE AND WILLIAM CARLETON

The first fully rounded tinker characters appear in Irish literature in the second quarter of the nineteenth century, when novelists develop a common interest in 'descriptive regionalism, the depiction of Irish classes and types, [and] the presentation of characteristic customs in all their unsullied picturesqueness and with all the charms of primitivism'.[85] Two examples of such works will be discussed here: George Brittaine's *Irishmen and Irishwomen* (1830), and William Carleton's *The Emigrants of Ahadarra* (1848).

George Brittaine was the protestant Rector of Kilcormack, County Wexford, whose eight novels were dedicated to showing the detrimental effects of Catholicism on the Irish peasantry. *Irishmen and Irishwomen*, first published in Dublin in 1830, is set in 'an inconsiderable village in one of the north-west counties of Ireland' called Derrynaslieve.[86] Its plot centres around the planned assassination of the local landlord, Mr Oglandby, by a committee organized by Mr Mulvaney, a 'middling farmer' (p.20), consisting of a group of farm labourers, including Connel St Leger and Wat Delahunt, and a tinker called Murtagh Cummusky. Delahunt, St Leger, and two others are to shoot Oglandby when he makes his way by coach to the estate of a neighbouring landowner. Delahunt expresses misgivings, since he knows that Oglandby's niece, Dora, to whom he is indebted for once having saved his life, will be travelling with her uncle. The others argue that death is only what the girl deserves, and that the blow will be struck 'for the glory of God, and the good of Ireland' (p.26). St Leger makes Delahunt swear on his life that he will take part in the attack.

In the event, a local teenager called Lanty is persuaded by Delahunt to prevent Dora from travelling on the day by tipping a bucket of mud over her dress as she is preparing to depart. The subsequent attack on Oglandby, moreover, goes awry when the assassins fire their guns over his head. The identity of the attackers remains unknown to the local upper echelon, although there is much speculation. As time goes by, the members of the assassination committee begin to worry that Delahunt, who had engaged Lanty to save Dora's life, will end up betraying them all. Delahunt begins to fear for his own life and takes shelter in the house of Ned Costigan, a local farmer. When Delahunt tells St Leger that he plans to emigrate, Mulvany persuades St Leger that Delahunt intends to buy his ticket to America with his informer's fee. One night, with the aid of the tinker's skills, the men imprison Costigan and Delahunt in their farm and set it on fire. Eventually the neighbours arrive to liberate them, but by then Delahunt has been shot by his former comrades while trying to escape from the flames. The tinker is killed by the rescuers, while the other conspirators are arrested.

Murtagh Cummusky, the tinker, is described as a resourceful and busy man, who travels the roads with his budget on his back. He first appears early in the story when he is hailed in the street by Costigan's servant Ileen, and scolded for not yet mending her mistress's tea-kettle. Cummusky explains he was travelling 'up the country' where the work kept him occupied (p.5). On a later occasion, he also mentions being 'up the country for the last three weeks' (p.255). Metal-work is not his only occupation, for 'to his other accomplishments ... [he] added that of a musician', with enough ability to relieve the regular blind fiddler from time to time at parties (p.60). Ileen suspects the tinker of having 'more ways nor one of turning a penny', since rumour has it that Murtagh is also 'a cliver hand at mending a gun, and firearms of that sort'. He does not deny it, but tells her off for faulting a struggling man 'for helping himself as well as he can, these hard times' (p.5).

In *Irishmen and Irishwomen*, the tinker freely consorts with the servants and labourers, although he is perceived by them as their social inferior. He is a far cry from the destitute beggars who, according to Ileen, wander the roads in large numbers, 'the oceans of poor coming to the house, that I darn't stretch out a hand to, barring six in a day' (p.199).[87] Within the assassination committee there is also a clear social hierarchy: while his co-conspirators sit around the table in the upper room of the publican's house, with the labourers at the lower end, the tinker squats on a stool 'close into the chimney-corner' (p.20). When Mrs Delahunt is entertaining acquaintances and fellow-servants in her kitchen, the tinker, who, looking for Wat Delahunt, 'had entered the house unperceived' (p.147), joins in their conversation, 'laying his budget on the dresser' (p.148). The servants welcome the tinker, make him sit at the table and feed him, but comment on his manners after he leaves:

> 'That's as pleasant company as I'd wish to sit in a room with', said Ileen, as the tinker left the house. 'I never thought that a man with so ornary a face, could be half so agreeable and lively as he is.'
>
> 'He has no more knowledge of being mannerly, in company', said Christian, with a very fastidious toss of the head, 'nor an East Indian. Did you notice how he never turned down his cup, or even put the spoon in it, when he was done; and how he ate up every bit was put before him, without leaving a small piece to shew he wasn't ravenish and half-starved?'
>
> 'Ah! How would you expect manners from a tinker', said Wat; 'where would he come by them?'
>
> 'And maybe the place he came from is not all as one as this', apologized Ileen. (p.259)

All the while, the tinker's business is to spy on Wat Delahunt for the assassination committee. Notwithstanding his ability to entertain the servants, Cummusky is generally depicted as cunning, hot-tempered, and ruthless, characteristics that are established during the first committee meeting. Impatient with St Leger for questioning their information about Oglandby's travel schedule, the tinker scolds him: 'Ah! Folly, man! ... I was told it by Will Travers, his own coachman, and I soldered one of the lamps where the top was crazy' (p.24). When some of the men object to attacking the niece, the tinker mutters 'an imprecation against cowards and informers' (p.25) and joins Mulvany in expressing contempt for the girl's life: 'and where's the spalpeen will dar to contradict it?' This annoys St Leger: 'you may fault your budget, and welcome; but it don't become you to put names on them that is your betters' (p.27). St Leger is further angered when Cummusky offers to take Wat Delahunt's place and pull the trigger himself. After Wat is persuaded to see the assassination through, the tinker upsets him, too, by suggestively referring to Dora as his 'sweetheart': '"you tinkering thief", cried Delahunt, in a rage, "if you don't stop your jibing at me, I'll brain you on the spot"' (pp.29–30). The tinker, then, is depicted as the most eager and ruthless participant in the assassination plot, but is not accepted as a full and equal member of the group.

At the end of the novel, Delahunt dies of the wound inflicted by his former comrades; they, in turn, are arrested; and Murtagh

Cummusky's death at the hands of the authorities is regretted by nobody. The protestant rector is informed of the events by one of the locals: 'As for Cummusky, the ugly tinker, he was shot by the police, right through the head, at once, and he is lying in the cow-house till the coroner comes. – Would you like to look at the shot? You never saw any thing go so fair, through and through, as it did' (p.275). The reputation of tinkers is such that one village gentleman wonders if Cummusky alone could be to blame for the night's events: '"The tinker, who I understand was shot", continued Mr. Fitzcarrol, "was like all of his trade, a great rogue; and is it not very probable that he was the whole and sole contriver of the burning, hoping to plunder securely in the confusion?"' (p.277). The final comment on Cummusky comes from Kitty, a housemaid, who explains to her mistress why she had been too upset to attend to her usual duties that morning:

> What did Barny Dilon do with me, Ma'am, the minute I came to the place, but gallopped me off to the cow-house, to look at the terrible tinker that mended the dripping-pan, and the colander, three times over, and you know they are wanting to be mended again now, Ma'am. There he was, lying stretched out on the straw. The ball went in at his cheek, and out near the top of his head, the other side. When I seen that, my heart came up into my mouth with fright, at the escape the unfortunate man had, that it didn't hit his eye, for it was within half an inch of it; and I won't recover it these twenty minutes and more, I am sure. (p.284)

Earlier in the novel, Cummusky's skills had been much in demand, and his pleasantness and versatility were commented upon. He was also credited with being able to see in the dark, and 'as well with the back of his head as the front' (p.197). The housemaid's comments on his ignominious end serve to discredit and demythologize the tinker on all fronts: for all its cunning, Murtagh's eye did not see the bullet coming, and in the end he is exposed not only as a traitor, but as an inferior craftsman to boot. George Brittaine's shifting representation of the tinker grudgingly acknowledges the rural community's dependence on the travelling craftsman, even as it exploits his outsider status to turn him into a scapegoat for society's ills.

William Carleton, born in 1794, the fourteenth child of Irish-speaking farmers, was educated in a hedge school, spent some time in the company of professional beggars, and was generally familiar with the 'lower orders' of society. Carleton converted to Protestantism, and began writing for a newspaper published by Church of Ireland clergyman Caesar Otway, whose influence manifests itself as an element of didacticism in an oeuvre that is otherwise heavily based in recollections of the stories, language and culture of his native Tyrone. Tinkers appear in his work on a number of occasions. 'The Midnight Mass', a story dating from the early 1830s, merely contains a fairly conventional reference to the inferior quality of tinkers' work: one character accuses another of being 'the very tinker of good manners – bekase for one dacency you'd mend, you'd spoil twenty'.[88] In *The Lough Derg Pilgrim* (1828), however, Carleton introduces a female character who is subsequently identified as a tinker, with all the negative characteristics suggested by the previous citation. While on his way to Station Island, the narrator of the story is taken in by an old woman who strikes him as sensible, intelligent and pious, and who lends him a hat and coat against the inclement weather, which she produces from 'a large pocket by her side (such as tinkers wore)'(p.804).[89] On the return journey from the island, she promises to look out for the narrator while he sleeps, but when he wakes up, his good clothes and his money are gone, along with the old lady. A priest tells him he has been duped by Nell McCollum, 'the most notorious shuler in the province – a gipsy, a fortune-teller, and a tinker's widow' (p.818).

Like Brittaine, Carleton makes a clear distinction between tinkers and beggars, even as there are also gradations within the community of mendicants. 'The Midnight Mass' suggests that the 'known beggar' differs 'so strikingly from the common crowd of beggars as to constitute a distinct species', which 'goes his own rounds, and has his own walk, always adapts his character to that of his benefactor', and knows how to flatter him successfully (p.859). The character of Darby More in the story, who is such a known beggar, also cures various ailments with charms and by rubbing the afflicted part, and makes money 'by a knack which he possessed of tatooing into the naked breast the representation of Christ upon the cross' (p.860). In *The Emigrants of Ahadarra* (1848), Peety Dhu walks the roads with his young daughter Nanny, depending on 'the large heart an' lavish hand' of his benefactors whose kitchen he frequents: 'Peety, who was well known and a great favorite on his rounds, received a warm and hospitable welcome from Jemmy Burke, who made him and the girl sit upon the hob, and immediately ordered them breakfast' (p.494). Even if they make money by other means than begging, known beggars like Darby and Peety are distinct from tinkers, whose primary occupation is metal-work, and whose sense of independence from the community endows them with a less favourable reputation than the known mendicants, whose business it is to ingratiate themselves with the patrons on whom they depend for a living.

Like George Brittaine's *Irishmen and Irishwomen*, Carleton's novel *The Emigrants of Ahadarra* is a story of betrayal, in which the tinkers play a pivotal role. Hyacinthus Burke, known as Hycy, a profligate farmer's son, has designs on his neighbour Bryan M'Mahon's land, as well as on his fiancée Kathleen Cavanagh. He sets out to ruin M'Mahon by having the tinkers build an illicit still on his property, a ruse financed with money stolen from his own father with the aid of the same tinkers. When the still is discovered, Bryan defends himself against accusations that he has broken the law, saying, 'I know nothing about this business, except that three ruffianly looking fellows named Hogan, common tinkers, and common vagabonds to boot – men that are my enemies – are the persons by all accounts who set up the still on my property' (p.576). Unable to prove that he did not employ the tinkers, Bryan remains a suspect who faces ruin and forced emigration. His name is only cleared when Nanny Peety is able to prove that Hycy Burke engaged the tinkers, stole his father's money with their help, and was the brains behind the plan to ruin Bryan. The honest 'known beggar' is thus the downfall of the 'ruffianly' tinkers.

Whereas in Brittaine's *Irishmen and Irishwomen* the tinker is a solitary traveller with no known family, the tinkers in Carleton's *The Emigrants of Ahadarra* are a group of extended relatives living in the grain kiln of the Cavanagh family, to whom they have a loyalty going back at least a generation. Jemmy Burke explains about the Cavanaghs:

> '... as to havin' the Hogans about them – they wor always about them; it was the same in their father's time. I remember ould Laghlin Hogan, an' his whole clanjamfrey, men an' women, young an' old, wor near six months out o' the year about ould Gerald Cavanagh's – the present man's father. ... At any rate, whatever bad qualities the vagabonds have, want of gratitude isn't among them'. (p.507)

The schoolmaster once entered the kiln and observed how the tinkers lived there:

> The place was nearly waste, and had a very desolate look. Scattered around, and littered upon shake-down beds of straw, some half dozen young besmutted savages, male and female, lay stretched in all posi-

> tions, some north, others south, without order or decency, but all seeming in that barbarous luxury which denotes strong animal health and an utter disregard of cleanliness and bodily comfort. (p.529)[90]

The tinkers travel around, but always return to this place, as Kate (Bat Hogan's wife) reminds her brother-in-law Philip: 'Wherever we went over the province, this you know was our headquarters. Here's where all belonging to us ... rests, an' I'd not like to go far from it' (p.553).

The tinkers' main occupation is metal-work, although the objects in their 'headquarters' indicate that they also work as 'horners' and menders of broken dishes: 'Over in one of the corners lay three or four budgets, old iron skillets, hammers, lumps of melted lead, broken pots, a quantity of cows' horns for spoons, wooden dishes that required clasping, old kettles that wanted repair' (p.529). In addition, Kate Hogan is not above stealing the odd goose from 'some neighboring farmer' to provide supper for her tribe (p.511). The Hogans are first seen in the Burke household, 'very busily engaged in soldering, clasping, and otherwise repairing certain vessels belonging to that ... establishment' (p.505). Tinkers' work, however, does not have a very high reputation; the schoolmaster – admittedly a pompous man – tells Philip Hogan: 'You stand in the same degraded ratio to a tradesman that a rascally quack does to a regular surgeon', being only 'a rascally sotherer of ould skillets and other anonymous utensils' who deserves no respect (p.528). As it is, however, the Hogans make an excellent working still for Hycy Burke; the narrator explains that the three 'most unadulterated ruffians ..., notwithstanding their savage brutality ... were each and all possessed of a genius for mechanical inventions and manual dexterity that was perfectly astonishing when the low character of their moral and intellectual standard is considered' (p.608). They use these skills for even less legitimate purposes, for in the end, their complicity in the betrayal of Bryan M'Mahon is hard to prove, but 'new charges of uttering base coin came thick and strong against them', so that justice can be served: 'instead of Bryan M'Mahon, it was they themselves that became "the Emigrants of Ahadarra" at the king's expense' (p.636).

Like many later writers, Carleton makes much of the physical characteristics of the tinkers, particularly their eyes. Kate Hogan is described as 'tall, lank, but powerful', with 'black piercing eyes' (pp.511; 517).[91] Philip Hogan, the tinkers' leader, has great strength and insolence, and is accompanied everywhere by a fierce bull-dog. His brother is described as 'a tall, smut-faced, truculent-looking young fellow, with two piercing eyes and a pair of grim brows' (p.509). The tinkers' brutality finds its most direct expression within their own circle. When the reader is first introduced to Kate, she is sporting a black eye, her husband's handiwork, but, she asks, 'who has a betther right?' (p.512). Kate is married to Bat Hogan; the other two brothers are widowers, 'owing, it was generally believed, to the brutal treatment which their unfortunate wives received at their hands' (p.553). Indeed, Kate accuses Philip of having murdered 'two wives' (p.579). The tinkers are heavy drinkers, and when Kate gets into an argument with Philip and he threatens her, she grabs him by the throat; in the ensuing struggle, she nearly kills him, until her husband feels compelled to intervene.

> Kate, however, heard him not, but still tugged and stuck to the throat of Philip's quivering carcass, until by a united effort they at length disentangled her iron clutches from it, upon which she struggled and howled like a beast of prey, and attempted with a strength that seemed more akin to the emotion of a devil than that of a women to get at him again and again, in order to complete her work. (p.579)

At a later time, Philip threatens to give Kate 'a clink wid one o' these sotherin'-irons', whereupon she shows him a large knife hanging from her belt, which she threatens to have soon 'greased in your puddins' (p.609).

While Carleton makes the Hogan brothers savage beyond salvation, he eventually allows Kate's feminine qualities to get the better of her more brutal characteristics:

> What an insoluble enigma is woman! ... In truth this fierce and furious woman who was at once a thief, a liar, a drunkard, and an impostor, hardened in wickedness and deceit, had in spite of all this a heart capable of virtuous aspirations, and of loving what was excellent and good. ... and, indeed, it is difficult to meet a woman in whose disposition, however corrupted by evil society, and degraded by vice, there is not to be found a portion of the angelic essence still remaining. In the case before us, however, this may be easily accounted for. Kate Hogan, though a hell-cat and devil, when provoked, was, amidst all her hardened violence and general disregard of truth and honesty, a virtuous woman and a faithful wife. Hence her natural regard for much that was good and pure, and her strong sympathy with the sorrow which now fell upon Kathleen Cavanagh. (p.580)

Kate is instrumental in persuading Nanny Peety to speak to the authorities, not just about the involvement of the Hogans, but also that of Hycy Burke: 'she must either state the *whole* truth or nothing, that is what I want, an' what she *must* do – put the saddle on the right horse, Nanny – since you *will* spake' (p.631). Thanks to the tinker woman and the beggar girl, the criminals are exposed and punished, and Bryan M'Mahon and Kathleen Cavanagh are married. They 'took Nanny Peety into their service; and ... Kate Hogan ... had always a comfortable seat at their hospitable hearth' (p.639).

The tinker characters in these texts published in the decades up to the Famine share a number of characteristics that reveal how Travellers were regarded by the sedentary population. They are not beggars, nor are they perceived as such by settled characters. They have a recognized function in the rural community where they fulfil a need by mending pots, kettles and crockery. Their status is somewhat below that of domestic servants and farm labourers, with whom they have regular dealings and social contact. The tinkers in both Brittaine and Carleton are predominantly makers and menders of pots and kettles, but they are shown to be versatile and to turn their hand to other occupations. Such alternative ways of surviving 'these hard times' are not always legal or approved of by the surrounding community: Ileen frowns upon Murtagh's gun-repairing activities, Kate is not above petty theft, and the Hogans are deported for forging coins.

While the tinker in *Irishmen and Irishwomen* travels his regular route by himself, the Hogans in *The Emigrants of Ahadarra* live in an extended family group comprising men and women. They also travel within the county, but always return to Ahadarra, where they have a traditional connection to one of the local farmers. It is possible that this difference represents an older distinction between different types of Travellers in Ireland. In her account of Dutch Travellers, Cottaar mentions that, while Dutch *Reizigers* often travelled in family groups after the middle of the nineteenth century, travelling tinkers (menders of kettles) in earlier times usually travelled alone.[92] Writing about the situation in nineteenth-century England, Mayall also distinguishes between males who travelled alone and often slept in barns and sheds, and families who travelled as a group, and who were more likely to stay in tents or caravans.[93] Such a distinction probably also existed in Ireland at one time, and may account for historical discrepancies that are otherwise difficult to account for (such as the clear difference between the 'plain tinkers' in Thomas Gainsford's account of 1619 and the 'tinklars' mentioned by the Antrim rector some sixty years later).

The tinkers in Brittaine and Carleton are engaged by settled persons to aid them in their unlawful enterprises; they may be willing accomplices, but they do not initiate the violent or devious practices in which they become tangentially involved. At the same time, they are consistently depicted as more blatantly violent, blasphemous and immoral than their settled employers, even though it is the latter who organize the criminal events depicted in the novels. This double standard is also revealed in the ambiguity with which the tinkers' trade is represented: while the illegal schemes depend for their success on the acknowledged skill and craftsmanship of the tinkers, that craftsmanship is simultaneously called into question by derogatory remarks made by other settled characters about the quality of the work. Moreover, even though the tinkers are only accomplices, they are dealt with harshly and definitively by the settled community: Cummisky is shot dead, the Hogans are deported, and nobody is sorry to see them gone. They are made to carry a disproportionate part of the blame, and would be made to shoulder the whole burden if settled society could get away with it.

Both plots, moreover, revolve around the possession of land. Oglandby, the target of the assassination in Brittaine's novel, is a local landlord, while Carleton's novel centres on Hycy Burke's attempt to appropriate Bryan M'Mahon's land. Although neither novel emphasizes the contrast between land ownership and the unsettled way of life of the tinkers, unease about one of the essential characteristics of the Travellers may nevertheless underlie the prominence given to the tinker characters in these particular plot configurations. Such unease may also lie at the root of William Carleton's treatment of Kate Hogan and Nanny Peety in *The Emigrants of Ahadarra*, which suggests the beginnings of a notion that 'rehabilitation' of the tinkers is desirable, and should begin with those members of the Travelling community considered most amenable to being domesticated: women. In this regard Carleton's work echoes the moralizing discourse of the Protestant tract societies with which he was unquestionably familiar, whose didactic tales were aimed at instilling in the lower classes the virtues of cleanliness, godliness and hard work in an occupation suited to their ordained station in life.

In the decades when Brittaine and Carleton were writing their novels, a movement for the settlement and rehabilitation of Travelling people already existed in Scotland.[94] The 'Committee for the Reformation of the Gipsies in Scotland' was formed in 1838, and argued that nomadism itself was a cause of immoral behaviour:

> So long as these Gipsies continue to wander about, no good can be done for them. ... If improvement is to be effected upon the Gipsy, his unsettled wandering life must be discontinued – he must cease to live as a savage – he must be civilised, educated, learn to stay at home and adopt the quiet, settled, industrious, and useful, though more commonplace life, of those around him.[95]

Fictional accounts of the period, such as Diana Mulock's *Two Little Tinkers* (1876), in which two charitable Scottish ladies 'save' a pair of young Traveller girls from 'the roughest, wildest, most wandering of lives',[96] reflect these sentiments. Although initially 'as uncivilised as Red Indians or Australian Bushmen',[97] and 'as ignorant of any of the restraints of civilised life as beasts of the field',[98] both girls are eventually taught the value of hard work, neatness and Christian observance in an Industrial School: 'Here was a place of safety, a place to learn in, where the two little tinkers might grow up to be decent and useful members of society after all.'[99]

In Scotland, the motivation behind this endeavour at the time was primarily religious, and its execution fell to evangelist missionaries; the concept of Traveller 'civilization', however, would later reappear in Catholic Ireland as part of the social and political trend to settle the Travellers, but in a different and secular context. When the Scottish tract was written, Ireland was about to experience the Famine, which would add hundreds of thousands of destitute people to an already impoverished population. Partly for that reason, the incipient notion of the rehabilitation of Travellers discernible in Carleton did not make it onto the social agenda in Ireland in his day, but it resurfaced with a vengeance a century later, at a time when the country was in the process of fashioning a modern image for itself that could not accommodate the Travellers' nomadic mode of existence. The endeavour would give prominence to the theory that the Famine had been directly to blame for creating the Travellers' way of life.

NOTES

1. Hayes, *Irish Travellers*, p.9.
2. Jane Helleiner, *Irish Travellers: Racism and the Politics of Culture* (Toronto: University of Toronto Press, 2000), p.30.
3. Quoted in Hayes, *Irish Travellers*, p.12.
4. Sinéad Ní Shuinéar, 'Apocrypha to Canon: Inventing Irish Traveller History', *History Ireland*, 12, 4 (2004). Accessed 14 July 2005: http://www.historyireland.com/magazine/features/12.4FeatA.html
5. Sinéad Ní Shuinéar, 'Irish Travellers, Ethnicity and the Origins Question', in McCann *et al.*, *Irish Travellers*, pp.70–1.

6. Dymphna McLoughlin, 'Ethnicity and Irish Travellers: Reflections on Ní Shuinéar', in McCann *et al.*, *Irish Travellers*, p.90.
7. Dorothy Wordsworth, *Journals of Dorothy Wordsworth: The Alfoxden Journal 1798; The Grasmere Journals 1800–1803*, ed. Mary Moorman (Oxford: Oxford University Press, 1971), p.26.
8. Pecker Dunne, *Parley-Poet and Chanter: Pecker Dunne*, transcr. and ed. Mícheál Ó hAodha (Dublin: A. and A. Farmar, 2004), p.3.
9. Ibid., p.13. Dunne notes that the inspiration for his song 'Sullivan's John' came from the marriage of Johnny Sullivan, a farm boy, and a Travelling girl. Sullivan joined the Travellers and started a tarmacking and trucking business in England. Dunne's explanation that '[i]n the song he doesn't adapt to the Travelling life because he is a settled person. But in reality he became a very successful businessman' (p.99) suggests that the Travellers' view of the incompatibility of Travellers and settled people may in part be a romanticization of their own uniqueness.
10. Sharon Gmelch, *Nan: The Life of an Irish Travelling Woman* (New York and London: W.W. Norton, 1986), p.30. All subsequent page references in the text are to this edition.
11. See Annemarie Cottaar, Leo Lucassen and Wim Willems, *Mensen van de reis: woonwagenbewoners en zigeuners in Nederland (1868–1995)* ['Travelling people: caravan-dwellers and Gypsies in the Netherlands, 1868–1995'] (Zwolle: Waanders, 1995), passim.
12. Michael H. Crawford, 'Genetic Affinities and Origin of the Irish Tinkers', in Elizabeth S. Watts, Francis E. Johnston and Gabriel W. Lasker (eds), *Biosocial Interrelations in Popular Adaptation* (The Hague and Paris: Mouton, 1975), p.101.
13. Kari E. North, Lisa J. Martin and Michael H. Crawford, 'The Origins of the Irish Travellers and the Genetic Structure of Ireland', *Annals of Human Biology*, 27, 5 (2000), p.463.
14. Ibid.
15. For example, the 'ragman' mentioned by 'Rose' in her dialogue with 'Nancy' in Mary Leadbeater's *Cottage Dialogues: Among the Irish Peasantry* (Philadelphia: Johnson and Warner, 1811), may be a Traveller: 'That is my rag bag. I put all the parings of my work, and all the rags that are good for nothing into it; and then when Thady the ragman comes, he gives me pins and needles for them, so that I never want to buy any' (p.180).
16. Quoted in P.J. Leese, B. Piatek, and I. Curyllo-Klag (eds), *The British Migrant Experience, 1700-2000: An Anthology* (London: Palgrave Macmillan, 2003), p.43.
17. Davie Stewart, interview with Alan Lomax, sound recording. *Davie Stewart: Go On, Sing Another Song*. Alan Lomax Collection: Portrait Series (Rounder CD1833, 2000).
18. William Cauley, *The Candlelight Painter: The Life and Work of William Cauley, Traveller, Painter and Poet*, transcr. and ed. Mícheál Ó hAodha (Dublin: A. and A. Farmar, 2004), pp.89–90.
19. Dunne, *Parley-Poet*, p.54.
20. Ní Shuinéar, 'Irish Travellers', p.72.
21. Dunne, *Parley-Poet*, p.58. Andrew McCormick recorded varieties of Travellers' Cant from the different districts of Scotland in *The Tinkler-Gypsies* (1906). A.T. Sinclair found evidence of 'a secret language spoken only by stone-masons' among 'old Irish masons' in the United States at the turn of the twentieth century. See 'The Secret Language of Masons and Tinkers', *Journal of American Folklore*, 22, 86 (1909), p.354.
22. Dunne, *Parley-Poet*, p.51.
23. Ibid., p.52.
24. Ní Shuinéar, 'Irish Travellers', p.58.
25. Bargoens – probably a corruption of 'Bourgondisch' ('Burgundian') – was first recorded in the early sixteenth century, and was used by groups outside of mainstream society, including beggars, pedlars and tinkers, in much the same way 'pedlars' French' was used in England during the same period.
26. See Dónall Ó Baoill, 'Travellers' Cant – Language or Register?', in McCann *et al.*, *Irish Travellers*, pp.155–69.
27. Alice Binchy, 'Shelta: Historical and Sociolinguistic Aspects', in Ciara Breathnach and Aoife Bhreatnach (eds), *Portraying Irish Travellers* (Newcastle: Cambridge Scholars Press, 2006), pp.105–15.
28. In a comparative instance, Ian Hancock's research into Roma origins suggests that, since the Roms' metal-working vocabulary is entirely derived from Greek, it must have been acquired after their arrival in Constantinople in the twelfth century.

29. Hayes, *Irish Travellers*, p.55.
30. Quoted in R.A. Stewart Macalister, *The Secret Languages of Ireland* (Cambridge: Cambridge University Press, 1937), p.xii.
31. Ibid., p.163.
32. Binchy, 'Shelta', p.110.
33. Leo Lucassen, 'Eternal Vagrants? State Formation, Migration and Travelling Groups in Western-Europe, 1350–1914', in Jan Lucassen and Leo Lucassen (eds), *Migration, Migration History, History: Old Paradigms and New Perspectives* (Bern: Peter Lang, 1997), p.228.
34. Quoted in Hayes, *Irish Travellers*, p.140.
35. Thomas Harman, *A Caveat for Common Cursitors*, in Gāmini Salgādo (ed.), *Cony-Catchers and Bawdy Baskets: An Anthology of Elizabethan Low Life* (Harmondsworth: Penguin, 1972), p.146.
36. A.L. Beier, *Masterless Men: The Vagrancy Problem in England 1560–1640* (London and New York: Methuen, 1985), p.64.
37. Ibid., p.62.
38. Seán MacGrath, 'The Tinkers of Ireland' I, *Irish Times*, 15 November 1955, p.5.
39. Robert Jütte, *Poverty and Deviance in Early Modern Europe* (Cambridge: Cambridge University Press, 1994), p.146.
40. Ibid., p.185.
41. Ibid., p.146.
42. Harman, *Caveat*, p.120.
43. Ibid., p.121.
44. Samuel Rid, *The Art of Jugling or Legerdemaine* (London: Samuel Rand, 1612), p.2.
45. Ibid., p.3.
46. Henry Morley (ed.), *Character Writings of the Seventeenth Century* (London: Routledge, 1891), p.54.
47. Beier, *Masterless Men*, p.90.
48. The wives of Dutch travelling chair-menders and knife-grinders hawked around the farms carrying baskets of thread, ribbon, pins, needles, laces, soap, shoe polish, etc. (Cottaar *et al.*, *Mensen van de reis*, p.95). Nan Donohoe's father worked as a chimney sweep, while 'Nan walked to the neighboring cottages and farms with her mother who carried scrubbing brushes, lace, needles, boot polish, and camphor balls in a basket over her arm. These she sold or bartered for potatoes, turnips, eggs, bacon, homemade bread and butter, and even flour, sugar, and salt' (Gmelch, *Nan*, pp.33–4). A recollection by Bridget Gilhooley of Carricknagava, County Armagh, was recorded by the Irish Folklore Commission in 1937/38: 'A woman would come from Newtown. They would have a donkey and a cart and she would be selling little things. She would collect some potatoes or milk and her husband was a tin-smith who would mend kettles, pots and pans. She would take them away with her and take them back mended.' Brian Sherry, Raymond McHugh, and Brian O'Flaitheartaigh (eds), *Along the Black Pig's Dyke: Folklore from Monaghan and South Armagh* (Castleblayney: Castleblayney Community Enterprise, 1993), pp.223–4.
49. John Awdeley, *The Fraternity of Vagabonds*, in Salgādo, *Cony-Catchers*, p.65.
50. Quoted in Leese *et al.*, *The British Migrant Experience*, p.82.
51. Beier, *Masterless Men*, pp.90–1.
52. See Henry Mayhew, 'Of the Street-Irish', in *London Labour and the London Poor*, vol. 1 (1851; New York: Dover Publications, 1968), pp.104–20.
53. Morley, *Character Writings*, p.54.
54. Harman, *Caveat*, p.145.
55. Ibid., pp.104–5.
56. Ibid., p.104.
57. Morley, *Character Writings*, p.65.
58. Patricia Fumerton, *Unsettled: The Culture of Mobility and the Working Poor in Early Modern England* (Chicago and London: University of Chicago Press, 2006), p.35.
59. Mark Netzloff, '"Counterfeit Egyptians" and Imagined Borders: Jonson's *The Gypsies Metamorphosed*', *ELH*, 68, 4 (2001), p.771.
60. Ibid., p.773.
61. Ibid., p.778.
62. Mayhew, *London Labour*, p.2.

63. Ibid., pp.2–3.
64. Thomas Dekker, 'The Wonderfull Yeare. 1603', ed. R.S. Bear. Renascence Editions. Accessed 10 October 2005: http://darkwing.uoregon.edu/~rbear/yeare.html
65. William Thomson, *Mammuth; or, Human Nature Displayed on a Grand Scale in a Tour with the Tinkers, into the Inland Parts of Africa* (1789), in Jeanne K. Welcher and George E. Bush, Jr. (intro.), *Gulliveriana*, 4 (Delmar, NY: Scholars' Facsimiles & Reprints, 1973), p.253.
66. Ibid., p.239.
67. Quoted in James M. Cahalan, *The Irish Novel: A Critical History* (Boston, MA: Twayne, 1988), p.8.
68. Maria Edgeworth, 'The Limerick Gloves', in *Popular Tales* (Paris: Baudry, A. and W. Galignani, Bobée and Hingray, 1827), p.185. The son of an English clergyman, Bampfylde Moore Carew (1693–1759) was a rogue and vagabond who claimed to be 'King of the Beggars'. His biography, *The Life and Adventures of Bampfylde Moore Carew* (1745), probably written by Robert Goadby but based on his own account, was a bestseller and was reprinted in numerous editions.
69. Ibid., p.199.
70. Ibid. A footnote in the text suggests that this part of the story was based on the actual case, cited in Colquhoun's *On the Police of the Metropolis*, of a man who was deceived by an astrologer in Shoreditch, London. Edgeworth quotes Colquhoun: '"The magistrate settled the matter by discharging the prisoner, reprimanding the accuser severely, and ordering the conjurer to be taken into custody, according to law, as a rogue and a vagabond"' (p.194 n.1).
71. Ibid., p.206.
72. Jonathan Swift, 'Prometheus', in Joseph Horrell (ed.), *Collected Poems of Jonathan Swift* (Cambridge, MA: Harvard University Press, 1958), vol.2, pp.518–19.
73. Maria Edgeworth, *Belinda* (1810; Oxford: Oxford University Press, 1999), p.224.
74. Mary Burke, '*Hidden Like a Religious Arcanum*: Irish Writing and Shelta's Secret History', in Kirk and Ó Baoill, *Travellers and Their Language*, p.80.
75. Ní Shuinéar, 'Irish Travellers', p.64.
76. Thomas Gainsford, *The Glory of England* (London: Edward Griffin, 1619), pp.148–9.
77. Ní Shuinéar, 'Irish Travellers', p.64.
78. William Chambers, *Exploits, Curious Anecdotes, and Sketches of the Most Remarkable Scottish Gypsies or Tinklers Together with Traits of Their Origin, Character, and Manners* (Edinburgh: William Chambers, 1823), p.15.
79. 'Outrage by Irish Shearers', broadside (1821), National Library of Scotland. Accessed 26 August 2006: http://www.nls.uk/broadsides/broadside.cfm/id/15300/transcript/1
80. Rev. John Baird, *The Scottish Gipsy's Advocate: Being a Short Account of the Gipsies of Kirk-Yetholm, etc.* (Edinburgh: John Lindsay and Co., 1839), p.12.
81. Committee for the Reformation of Gipsies in Scotland, *First Report of the Committee for the Reformation of the Gipsies in Scotland* (Edinburgh: Thomas Constable, 1840), p.30.
82. Quoted in Sharon Gmelch, *Tinkers and Travellers* (Dublin: O'Brien Press, 1975), p.10.
83. John O'Donovan, *Ordnance Survey Letters: Donegal*, ed. Michael Herity (Dublin: Four Masters Press, 2000), p.26.
84. Ibid., p.94.
85. Patrick Rafroidi, *Irish Literature in English: The Romantic Period (1789–1850)* (Gerrards Cross: Colin Smythe, 1980), vol. 1, p.122.
86. George Brittaine, *Irishmen and Irishwomen* (1830; Dublin: Richard Moore Tims, 1831), p.1. All subsequent page references in the text are to this edition.
87. In 1834 the Royal Commission on the Poor Laws 'estimated that there were 2,385,000 beggars (including dependents) on the roads of Ireland at least part of the year' (Gmelch, *Tinkers and Travellers*, p.10).
88. William Carleton, *The Works of William Carleton* (1881; Freeport, NY: Books for Libraries Press, 1970), vol. 2, p.872. All subsequent page references to Carleton's works in the text are to this edition.
89. The traditional 'beady pocket', decorated with buttons, holy medals and the like, was tied around the waist and worn underneath the apron or skirt. It was used to hold small items (a comb, needle and thread, etc.).
90. The 'strong animal health' of the Irish tinkers was also noted by English writer George Borrow during his travels in Wales in 1854, recorded in *Wild Wales: Its People, Language and Scenery* (1862; London: John Murray, 1923):

> As I was standing in the middle of one of the business streets [of Bangor] I suddenly heard a loud and dissonant gabbling, and glancing around beheld a number of wild-looking people, male and female. Wild looked the men, yet wilder the women. The men were very lightly clad, and were all barefooted and bareheaded; they carried sticks in their hands. The women were barefooted too, but had for the most part head-dresses; their garments consisted of blue cloaks and striped gingham gowns. All the females had common tin articles in their hands which they offered for sale with violent gestures to the people in the streets, as they walked along, occasionally darting into the shops, from which, however, they were almost invariably speedily ejected by the startled proprietors, with looks of disgust and almost horror. Two ragged, red-haired lads led a gaunt pony, drawing a creaking cart, stored with the same kind of articles of tin, which the women bore. Poorly clad, dusty and soiled as they were, they all walked with a free, independent, and almost graceful carriage. ... I thought that in many respects they were fine specimens of humanity. (pp.188–9)

91. The reference to the 'black, piercing eyes' of tinkers is a recurring one in Irish texts. Sinéad Ní Shuinéar ('Irish Travellers', p.64) mentions a reference to 'tinklars' in the account books of a late-seventeenth-century vicar from County Antrim, in which the women are described 'as being strikingly distinct from the general population, with very dark hair and eyes and brightly coloured plaid skirts'. Many other texts describe the 'tinkers' as having striking red hair.
92. Cottaar *et al.*, *Mensen van de reis*, p.14.
93. David Mayall, *Gypsy-Travellers in Nineteenth-Century Society* (Cambridge: Cambridge University Press, 1988), p.25.
94. The movement to 'reform' Gypsies dated from 1780, when the hanging of a number of young Gypsies in Northampton led to the realization that persecution was no way to solve the perceived Gypsy 'problem' (ibid., p.97).
95. Committee for the Reformation of Gipsies, *First Report*, p.7.
96. Diana Maria Mulock (Mrs Craik), *Two Little Tinkers: A Simple Story*, in *The Laurel Bush* and *The Two Tinkers* [*sic*] (Leipzig: Tauchnitz, 1876), p.242.
97. Ibid., p.242.
98. Ibid., p.255.
99. Ibid., p.286.

CHAPTER 2

Alternative States: The Literary Revival

Ae day, upon the border bent,
The tinkers pitched their gipsy tent,
An' auld an' young, wi' ae consent,
Resolved to have a weddin' O.
'The Tinker's Wedding', traditional ballad

The second half of the nineteenth century was not a period in which Irish literature flourished; indeed, it was 'in many ways the bleakest of all for the Irish novel'.[1] The tinkers, who had made a tentative appearance as characters in the literature of the 1830s and 1840s, are not much of a literary presence in the second half of the nineteenth century, and only re-emerge – albeit with a vengeance – at the turn of the twentieth. In large part their renewed invisibility was a consequence of the unsettling effect, literally as well as figuratively, of the Famine on Irish society. Jim MacLaughlin argues that one reason 'why it is so difficult to clearly distinguish between the "settled" population and "Travellers" in nineteenth- and early twentieth-century Ireland is because large sections of the so-called "settled" population were extremely mobile'.[2] Emigration was widespread, and seasonal migration to the harvests of England and Scotland was a common way for sons and daughters from the poorer regions to supplement their family's income. In the eyes of more affluent farmers and town dwellers, the poverty and survival strategies of such migrant workers 'tended to identify them with, rather than distinguish them from, "tinkers" who similarly looked on the "travelling life" as a strategy for survival'.[3]

Tinkers once more made a distinctive appearance as literary characters at the end of the nineteenth century, when the landless and mobile population decreased, and 'the proportion of middle and larger farmers was greatly increased', in part due to the land legislation of the early 1880s, resulting in 'a general if uneven process of "rural embourgeoisement" throughout the island'.[4] The new emphasis on land and property may have contributed to an increasing suspicion among settled people of the mobility of the tinkers, whose population, reduced in the aftermath of the Famine, may also have increased to the point of greater visibility by the final decades of the nineteenth century. John Sampson claimed in 1890 that the tinkers were at that time 'uniquely "tabooed and dreaded"',[5] but Jane Barlow suggests in one of the 'idylls' in her collection *Strangers at Lisconnel* (1895) that the unfavourable reputation the tinkers have 'begun to develop'[6] is a relatively recent phenomenon.

The 'tinkers' who are the focus of Barlow's story are, in fact, dispossessed settled people, who are not on the road by choice. Thady and Judy Quinlan make their camp in 'the driest end of ... [an] un-roofed cabin' (p.51), but their father had at one time 'kept a little shop in Bantry, before he was stone broke one bad year and took to carrying the remnant of his stock-in-trade about in a basket as a higgler, which eventually led other members of his family to wander, less reputably, for their livelihoods' (p.53). When Thady passes through Lisconnel and steals the heavy blue cloak that is Mrs Kilfoyle's prized possession, he confirms the villagers in their bad opinion of the tinkers:

> Their very name has become a term of reproach among us, so that 'an ould tinker' is recognised as an appropriate epithet for any troublesome beast or disagreeable neighbour. ... The approach of the two queer vehicles in which they now generally travel is watched by displeased eyes all over our country-side, and they are so to speak lighted on their way by the gleam of suspicious or resentful glances. And it must be admitted that their evil reputation has not been bestowed upon them gratuitously. (p.28)

Barlow's narrator later qualifies the claim that the tinkers deserve their negative reputation by admitting that 'there are tinkers and tinkers', and that 'some few' are indeed honest and harmless enough (p.47).

Barlow further qualifies the 'evil reputation' of the tinkers by making them part of the Irish national narrative, suggesting that, while they may generally be villains, they are at least *native* villains. The

Lisconnel police, on the other hand, who, in the eyes of the villagers, 'belonged completely to the category of pitaty-blights, rint-warnin's, fevers, and the like devastations of life', receive no assistance from them in looking for the thieving tinker, for that would have been 'a condoning of great permanent wrongs for the sake of a trivial temporary convenience' (pp.40–1). Moreover, Barlow's narrator reflects that the 'pickings and stealings' of the tinkers 'have at worst never been so serious a matter as those of another flock, finer of feather, but not less predacious in their habits, who roosted, for the most part, a long way off, and made their collections by deputy' (p.47). In any case, the narrative goes on to reveal that Thady's motives for stealing the cloak were entirely altruistic, since the garment was intended to save his sister Jane from perishing in the bone-chilling cold. The theft of the big cloak, indeed, to some extent makes up for past evictions since, according to Jane, 'it's as good as a little house of your own' (p.59). However, the fact that the heavy cloak eventually drags her down to her death when she is caught in a flash flood serves as a warning that 'predacious habits' never pay, whether one is an absentee landlord or a tinker.

Writing around the same time as Barlow, but from the perspective of the declining Anglo-Irish Ascendancy rather than rural villagers, Edith Somerville and Martin Ross depict the tinkers as a more seductive but also more insidiously corrupting presence. In 'The Tinker's Dog', one of the sketches collected in *All on the Irish Shore* (1903), the duo ironically describe the Traveller in question, Willy Fennessy, as 'a very good-looking young man, almost apostolic in type, with a golden red aureole of hair and beard and candid blue eyes'.[7] Mrs Alexander and her son Freddy, the Anglo-Irish owners of the Craffroe estate, fall under 'the fatal spell of the fascinating tinker' (p.10), who persuades them that he has been 'goin' the roads' for only three months: 'Indeed, me lady, I think the time too long that I'm with these blagyard thravellers' (p.9). Employed as an estate hand, Fennessy soon makes himself indispensable, and '[s]ave for the incessant demands upon his skill in the matter of solder and stitches, his recent tinkerhood was politely ignored, or treated as an escapade excusable in a youth of spirit' (p.11). 'Tinkerhood', then, is here again constructed almost entirely in terms of reputation and not occupation. Fennessy's ineradicable past, however, literally begins to haunt the Big House, in the 'spectral' form of the dog the tinker claimed to have disposed of; one afternoon, the elusive animal reveals itself and leads Mrs Alexander from her unusually deserted Big House to the

Craffroe gate lodge, where the outraged lady discovers her servants, including her English cook, carousing with the tinker: 'Was that the immaculate Barnet seated at the head of a crowded table, in her – Mrs Alexander's – very best bonnet and velvet cape, with a glass of steaming potheen punch in her hand, and Willy Fennessy's arm around her waist?' (p.29). Barnet, now Mrs Fennessy, ends up paying 'the fines inflicted upon her husband for potheen-making and selling drink in the Craffroe gate lodge without a licence' before taking him away to America (p.30). Upon his subsequent return to Ireland, Fennessy sets himself up as a publican and smallholder, the latest instalments in a 'varied career' not 'bound by convention', as the narrator euphemistically phrases it (p.81). The narratives by both Barlow and Somerville and Ross, while constructing the tinkers as a bad influence on settled society, also show them as fluidly related to that society, in a discourse of eviction, dispossession, migration and reintegration. The writers of the Revival moved that discourse in a radically different direction.

THE TIME OF THE TINKERS

If Somerville and Ross's warning against the 'fatal spell of the fascinating tinker' was aimed at the address of their fellow Anglo-Irish writers, it fell on deaf ears, for many of their colleagues were already mesmerized by the Travellers, as were others across the Irish Sea. According to Mary Burke, the nineteenth-century '"Irish tinker" fad among writers of the British Isles' was 'the late and localized flowering of an eighteenth-century European academic craze centred on the investigation of Gypsy origins'.[8] Indeed, late in the nineteenth century the British *Journal of the Gypsy Lore Society* devoted a number of articles to the Irish tinkers as part of a debate about the origins of the Gypsies. In contrast with the English literature of the first half of the nineteenth century, which had idealized 'the solitary, apparently celibate scholar-gypsy',[9] the late nineteenth-century Gypsy Lorists constructed the Gypsies and tinkers in a way that reflected their own bohemian penchant for 'sexual heterodoxy' and 'self-conscious unconventionality'.[10] This fostered the general perception in the early twentieth century that Travellers were 'sexually and (to all intents and purposes) humanely Other'.[11] J.M. Synge, for example, was told by an informant that the tinkers of Wicklow had unorthodox marital practices, and one man might 'swap the woman he had with one from another man, with as much talk as if you'd be selling a cow'.[12] Liam

O'Flaherty's story 'The Tent' depicts a tinker 'and his two wives',[13] one of whom becomes the object of desire for a passing stranger, until the tinker violently puts a stop to the man's amorous advances. The Gypsy Lorists also drew attention to the existence of 'Shelta', the tinkers' language, the study of which was subsequently taken up by Celticists like John Sampson and Kuno Meyer, who constructed Travellers' Cant as a language of great antiquity harking back to an ancient Celtic past. This brought the tinkers into the discourse of Irish cultural nationalism.

As Paul Botheroyd was among the first scholars to point out,[14] the first decade of the twentieth century in particular produced a large number of literary and dramatic texts featuring tramps, tinkers and Travellers. Literary Revivalists like Yeats, Synge and Lady Gregory inscribed such figures with 'an anarchic and vigorous potential which was supposedly at odds with the material interests of the emerging bourgeoisie'.[15] They represented Travellers as living remnants of an ancient, pre-English, traditional way of life. Many if not all of the dramas and stories about tinkers of the Revival period are based to some degree on folk tales or traditional anecdotes; they therefore form part of the Revivalists' endeavour to find material for a national literature in the mythology and folktales of Ireland. In 'The Wandering Tribe', for example, Lady Gregory describes how she collected stories about tinkers from her local informants in much the same way that she would have collected folk tales. Douglas Hyde included two stories about tinkers, 'Shaun the Tinker' and 'The Buídach, the Tinker, and the Black Donkey', in his *Legends of Saints and Sinners*, a collection of 'folk-stories and folk-poems'.[16] The latter story involves a gentleman who dies and is reincarnated as a black donkey, to atone for his sins. He spends seven years with an aggressive tinker, who beats him often. Killed by the 'buídach' (a 'little lad'), the tinker is himself reincarnated as an ass and has to endure twenty-one years with a tinker from Munster. In 'Shaun the Tinker', collected from an Irish native-speaker in County Galway, the tinker is a trickster who outwits first the Devil and then Death himself. A number of the plots of Revival dramas and stories involve tinkers playing tricks on settled people, or vice versa: examples include P.T. McGinley's one-act play *Lizzie and the Tinker* (1901) – actually 'beggar woman' (*bean déirce*) in the original Irish-language version – and several stories by Seumas MacManus featuring tinkers, like 'The King of the West Indies' and 'The Tinker of Tamlacht'. Stories like Patrick Boyle's 'Myko' and Seumas O'Kelly's 'The Can with the Diamond Notch', both from the 1960s, also fall within this category.

The founders of the Irish Literary Theatre and their circle of associates were, barring a few notable exceptions, protestant Anglo-Irish nationalists. They belonged to an Ascendancy class that was doomed to become a marginalized and disempowered minority in the bourgeois Catholic state that would be the inevitable outcome of the decolonizing process that had been set in motion by the laws and reforms passed by the British government towards the end of the nineteenth century. For these nationalist playwrights, imagining the future nation as not English was self-evident; the spectre of a state dominated by Catholic peasants and shopkeepers, however, was one they were hardly prepared to contemplate. Paul Murphy has argued that the strategy of Yeats and his associates was 'to create a feudal dramatic fantasy space as the alternative to modernity based on Catholic *bourgeois* nationalism', which floundered on the 'key issue of representing the Irish peasant'.[17] Before they attempted to represent the peasant, however, these writers sought to avoid him altogether by focusing on the figure of the Irish tinker as a representative of the pre-colonial past and 'the antithesis of what was considered to be the materialism, stultifying Catholicism, and repressed sexuality of post-Famine Ireland'.[18] Yet if, as Kathleen Raine suggests, the tinkers 'were the true heirs of the Ireland of the kings and the bards',[19] they were nevertheless unlikely candidates to lead the new nation into the twentieth century. After all, J.M. Synge suggested that what was attractive about the tinkers was precisely their detachment from the modern world.

THE YEAR OF THE TINKER'S WEDDING

In 1902, a number of writers associated with the Irish Literary Theatre produced plays based on the Celtic myth of the Sovereignty Goddess. The first and best-known of these, *Cathleen Ni Houlihan* by Lady Gregory and W.B. Yeats, was performed in April of that year.[20] In Celtic mythology, the Sovereignty Goddess, a representation of the land, marries the rightful king (the land's ruler) in a ceremony at Tara by pouring him a drink, thereby bestowing the kingship of Ireland upon him. Before the marriage she appears as a hideous old hag or an old beggar woman (the fallow land), but the union rejuvenates her and transforms her into a beautiful queen. *Cathleen Ni Houlihan*, of course, famously desexualizes the myth by replacing the wedding with a blood sacrifice. In the play, a young man is about to get married, when a poor old woman appears at the door of his father's cottage, complaining about the loss of her four green fields and the strangers in her house. Having absorbed her message, the young man abandons his bride to fight the British and shed his blood for the old woman, who is rejuvenated as a consequence of his martyrdom.

In *Cathleen Ni Houlihan*, the poor old woman does not bestow the kingship on the young man whose marriage she thwarts, nor indeed on his younger brother, who witnesses her transformation as the result of his brother's sacrifice. That transformation, moreover, takes place off-stage. In this way, the answers to two thorny questions are symbolically evaded and left to the imagination of individual spectators: what the newly transformed nation will look like, and who will be its rightful ruler. The independent nation will not be in British hands when the strangers leave, but the exact nature of its new rulers remains undefined. The tramps and tinkers who wander in large numbers through the plays of the Revival period are a manifestation both of the need and the hesitation of the Anglo-Irish playwrights to fill in that blank space. Theirs could be constructed as an alternative form of Irishness: neither landlords, peasants nor shopkeepers, they had no apparent interest in material possessions or land ownership, but could be seen as a class apart, or no identifiable 'class' at all. As presumed remnants of 'pagan' times, moreover, they were imagined as having rituals and superstitions that were neither Catholic nor Protestant. For Anglo-Irish nationalists, then, tinkers appeared to provide a way of speaking about the Irish nation without having to address the problematic issues of class and religion.

Once the tinker had been inserted into the Sovereignty myth in this symbolic way, however, Anglo-Irish writers found themselves resisting the implications of their own metaphor: that the tinkers would be the rulers of Ireland. Moreover, they ran into a paradox: can a tinker who is made 'king' by way of marriage to a noble lady or queen still represent desirable alterity, or is he inevitably metamorphosed by his new position into a replica of the ruling figures whom he was meant to replace? The many reversals and contradictions within Douglas Hyde's short one-act play *An Tincéir agus an tSídheóg* are indicative of some of these tensions.

DOUGLAS HYDE'S *THE TINKER AND THE SHEEOG*

Hyde's little play, translated at the time by Belinda Butler as *The Tinker and the Fairy* and some years later by Lady Gregory as *The*

Tinker and the Sheeog, was first performed in May 1902, a month after *Cathleen Ni Houlihan*, although Hyde had begun it in August 1900.[21] It stays closer to the original configuration of the Sovereignty myth than its predecessor. Although the medieval tale 'The Adventures of the Sons of Eochaid Mugmedon' was not published in the *Revue Celtique* until 1903, in an edition by Whitley Stokes, Hyde clearly was familiar with it, for he broadly follows its plot. In the story, the five sons go on a hunting trip and become thirsty. One of them goes to look for water and finds a well guarded by a hideous old hag, who offers to give him a drink in return for a kiss, which he refuses. Three more brothers set out, with similar results. However, when the fifth brother, Niall, arrives at the well, he agrees not only to kiss the hag, but to have intercourse with her, whereupon she turns into a beautiful young woman who declares that she is the 'Sovereignty of Erin' and pronounces him king of Ireland.[22]

The 'Old Hag of the World'[23] in Hyde's play is an otherworldly being from Irish mythology, a Sheeog or 'fairy', who was condemned by the jealousy of the queen of her own people to grow old and die. Now 1,000 years of age, she has only an hour left to live, unless 'she finds in that day a man that will kiss her mouth willingly' (p.195). In Hyde's configuration, the Sheeog seems almost to be a personification of the Irish Home Rule Bill, which had been defeated so many times in the British parliament that its fate seemed to be at the mercy of an irrational and vindictive ruler. What rightful king, then, will arrive to liberate Ireland from the fate imposed on her by an evil queen in another world? The dying Sheeog first encounters a young man with a gun and a hound: a representative of the Anglo-Irish landed gentry. At her request for a kiss, the gentleman declares her 'cracked', gives her a piece of money, and departs (p.195). A young farmer enters next, in pursuit of an ass, and proceeds on his quest without so much as taking notice of the old woman; it appears that neither the Ascendancy nor the Irish peasantry can be relied upon to act as Ireland's saviours. The Sheeog is encouraged by the 'gladness' and lightness of heart of the cheerful, ragged tinker who enters next, with a song on his lips and a healthy appetite (p.196). He offers to give her anything he has to give, seeing that he has very little, which he will not begrudge her. When she asks for a kiss, however, he is taken aback, but complies because he is unwilling to break his word, whereupon the Sheeog is transformed into a beautiful young woman.

The tinker is much intimidated by the *bean uasal* or 'noble lady' suddenly confronting him, and even more confused by her offer of marriage. He decides to speak to her in poetry to placate her, since he has nothing else: 'A couple of sacks, and they raised on a couple of old sticks; devil a house have I but that. But I will put a clothing of poetry on it' (p.198). Satisfied by his metaphors, which turn nothing into something, the Sheeog offers to kiss him, and he is now willing to accept her advances. Just when the idea of marrying her begins to appeal to him, however, the music of the Sidhe calls the Sheeog back to the otherworld, as her sisters chant that 'An earthly clown like that / Would not be a right mate for you' (p.201). The tinker reminds her that he had saved her from death, and that she would get in him the King of the Tinkers, capable of earning at least 'half a crown' per day (p.202). As if spurred by the word 'crown' into realizing that she is about to bestow the kingship of Ireland on an improvident tinker, the Sheeog thanks him for his assistance and returns to her own people, the ones ruled by the vengeful queen, with whom, after all, she had shared 'a thousand years of company' (p.203).

The tinker indirectly compares himself to Wandering Aengus: 'Nothing before me but to be walking and ever walking the whole world till I get sight again of that woman that is after destroying me', and he declares himself 'heir to Cuchulain long ago when he said "I am the apple on the top of the tree. / It is little I thought of falling"'(p.203). But he is neither an ancient god nor a hero, of course, and being a tinker he would be walking the world anyway, so he is soon over his grief. He dismisses the Sheeog as a 'slut', complains that she left him no magical purse of money, and finds comfort in his bottle. 'I thought she was going to give me the kingdom of Ireland when she kissed me – the deceiver!' he grumbles, but he is also relieved, and hopes never to see one of her kind again (p.203). The Sheeog has betrayed the tinker who saved her, and the tinker curses the Sheeog for not giving him the kingship he does not want in the first place. In the end, it was all 'a dream of a summer day' (p.204) – a play performed in George Moore's garden. 'If it was all written in a book my fortune would be made in a minute', exclaims the tinker (p.204): and it is, of course, in the 'books' of the Anglo-Irish writers of the Revival that the tinker's 'fortune' is made, and not in the real world. In those plays, it is what the tinker is *not* (a landowner, a peasant, a shopkeeper, a Catholic, a Protestant) that makes him such an attractive would-be saviour. The abstract 'tinker' is therefore potentially the ideal future king of Ireland, but that potential can never be actualized, because the very act of crowning him, of putting him in a position of authority, leadership, and responsibility, turns him into his own opposite and destroys the 'tinkerish' qualities that make him potentially so perfect.

The six letters George Moore sent to Douglas Hyde in the months before the play's performance reveal something of this paradoxical quality of the tinker. Moore pestered Hyde with suggestions for improvement to Belinda Butler's translation of the play, while all the time stressing how much he liked the work. Reading the encounter between the tinker and the fairy as humanity's fleeting encounter with Otherness, Moore wanted the tinker's final soliloquy to be more philosophical: 'He is no longer a tinker, he is abstract humanity' ... 'a fairy comes to us [but for] half an hour, and ... this half hour is what we remember all [our live]s'.[24] Hyde resisted Moore's argument and did not change the tinker into an abstraction at the end of the play, because Moore got it backwards: the tinker is an idealized abstraction only at the play's beginning, when he is a potential saviour, but it is the Sheeog's realization of his actual, real-life tinker status that makes her turn away from him in the end.

The performance of *An Tincéir agus an tSídheóg* in Moore's garden was attended by over 300 people, including Lady Gregory, Jack Yeats, Æ, Edward Martyn and delegates to the annual *Oireachtas* of the Gaelic League, who arrived late and delayed the performance. The idea was to make the Irish language the focus of a main event of the Dublin social season, but Joseph Hone reports that Moore's neighbours made fun of the sounds they heard emanating from next door.[25] The *Irish Daily Independent* called the play 'a clever sketch amusingly played',[26] and the *Gael* described it as a 'charming little woodland idyll'.[27] One wonders how many of the respectable attendees understood this 'idyll' in terms of the Sovereignty myth, and more specifically as a depiction of the narrowly averted spectre of a 'tinker's republic', something made all the more ironic by the fact that the tinker's part was performed by Douglas Hyde himself, who was to become the Irish Republic's first president, while the part of the Sheeog was played by Sinead O'Flanagan, wife-to-be of the future president of the Republic, Eamon de Valera.

The performance of Hyde's play in his garden appears to have inspired George Moore, for a few months later, on 3 July 1902, he 'produced a draft scenario about a young intellectual who adopts the life of a tinker, spurns civilization as barbaric, attempts to found his own religion, endures many vicissitudes ... and is eventually killed by outraged villagers'.[28] Yeats was supposed to collaborate on the play with Moore, but when the two fell out, Moore informed him that he was using the plot for a novel, whereupon Yeats 'frantically set to writing, and by 26 September [1902] had completed the play, *Where There Is Nothing*',[29] with help from Douglas Hyde and Lady Gregory. It was published as a supplement to the *United Irishman* of 1 November 1902, though it was revised in 1903 before eventually being entirely rewritten as *The Unicorn from the Stars*.

W.B. YEATS'S *WHERE THERE IS NOTHING*

The play's protagonist, Paul Ruttledge, a member of the Ascendancy, is despondent about his life, and dreams of pulling down his own house and even the whole world: 'I only know that I want to upset everything about me. Have you not noticed that it is a complaint many of us have in this country? And whether it comes from love or hate I don't know, they are so mixed together here.'[30] Yeats's play is less about depicting the new Ireland than escaping from or destroying the existing one, and Paul expects to find an alternative in the 'freedom' and 'lawlessness' of the tinkers, whom he decides to join. His first act upon doing so is to exchange clothes with Charlie Ward, one of the tinkers. The exchange, apart from showing that the transformation is largely cosmetic, indicates the problem Paul keeps encountering: by giving the tinker his own clothes to wear, he does not eradicate the society he wants to 'tear down', but merely succeeds in displacing it. By defining the tinker as the opposite of a gentleman, the gentleman remains the norm. Paul ends up staging a carnival in which the world is turned upside down, but such a reversal only ends up endorsing the model he is attempting to leave behind. This is also illustrated by the fact that the 'lawless' tinkers are, in fact, obsessed by the police and the law. The tinkers are attractive to Paul because they 'go about like the crows' (p.1074), but once Paul has joined them he observes that crows 'fly home' at the end of the day, and Charlie Ward tells him that they have nests 'among those big trees about Tillyra Castle' (p.1102). The tinkers may have 'the happiness of men who fight ... the endless battle' (p.1097), but they keep their fighting cocks locked up in baskets and hidden under sacks. Wildness and freedom are therefore also not all they appear to be.

As soon as Paul has, rather imperiously, joined the tinkers, he sets about remaking himself by putting on a common accent and learning how to use a soldering iron. The tinkers are polite but address him as 'sir' and refer to him as 'the gentleman'. When told by Charlie Ward that the only thing that would turn a gentleman into 'one of ourselves' is marriage to a tinker, Paul decides to take Sabina Silver as his wife. Old habits die hard, however, and when he calls for a priest to perform the wedding ceremony, Charlie corrects him: tinkers 'hate priests and friars', and he should marry Sabina 'by lepping over the budget the same as the rest of us marry' (p.1095). The tinker's wedding simultaneously makes Paul a 'real' tinker and propels him into a leadership position among them, effectively making him their 'king', with the paradoxical results Douglas Hyde had only hinted at in *The Tinker and the Sheeog*. From then on Paul is in charge of the tinkers, and proceeds to recreate the very structures of authority and responsibility he had wished to tear down by joining the tinkers. The wedding is celebrated with an orgy of drunkenness in which the entire village participates, paid for with money from Paul's deep pockets; policemen and domestic servants are incapacitated by the week-long revel, but it is ironic that the social system whose mainstay they are, and which is so despised by Paul, can only be brought to a standstill with the help of his own inherited Ascendancy fortune.

When Paul's former friends, the magistrates, arrive to talk him out of his foolishness, he orders the tinkers to put them on trial, instructing the pagan Travellers to behave as if they were in a court of law, and to judge the magistrates on whether they had led 'a Christian life'. But he also tells the tinkers that this is not 'their show', and that their evidence is not wanted. Paul himself finishes the trial of the world he has 'left' (p.1118), proving by that very act that he has not left it at all. At the beginning of the play's next act, the tinkers drop Paul off at a monastery, since life on the road has left him bent and limping. Courteous as ever, the tinkers are also edgy, and apparently on the run because their leader's breezy quest for 'irresponsibility' had led them into trouble with the law.

In Yeats's play, the tinkers are, for Paul, a representation of a life 'where there is nothing that is anything, and nobody that is anybody; one can be free there, where there is nothing' (p.1091). In spite of cursory references to budget-leaping and tinsmithing, the tinkers have no culture of their own but are only defined negatively by what they are not: they constitute a blank space that Paul proceeds to fill in. Curiously passive and accommodating of their new companion, they allow him to order them about and run their lives. They seldom argue with him and never abandon him, even when he is a burden or gets them into trouble. As Hyangsoon Yi has pointed out, the tinkers are merely there as 'mute props' or 'dumb actors' to lead Paul to the very belated realization that 'a true revolution should take place in the minds of people, not in the physical domain'.[31] Yet perhaps Yeats's tinkers have revealed something about the physical world after all: if everyone followed their example and Paul's creed of not working and abandoning all social structures, there would indeed soon be nothing: nothing to eat, and nobody to beg from. Paul's martyrdom at the end of the play, his ceasing to be, is the only logical outcome of his philosophy, and his tinker wife and Charlie Ward dutifully return one more time to mourn his demise. By then, the tinkers are themselves a diminished force, and once Paul is dead there is no further use for them: 'There'll soon be none of us left at all,' Charlie predicts (p.1164).

Roy Foster suggests that a transcendentalist friend of George Russell's, Philip Francis Little, may have been one of the inspirations behind the figure of Paul Ruttledge. Little used to harangue the passing bourgeoisie from the sea-wall at Bray 'about vision and reality, attacking the assumptions of respectable life; he wanted to live, Diogenes-like, in an overturned truck at Kingstown'.[32] Yeats combined Little's iconoclasm with Moore's idea about the young intellectual who adopts the life of a tinker. Afterwards, the two sources of inspiration seem to have merged into one in the imagination of their friends. John Quinn wrote to John Lane in October 1902: 'Russell told Yeats and Moore a story about a member of a well-connected family who had joined the tinkers in Ireland, and had related various of his experiences.'[33] That story then took on a life of its own. William Bulfin, in the accounts of his bicycle ride through Ireland in 1902 published in the *United Irishman* as 'Rambles in Eirinn', records a roadside encounter with an unidentified tinker, who tells him he has been '[i]n throubles and in melia murdher ... on account of what a pote up in Dublin wrote about the tinkers'.[34] His particular objection to *Where There Is Nothing*, about which he apparently argued with another man, is the notion of the wedding between Paul Ruttledge and 'one of the girls of the Wards', because 'the Wards is relations of mine, and I know them, and I know that none of 'em would marry an *amadan* that couldn't earn his bread'. Indeed, he goes on, 'the story about the marriage is all in me eye', since 'no such boy as this young Misther Ledwitch, or whatever you call him, ever joined us, or would be let join us, much less marry one of us – a good-for-nothin' madman ... that couldn't tell a sodherin' iron from a pot stick'.[35] According to Bulfin's informant, one of the Wards raised the issue of the offending play when he was brought up before the magistrate for allowing his asses to trespass in a field of oats, incongruously bringing up the poet's unauthorized use of his name as evidence in his defence and threatening to sue for damages. Bulfin disingenuously asks his tinker informant to which part of the play Mr Ward objected specifically, and receives the reply: 'To the whole of it, sir. ... It's all wrong, lock stock and barrel. Neither that pote nor anybody else who isn't a tinker knows our saycrets ... and never will.'[36]

It is not entirely unlikely that William Bulfin made up the conversation with the tinker to poke fun at Yeats's rather unearthly and idealized representation of the tinkers, but whether his account was reportage or pure fiction, the story persisted. In August 1904, Lady Gregory wrote to J.M. Synge:

> I hear that some man of a fairly respectable class was taken up with a lot of tinkers somewhere in Munster, and that the Magistrate compared him to 'Paul Ruttledge'. The next night one of the Tinkers seems to have said something to the others about being in a book; the others resented this in some way, and there was a fight which brought them all into Court again. I am trying to get the papers.[37]

Synge himself had begun writing his play *The Tinker's Wedding* in the summer of 1902, when Hyde and Yeats were producing their own versions of the tinker's wedding, but he struggled with it for a long time. He was still working on it in 1905 when Yeats wrote to him: 'Bring if you can ... the M.S. of the Tinkers. ... We are rather hard up for new short pieces, and you have such a bad reputation now it can hardly do you any harm. But we may find it too dangerous for the Theatre at present.'[38] Robert Rhodes writes that 'the fact that Synge worked with it through several versions, revising characterizations of the priest, the tinkers, and their interactions until it was published in 1907, argues for a struggle to find appropriate expression for what he knew was a chancy enterprise that, on balance, does not succeed'.[39]

Paul Murphy makes the point that the Anglo-Irish writers of the Irish Literary Theatre and the Irish National Theatre Society 'produced plays that evoked an Ireland where the peasantry lived in union with nature in a pre-modern and specifically pre-*bourgeois* society'.[40] Synge's critique of the Catholic bourgeoisie, he argues, comes from 'the perspective of an Ascendancy figure who can fetishize the miserable lifestyle of wandering tramps and indulge in their social exclusion, safe in the knowledge that his "small private income" will put food in his mouth and a roof over his head'.[41] That description makes Synge sound a lot like Paul Ruttledge. But if Paul fetishized the tinkers, Synge made a distinction between tramps and tinkers, endowing the former with courteousness and vitality, whereas tinkers were always dangerous outcasts with a reputation for violence. In *The Well of the Saints*, 'the tinker girls is above running the hills' are on a par with 'the sluts of the town',[42] and in *The Playboy of the Western World*, Pegeen claims to be afraid of 'the ten tinkers is camped in the east glen',[43] and the first question she asks Christy is whether he is one of them. *The Tinker's Wedding*, then, while critiquing Catholic bourgeois nationalism, also problematizes Hyde's and Yeats's vision of the tinker as a kind of abstract, if intermediary, saviour of the nation from the strictures of class and religion. Hyde's and Yeats's plays start out optimistically but end in paradox: in *The Tinker and the Sheeog*, the 'noble lady's' offer of marriage and kingship to the tinker threatens to make him respectable and turn him into the kind of young man who had previously rejected and ignored her; in *Where There Is Nothing*, Paul Ruttledge transforms the world of the tinkers into a copy of the society he wished to leave behind. Synge's *The Tinker's Wedding* starts out with a paradox, as if to question the very premise used by Hyde and Yeats. If the tinkers are implicitly used by Hyde and Yeats as an antidote to the Catholic bourgeoisie, Synge seems to ask, what happens if representatives of these opposite ends of the social spectrum (in the form of a priest and three tinkers) are put on the same stage? What happens is that the plot has nowhere to go, leading inevitably to what Mary King calls 'the play's notoriously "illogical" resolution'[44] in which everything falls apart and nothing is resolved.

J.M. SYNGE'S *THE TINKER'S WEDDING*

The premise of *The Tinker's Wedding* is that Sarah Casey, a young tinker woman, wishes to be married to Michael Byrne, her longtime companion, by a Catholic priest. She has no real motivation other than that it is spring, which gives her 'queer thoughts', although her general sense is that marriage will make her respectable. Indeed, there is a suggestion that marriage is incompatible with disreputable tinkerdom, when Michael complains that making a wedding ring will destroy his ability to make tin cans, and Sarah complains that the ring squeezes and cuts her finger when she tries it on for size. The play begins in carnivalized topsy-turviness: since Sarah has lived with Michael for a long time and they have a number of children together, marriage at this stage seems rather like closing the gate after the horse has bolted. Sarah's desire for upward mobility is balanced by the priest's lack of decorum: when he first enters the stage, he is slightly the worse for drink, having played cards all night at the doctor's house. The ironic inversions present from the very outset introduce a satirical plot involving multiple parodies and reversals, in which diametrically opposed characters and points of view are placed in contention with each other without ever leading to a satisfactory resolution. When Sarah politely asks the priest to marry her to Michael, he rudely demands money, which is offered to him by Sarah in the form of 'half a sovereign' bearing the imprint of Queen Victoria's face, 'the living king's mamma'.[45] The queen of the British Empire, in this carnival of opposites, is also half a Sovereignty Goddess, representing Sarah Casey's Anglo-bourgeois marital aspirations; the other half of the Sovereignty Goddess is embodied by the tinker's 'mamma', Mary Byrne, who likens Sarah to the great queens of Ireland. In Mary's view, Sarah should not be 'fooling' with notions of marriage and respectability. Mary herself is drunk and thoroughly disreputable.

Mary's liking for porter gives her something in common with the priest, however, and she is soon sharing the contents of her jug with him and listening to his complaints about the bishop. The Sovereignty Goddess of Celtic mythology married the rightful king by pouring him a ceremonial drink, thereby bestowing the kingship of Ireland on him. Synge provides us with a parody of this ritual, in which Mary pours the priest a drink and thereby joins his fate to hers and to the nation, which both presages the dominant role of the Catholic church in a future independent Ireland, and savagely mocks its detrimental effects. Mary King argues that there are in fact two potential ceremonies in *The Tinker's Wedding*, a wedding (between Sarah and Michael) and an anti-wedding (between Mary and the priest), which together act as a caveat against too easy identification of the tinkers with freedom and the priest with conventional morality.[46] One could, however, argue that there are three potential weddings in the play: tinker to tinker; priest to tinker; and celibate priest to himself, when Sarah rejects bourgeois respectability and puts the wedding ring on his finger at the end to confirm his oath that he will never meddle with the tinkers again.

To be sure, the tinkers and the priest have a lot in common in spite of their opposite positions on the social spectrum. Sarah and Michael share with the priest an interest in money (representing bourgeois values), while Mary and the priest have a common thirst (representing 'tinker' values). The confusion of priestly and tinkerish characteristics eventually leads the plot back to where it began. At the beginning of the play, the priest *refuses* to perform Sarah's wedding, but at the end of the first act, he *agrees* to marry Sarah and Michael in order to prevent Sarah from becoming an immoral old hag like Mary, even though the latter had plied him with drink and sympathy only a few minutes before. The next day, however, when he unwraps what he thinks is a gallon can from a sack and finds empty beer bottles instead, and is thereby confronted both with the absence of drink and the reminder of his involvement with Mary the night before, he furiously *refuses* to marry Sarah and make her respectable.

At this point, the plot returns to square one. The priest accuses the tinkers of being thieving rapists, while the tinkers accuse him of being a lecherous drunk. All they can do is revert to type: the priest evokes the authority of the police and Almighty God, while the tinkers resort to physical violence by stuffing the priest into the sack that had previously held the gallon can and the empty bottles. Declan Kiberd has noted that the origin of this scene, which Synge added to the play in 1906, may be found in an Irish poem collected by Douglas Hyde, entitled 'The Lout and His Mother', in which the Lout proclaims, 'If you were dead to-morrow morning / And I were to bring you to a priest tied up in a bag, / He would not read a Mass for you without hand-money.'[47] The lines are ambiguous as to whether it is the mother or the priest who is tied up in the bag, but either way, the reference is to the use of canvas cloth by the Irish poor to bury their dead instead of coffins, which they could not afford. At the end of *The Tinker's Wedding*, the priest is therefore associated with a funeral rather than a wedding. Sarah is cured of her bourgeois aspirations and puts the wedding ring on the priest's finger, paradoxically as a token of her *refusal* to get married. She thereby leaves the kingship of Ireland in his celibate hands, without the promise of renewal or rejuvenation. Synge's ending reverses that of Hyde's play, when the tinker cursed the Sheeog who had so precipitously abandoned him, in that it is the priest who curses the tinkers, and the tinkers who make a hasty getaway. The representative of Catholic bourgeois orthodoxy is ridiculed, the tinkers remove themselves from involvement with the settled community, and no alternative is provided to these representatives of two unviable and undesirable national prospects. If, as Paul Murphy contends, Synge's own preference is 'a society where Ascendancy landlord and peasant "tenantry" live in pre-lapsarian harmony',[48] it is not a vision he is willing to articulate here, but one that exists only by default.

The Tinker's Wedding was not performed in Synge's lifetime, and in fact did not receive its first Irish production until 1963. The depiction of the priest on stage made the play 'too dangerous' for the directors of the Abbey Theatre to consider, a view confirmed by a 1908 review of the published version of the play which referred to it as 'an abominable libel upon the priesthood'.[49] Staging *The Tinker's Wedding* is still problematic today, but for very different reasons, as Garry Hynes, who directed the play as part of Druid's Synge cycle in 2005, discovered during her own experiments with the representation of the play's tinker characters. Initially, Hynes set the play in the mid-twentieth century, leading Helen Meany, in a review for the *Guardian* newspaper, to call the staging 'twee' and to wonder if the approach 'was to historicise and romanticise its depiction of tinkers'.[50] Hynes subsequently changed her interpretation and presented the characters 'done up unmistakably as contemporary travellers, fulfilling every stereotype that still persists about traveller culture', an approach that made another reviewer uncomfortable: 'I found it discomforting to sit amongst a contemporary cosmopolitan audience laughing at travellers, given that the problems of bias against travellers and their living conditions persist in Ireland today. ... A framing device or some other form of directorial commentary would not have gone amiss, to acknowledge and distance the production from the stereotypes it replicated.'[51] A century after its initial publication, then, producing *The Tinker's Wedding* on stage remains a problematic undertaking, although the altered nature of the problem signifies the extent to which the public's attitude towards authority figures as well as ethnic minorities has shifted.

FROM FASCINATION TO HORROR

As the plays by Hyde, Yeats and Synge demonstrate, the year 1902 can be called the year of the tinker's wedding. The tinker soon disappeared from the work of these writers, however, although in *The Demi-Gods* (1914) James Stephens would reprise Yeats's early idealism to some extent when he created an alliance between tinkers and angels: 'They had no property and so they had no prejudices, for the person who has nothing may look upon the world as his inheritance, while the person who has something has seldom anything but that.'[52] For Stephens, 'Traveller characters offer unorthodox perspectives with which to examine – and critique – received assumptions and dominant prejudices', including 'attitudes towards labour, theft, property and possession'.[53] In subsequent plays by Yeats and Synge, however, for example the revision of *Where There Is Nothing* as *The Unicorn from the Stars*, or Synge's *The Shadow of the Glen*, the tinkers are replaced by tramps or vagrants, who, as individual wanderers, are more easily romanticized and imbued with aristocratic features than tinkers. That general shift away from the fetishization of the tinkers is also apparent in Lady Gregory's disapproving choice of language when she wrote in 'The Wandering Tribe', published in *Poets and Dreamers* in 1903, that Paul Ruttledge, in his effort to leave the world of law and order behind, 'fell among tinkers'.[54] She went on to note that the reputation of the tinkers among the peasantry differed considerably from that of other travelling people: 'I wondered why our country people – who are so kind to one another, and to tramps and beggars ... – speak of a visit of the tinkers as of frost in spring or blight in harvest.'[55] Her informants give a number of reasons for their ill opinion of tinkers: that the tinkers had unorthodox marriage practices, including wife swapping, or no marriage at all; that they had religious beliefs all their own, or no religion at all; that they were deceitful; and that they had 'no control'.[56] Paul Delaney points out that the Travellers in Gregory's report are observed but never heard, and are 'made to embody many of the fears and anxieties of a dominant cultural imaginary'.[57] Such fears are also evident in remarks made about the tinkers by A.T. Sinclair in an article in the *Journal of American Folklore* of 1909:

> In Ireland they bear a hard reputation, as quarrelsome, hard drinkers, and given to every kind of deception and low trick. A woman with a sick baby appears at some respectable farmhouse and begs to be taken in for the night. As soon as all are asleep, she gets up and opens the door, and the house is filled with the whole ragged and perhaps drunken band. Sometimes even the poor farmer and family are practically driven out for the night.[58]

A particularly extreme example of this form of cultural anxiety can be found in *Doctor Danny* (1918) by American writer Ruth Sawyer, who had a degree in folklore from Columbia University, and spent the summers of 1905 and 1907 collecting folk tales in Ireland. Set in a year of 'comparative abundance' shortly before the Famine, when 'tinkers were plentiful everywhere',[59] *Doctor Danny* manages to imply that some of the blame for the Great Hunger should be put on the Travellers: 'As a plague they will surpass any that visited Egypt in Moses's time. They are worse than the locusts or the swarm of flies, and more terrifying than the hail and darkness could ever have been. They come in droves, and sweep through the land, spreading fear and desolation' (p.36). In one village, they 'settled for nearly a two-month, bringing famine to many a hearthside there' (p.37). When the tinkers eventually depart, they leave behind a baby girl, and the villagers debate whether she might, with careful raising, turn out well, or whether her tinker origins will make her a lost cause. The girl turns out to be deaf and dumb, however, and with the tinker's voice thus literally erased, the villagers proceed to raise her as a 'serenely happy' child (p.40). One spring, however, the 'vagabond blood' masters her, and she runs away like 'some hunted creature' (p.52). When she is eventually found she is pregnant, but the child is still-born. The villagers trick her into believing that the child's father has declared his love for her, sent her a wedding ring, and will one day return. Rescued from origins she can never quite overcome, and cut off, except in make-believe, from the marital and family life that spell female fulfilment in the sedentary world, she can only find respectability in service to that world, as she 'tends the wee children, nurses the sick, and sews the shrouds for the dead' (p.64).

The tramps who soon come to replace the tinkers in the literature of the Revival represent not the potential future leaders of the nation, but the declining Anglo-Irish Ascendancy that was about to be stripped of its power and possessions by the bourgeois rulers of the new state. The tramp's task is no longer to stand in for the king, but to represent a way of life that has become unviable and is already beyond the pale. In Synge's *The Shadow of the Glen*, for example, the young 'queen', Nora, and the tramp who links up with her, are unceremoniously expelled from the house (emblematic of the nation) by the money-counting peasants who claim possession of it. The over-determined characteristics of the tinkers in Hyde, Yeats and Synge led their Anglo-Irish creators not towards freedom and open-ended possibility, but into the dead end of paradox, where the tinkers could only be abandoned, much as they were virtually abandoned in life by successive governments of the newly created Catholic bourgeois state. That much, at least, the tinkers had in common with members of the Anglo-Irish Ascendancy.

TINKERS AND REVOLUTIONARIES

In his story 'Midsummer Night Madness' (1932), Sean O'Faolain depicts the fate of both marginalized minorities in the Irish Free State as the shot-gun wedding of a young tinker girl to an ageing and decrepit member of the Ascendancy, enforced by an Irish nationalist rebel. During the War of Independence, the story's narrator, John, is sent to find out why the battalion commanded by Stevey Long, with whom he had been friendly 'ever since the chances of revolution threw us together',[60] has been entirely inactive for a number of months. Long is stationed at a Big House known as Henn Hall, where John finds his friend more interested in the local pub and in his lover, a tinker girl named Gypsy Gammle, than in curbing the Black and Tans who are terrorizing the local population. The Big House owner, Alexander Henn, a man with a long-standing reputation as a libertine and always known for living 'by the things of the body' (p.10), also has a relationship with Gypsy, who is in an advanced state of pregnancy when John arrives at the house.

To the narrator who, like Long, is 'one of our new patriots', as Henn sarcastically calls him (p.20), both the Anglo-Irish landowner and the tinker girl are stereotypically pre-defined in his imagination by their perceived antithetical attitude towards the Irish Catholic bourgeoisie. John has imagined Henn since childhood as 'more terrifying than any of the ogres in the fairy-books' (p.10), and hates him as 'one of the class that had battened for too long on our poor people' (p.12). Gypsy's surname, that of 'a well-known tinker tribe', is categorized by John as one that 'few decent men or women ever bore' (p.29). Before he has met either of them, he has already, in his mind, condemned the decrepit owner of the fading, crumbling Big House and the abject tinker girl to each other in a sexual union: considering Henn now beyond charming 'even the coarsest woman', the narrator contemplates that the old libertine might have to 'descend to the women of the passing tinkers', although when he thinks of the 'big Red House' he 'could not believe that even such a house would fall so low' (p.13).

In spite of his mission to investigate Stevey Long's dereliction of duty, the narrator instinctively allies himself with his revolutionary comrade – indeed, he is even mistaken for him by Gypsy upon his arrival at the house – to the point where his loyalty and his own lack of initiative prevent him from taking his friend to task for his inactivity. Although John notes the disreputable aspects of Long's character, he merely registers them without the kind of explicit anger he reserves for Henn, or the desirous contempt he feels for the tinker girl, letting pass without rebuke the coarseness of Stevey's comment on Gypsy's 'titties' and the suspicion that 'Stevey's girl' is more likely only 'one of his girls' (p.18). John is mesmerized by Gypsy's voluptuousness and by Henn's sensuous interest in her, and notes that Stevey's voice 'was rough and coarse beside the rich voice of the girl and the cultured voice of the old man' (p.26). Driven to seek comfort in each other's presence by the 'coarse' voice of the 'patriot', the 'unequal pair' of the landowner and the tinker are voyeuristically observed by John, as they look at each other 'so silently, seeming not to say one word to each other' (p.31). With their voices now erased, their mutual sorrow, to their observer, makes 'country and freedom' seem 'a small thing' (p.32).

In a debate with the narrator about the past and future of Ireland, Henn distances himself from the nation by claiming that he is 'not an Irishman' (p.23), and argues that the Irish have always lacked an enterprising spirit and conveniently blame their individual and national failure to prosper on 'people like us' (p.22): 'It's always the same. This ruined us, and that ruined us, and the other ruined us' (p.23). To be sure, once Stevey Long is finally spurred into action by the narrator's arrival, his first deed is to blame the Ascendancy for both the public and private consequences of his own indolence and self-indulgence. His men burn down the Big House across the valley in retaliation for the murderous rampage of the Black and Tans in the nearby village – which Long had done nothing to prevent – and threaten Henn Hall with the same fate, unless its owner agrees to marry the pregnant tinker girl, because, or so Stevey claims, it was Henn who 'ruined her' (p.39). As a type of Cathleen Ni Houlihan, but one who, unlike the character created by Gregory and Yeats, is a dispossessed 'tramp' and a young queen at the same time, Gypsy becomes both the repository of legacies from the past for which the Ascendancy is forced to take sole responsibility, and an embodiment of the future nation that will be betrayed and abandoned by the very agents who help bring it into existence. Once Stevey has arranged the forced marriage, 'all Henn could say was, "You liar, you liar!" And all the girl could do was weep and say, "My misfortune. My misfortune. My misfortune"' (p.41). The narrator does not believe Long's accusations, but places himself in a position of neutrality, thereby betraying his own spinelessness. When Stevey disappears, John simply replaces him with a new commandant, and when Henn questions him about what has taken place, he replies that he has no cause 'to believe or disbelieve anybody'. After the wedding, Henn takes himself and his 'tinker wife' away from Ireland, to Paris, where the narrator finds it 'too painful' to think of them (p.43).

Paul Delaney observes that it is significant that Henn and Gypsy are bullied into marriage by a representative of the emerging Free State, and that it is 'through the transference of his appetites onto "the old libertine", Henn, that Stevey is able to assume for himself the role of a moral enforcer' so that his nationalist discourse can 'represent itself to itself as pure and as honourable'.[61] The language of the story, however, implies that the rebels are no better than 'tramps' themselves, and therefore no more fit to be stewards of their inheritance than the old order they so routinely accuse of ruining the nation. John's arrival in the countryside gives him a sense of relief from the claustrophobic city where he had to contend with the 'roaring' of the Black and Tans' Lancias and the 'funereal tramp-tramp, tramp-tramp' of their patrols (p.19). However, as soon as he arrives at Henn Hall, he is arrested by Gypsy, another kind of 'tramp', who questions him about Stevey's other girlfriend and fulminates against his betrayal of her in spite of his 'grand talk', leaving John 'with the feeling that this Hall and estate and countryside had an unpleasant, real life of its own' (p.15).Once John is invited into the drawing-room of the Big House – the crumbling emblem of Ascendancy power – he finds it just as he expected, 'a good room but battered and unkempt like a tramp' – 'drab' and 'dirty' and falling apart (p.21), like its occupant. But, as we learn from the narrator of the story 'Fugue' that follows 'Midsummer Night Madness' in the same collection, the rebels in the War of Independence also lead a 'vagabond life' (p.52) consisting of endless 'tramp[ing] up and down and up and down' (p.49). After they have forced Henn to accept the tinker girl as his bride, Stevey and his soldiers go 'tramping down the avenue', while the narrator 'tramped upstairs' to his bedroom (p.42). Just as Henn's scathing reference to the 'new patriots' implies the existence of an older, superior type of patriot, so the different uses of the word 'tramp' suggest that the new variety of tramp is characterized by ruthlessness, while the older type is more reminiscent of Synge's noble vagrant. Henn maintains his dignity and puts a brave face on his forced union, calling Gypsy 'as good as the next, and better than some, even though she *is* only a tinker's daughter' (p.43), and arguing that the child, if a boy, might even 'keep the name alive'. The narrator can only scoff at him dismissively: 'As if he were a Hapsburg or a Bourbon!' (p.43).

Sean O'Faolain was not alone in his disillusionment at the inability of the revolutionary leaders to form a state that lived up to the rhetoric of honour and heroism that had helped inspire its creation. For W.B. Yeats, the replacement of the old Ascendancy order by the democratic institutions of the Free State became an increasing source of bitterness and regret. By 1938, when Yeats wrote the short play *Purgatory*, Paul Ruttledge's idealization of the 'alternative' tinkers in *Where There Is Nothing* had been replaced in his work by a sentiment more akin to horror. In *Purgatory*, an Old Man and a Boy, his son, visit the ruin of a 'big old house that was burnt down',[62] where the Old Man was born from the union between an Ascendancy lady and the stable-groom she married, who 'was not her kind' (p.1047) and 'squandered everything she had' (p.1043). She died giving birth to her son, who, when he became a young man, killed his father for setting fire to the Big House and everything in it: 'to kill a house / Where great men grew up, married, died, / I here declare a capital offence' (p.1044). Dispossessed and under suspicion, he then 'became a pedlar on the roads' (p.1045), where his own son was born, '[a] bastard that a pedlar got / Upon a tinker's daughter in a ditch' (p.1044). Now an Old Man, he revisits the 'symbolical' ruined house (p.1041) and the moment of his own begetting by the ghosts of his parents, seeking to arrest the 'consequence of those transgressions' (p.1042) – in vain, as it turns out – by killing the Boy with the same knife that had stabbed his father: 'I killed that lad because had he grown up / He would have struck a woman's fancy, / Begot, and passed pollution on' (p.1049). As Terence Brown suggests, '[e]litist ideals and eugenic panic' find expression in *Purgatory*, while the destruction of 'what is manifestly an Anglo-Irish, eighteenth-century house'[63] adds a specific social and political dimension, making the Old Man 'the voice of urgent ... contemporary Protestant anxieties, expressing in local terms the crisis for social privilege implicit in democratic mass society in the twentieth century'.[64] The Old Man's implication in the very 'ineluctable pollution' he is seeking to eradicate points to the play's 'despairing cynicism that not even a tragic redemption can be imagined in the modern world'.[65] In the span of less than forty years, Yeats's tinkers have gone from being pre-modern embodiments of freedom and irresponsibility to symbols of a destructive mass modernity.

THE TINKER WITHIN

O'Faolain's suggestion that every character in 'Midsummer Night Madness' is a 'tramp' has a counterpart in Yeats's *Purgatory* in the idea that the 'tinker' identity is ineluctably associated with modernity. The notion that beneath the civilized veneer of every modern Irish citizen there lies a 'tinker' core runs through much of Irish literature in the twentieth century. The 'tinker beneath the skin' as part of the national self-image already began to emerge in the decades before the creation of the Free State. Two slightly different versions of William Bulfin's account of his encounter with the tinkers of Abbeyshrule during his bicycle trip through Ireland in 1902 are illuminating in this regard: the sketch originally published in the *United Irishman*, cited by James Woods in his *Annals of Westmeath*, and the revised version subsequently published in Bulfin's *Rambles in Eirinn*.

As he was cycling along the Royal Canal, Bulfin approached Abbeyshrule in County Longford from the direction of Mill Lane, where the labourers who constructed the canal in the early decades of the nineteenth century had lived in mud cabins. In *Annals of Westmeath*, before he goes on to cite Bulfin, James Woods describes this 'classic locality', now inhabited by 'chimney sweepers, tinkers, marine dealers, and a small sprinkling of sieve makers', as being

> in a state of chronic revolt against authorities, civil and sanitary. The houses are low structures formed into tenements separated by partitions about six feet high, which form admirable barricades for offensive or defensive operations whenever the war hatchet is exhumed. In times of feud these artless people amuse themselves by throwing large quantities of water, stones, and other missiles across the walls at each other, and such is the dexterity of these untutored children of nature, that a favourite boast of theirs is – that a neighbours [*sic*] hen can be stolen, cooked and eaten, before the owner discovers the loss.[66]

William Bulfin, in the original sketch reprinted in *Annals of Westmeath*, tells his readers at the outset that Abbeyshrule is 'quite respectable despite its unenvied possession of Mill Lane', which, he is told by a small boy, also goes by the name of 'Tinker's Hollow'.[67] Realizing that he is in the 'notorious' Mill Lane, Bulfin recalls hearing about the place many times in the past, and as far away as Argentina, when 'the sun-tanned exiles of Longford and Westmeath recalled some story of "The Tinkers of Abbeyshrule"'.[68] In the revised version of his sketch, published in *Rambles in Eirinn*, Bulfin withholds the information about the tinkers until a later point in the story, thereby creating ambiguities not present in the original version.

In the revised account, Bulfin does not mention Mill Lane up front, and presents himself as simply entering Abbeyshrule, unaware of the fact that he has strayed into a tinker encampment. His initial impressions are described with mock-horror:

> my attention was forcibly drawn to certain remarks made by a man who was sitting beside the towing path, fishing. He was calling upon a boy to bring him another maggot, and the qualifying parts of speech which he applied to the maggot and to the boy were more than vigorous. They were lurid. An aged female, with a rather reckless air of unconventionality, stood smoking at a door of a hovel near the canal, and she called to the man who was fishing – called him to come to his tea in terms which were peculiar and drastic and profane. A small boy rode a very hairy donkey along the road. In his small right hand he carried a large club with which he belaboured the donkey, cursing that unhappy quadruped at the same time with a fluency and a vehemence which were shocking.[69]

Believing himself to be among 'regular' Irish citizens, Bulfin agonizes over the unexpected moral decline of the locality – 'it would appear as if the general moral tone of the inhabitants has, in some respects, deteriorated since the olden pious days' – until he perceives his error, to his relief: 'This part of the Canal bank has been frequented by tinkers from the earliest ages of tinkerdom, and the good people of Abbeyshrule keep clear of it as much as possible.'[70] Contrary to his initial assumption, then, these are not, after all, 'good people', but tinkers, of whom such behaviour is to be expected. Yet the momentary confusion of the tinkers with the good people of Abbeyshrule is troubling, since Bulfin's initial supposition suggests that the invisible barrier that keeps these population groups apart is by no means impermeable. To allay his (and his readers') anxiety that it might actually be possible for Irish people to regress to such moral primitivism, Bulfin proceeds to construct the tinkers as not Irish at all:

> They are a puzzling people, and I have never met anyone who could give a satisfactory account of their origin. They have little in common with the gypsies, outside the mania for vagrancy. They have names borrowed from Irish clans, but they have a hundred characteristics which differentiate them from the Irish people. Are they some remnant of the Firbolgs or degenerated Tuatha de Danann? Or are they descendants of some wandering tribe that strayed in to Ireland when the land was empty after one of the great massacres? Nobody knows.[71]

In accounts like these, the Travellers are neither authentic Gypsies, nor are they genuinely Irish; the 'hundred characteristics' that set them apart from the general population, however, do not prevent Bulfin from 'misjudging the good people of Abbeyshrule'[72] by confusing them with the tinkers. The fact that he deliberately constructed the confusion for the entertainment of his (settled) readership, only to deconstruct it subsequently, serves to highlight the deep ambivalence felt towards the 'tinkers' by the majority population at the beginning of the twentieth century.

NOTES

1. Cahalan, *The Irish Novel*, p.46.
2. Jim MacLaughlin, *Travellers and Ireland: Whose Country, Whose History?* (Cork: Cork University Press, 1995), p.11.
3. Ibid., p.12.
4. Helleiner, *Irish Travellers*, p.42.
5. Quoted in ibid., p.43.
6. Jane Barlow, *Strangers at Lisconnel: A Second Series of Irish Idylls* (1895; Freeport, NY: Books for Libraries Press, 1971), p.34. All subsequent page references in the text are to this edition.
7. E. Œ. Somerville and Martin Ross, *All on the Irish Shore: Irish Sketches* (New York: Longmans, Green, and Co., 1903), p.8. All subsequent page references in the text are to this edition.
8. Burke, 'Eighteenth-Century European Scholarship', p.205.
9. Nord, *Gypsies and the British Imagination*, p.131.
10. Ibid., p.132.
11. Paul Delaney, 'Representations of the Travellers in the 1800s and 1900s', *Irish Studies Review*, 9, 1 (2001), p.55.
12. J.M. Synge, 'The Vagrants of Wicklow', *The Shanachie*, 1 (1906), p.95.
13. Liam O'Flaherty, *The Tent* (London: Jonathan Cape, 1926), p.7.
14. See Paul Botheroyd, 'The Years of the Travellers: Tinkers, Tramps and Travellers in Early Twentieth-Century Irish Drama and Society', in Heinz Kosok (ed.), *Studies in Anglo-Irish Literature* (Bonn: Bouvier, 1982), pp.167–75.
15. Paul Delaney, 'Migrancy and Cultural Disappearance', in P.J. Mathews (ed.), *New Voices in Irish Criticism* (Dublin: Four Courts Press, 2000), p.179.
16. Douglas Hyde, *Legends of Saints and Sinners* (London: Gresham, 1915), p.vii.
17. Paul Murphy, 'J.M. Synge and the Pitfalls of National Consciousness', *Theatre Research International*, 28, 2 (2003), p.126.
18. Helleiner, *Irish Travellers*, p.41.
19. Quoted in ibid., p.41.
20. W.B. Yeats, *Cathleen Ni Houlihan*, in Russell K. Alspach (ed.), *The Varorium Edition of the Plays of W.B. Yeats* (New York: Macmillan, 1966), pp.214–35.
21. See Janet Egleson Dunleavy and Gareth W. Dunleavy, *Douglas Hyde: A Maker of Modern Ireland* (Berkeley, CA: University of California Press, 1991), p.221.
22. For a translation of 'The Adventures of the Sons of Eochaid Mugmedon', see Tom Peete Cross and Clark Harris Slover (eds), *Ancient Irish Tales* (1936; New York: Barnes and Noble, 1969), pp.508–13.
23. Douglas Hyde, *The Tinker and the Sheeog*, trans. Lady Gregory, in Lady Augusta Gregory, *Poets and Dreamers* (1903; New York: Oxford University Press, 1974), p.195. All subsequent page references in the text are to this edition.
24. Letter from George Moore to Douglas Hyde, 25 March 1902. Quoted in Gareth W. Dunleavy and Janet Egleson Dunleavy, 'Editor Moore to Playwright Hyde: On the Making of *The Tinker and the Fairy*', *Irish University Review*, 3, 1 (1973), p.21.
25. Dunleavy and Dunleavy, 'Editor Moore to Playwright Hyde', p.29.
26. In Robert Hogan and James Kilroy, *Laying the Foundations, 1902–1904*, vol. 2 of *The Modern Irish Drama: A Documentary History* (Dublin: Dolmen Press, 1976), p.27.
27. Quoted in Dunleavy and Dunleavy, 'Editor Moore to Playwright Hyde', p.29.
28. R.F. Foster, *The Apprentice Mage*, vol. 1 of *W.B. Yeats: A Life* (Oxford: Oxford University Press, 1997), p.267.
29. Ibid.
30. W.B. Yeats, *Where There Is Nothing*, in Russell K. Alspach (ed.), *The Variorum Edition of*

the Plays of W.B. Yeats (New York: Macmillan, 1966), p.1072. All subsequent page references in the text are to this edition.

31. Hyangsoon Yi, 'The Traveler as "Noble Savage" in W.B. Yeats's *Where There Is Nothing*'. Accessed 10 November 2006: http://plaza.snu.ac.kr/~ed705/data/sun24/24-29.hwp
32. Foster, *The Apprentice Mage*, p.267.
33. Ibid., p.583 n.55.
34. William Bulfin, *Rambles in Eirinn* (1907; Dublin: Roberts Wholesale Books, n.d.), pp.296–7.
35. Ibid., p.297.
36. Ibid., p.298.
37. Ann Saddlemyer (ed.), *Theatre Business: The Correspondence of the First Abbey Theatre Directors: William Butler Yeats, Lady Gregory and J.M. Synge* (Gerrards Cross: Colin Smythe, 1982), p.54.
38. Ibid., p.80.
39. Robert E. Rhodes, '"More Matter for a May Morning": J.M. Synge's *The Tinker's Wedding*', in Alexander G. Gonzalez (ed.), *Assessing the Achievement of J.M. Synge* (Westport, CT: Greenwood Press, 1996), p.103.
40. Murphy, 'J.M. Synge', p.126.
41. Ibid., p.136.
42. J.M. Synge, *Plays*, ed. Ann Saddlemyer (Oxford: Oxford University Press, 1969), p.85.
43. Ibid., p.110.
44. Mary C. King, *The Drama of J.M. Synge* (London: Fourth Estate, 1985), p.88.
45. Synge, *Plays*, p.39. All subsequent page references in the text are to this edition.
46. King, *The Drama of J.M. Synge*, p.88.
47. Declan Kiberd, *Synge and the Irish Language* (Totowa, NJ: Rowman and Littlefield, 1979), p.143.
48. Murphy, 'J.M. Synge', p.138.
49. According to Joseph Holloway's diaries. Quoted in Delaney, 'Representations of the Travellers', p.61.
50. Quoted in Karen Fricker, 'Expanding the Cottage Walls', *Irish Theatre Magazine*, 5, 24 (2005), p.28.
51. Ibid., p.28.
52. James Stephens, *The Demi-Gods* (1914; Dublin: Butler Sims, 1982), p.50.
53. Paul Delaney, 'Privileged Perspectives and Subverted Types: James Stephens' *The Demi-Gods*', in Breathnach and Bhreatnach, *Portraying Irish Travellers*, pp.62–3.
54. Lady Gregory, *Poets and Dreamers*, p.94.
55. Ibid., p.94.
56. Ibid., p.95.
57. Delaney, 'Representations of the Travellers', p.58.
58. Sinclair, 'The Secret Language', pp.357–8.
59. Ruth Sawyer, *Doctor Danny* (New York and London: Harper, 1918), p.36. All subsequent page references in the text are to this edition.
60. Sean O'Faolain, *The Collected Stories of Sean O'Faolain* (London: Constable, 1980), p.10. All subsequent page references in the text are to this edition.
61. Paul Delaney, '"A Marginal Footnote": O'Faolain, the Subaltern, and the Travellers', *Irish Studies Review*, 11, 2 (2003), p.161.
62. W.B. Yeats, *Purgatory*, in Alspach (ed.), *Variorum Yeats*, p.1043. All subsequent page references in the text are to this edition.
63. Terence Brown, *The Life of W.B. Yeats* (Dublin: Gill and Macmillan, 1999), p.372.
64. Ibid., p.373.
65. Ibid.
66. James Woods, *Annals of Westmeath, Ancient and Modern* (Dublin: Sealy, Bryers and Walker, 1907), pp.174–5.
67. Ibid., pp.180–1.
68. Ibid., p.181.
69. Bulfin, *Rambles in Eirinn*, pp.293–4.
70. Ibid., p.294.
71. Ibid., pp.295–6.
72. Ibid., p.294

CHAPTER 3

Catching Them Young: Reading for Children and Young Adults

> My mother said I never should
> Play with the gypsies in the wood.
> If I did, she would say,
> Naughty girl to disobey.
>
> Skipping song

In the decades after the declaration of Irish independence, authors like Patricia Lynch and Eilís Dillon were pioneers in creating a new national children's literature and shaping the distinctive characteristics that would instil in Irish children a sense of Irish identity. A writer who had 'very traditionalist ideas about Ireland, and what it means to be Irish',[1] Lynch in particular was a major force in establishing a literature that Irish children could relate to by creating a recognizable, fictional world 'rooted in the situations in which they lived'.[2] The author herself characterized most of her books as 'stories, with an Irish background, stories of fairs and firesides – with the turf glowing on the hearth – of journeys and of home'.[3] Under her influence, Irish children's literature came largely to reflect the dominant Catholic, rural ideology, 'and indeed continued throughout much of the twentieth century, despite major changes in Irish society, to perpetuate an image of Ireland remarkably similar to the over-simplified pastoral envisioned by de Valera in 1943'.[4] At the same time, Lynch populated her fictional world with leprechauns, changelings, and characters from Irish heroic legend, which, while representing a facet of Irish traditionalism, also reveal a 'wild and unruly subconscious' beneath the conservative surface: the supernatural provides 'a way out or escape, a place where pent-up emotions can be released'.[5] Growing up in Cork, Lynch was inspired by the folktales and legends told by a local 'shanachie', and as a writer who styled herself in that tradition, she felt that the line between the real and the fantastic should not be too strictly drawn: 'It is time we saw life as a whole and realized its magic. What I have tried to do in my books is to reveal the magic of ordinary life.'[6]

Travelling people or 'tinkers' play a prominent role in a number of Patricia Lynch's books, including *The Turf-Cutter's Donkey* (1934), *King of the Tinkers* (1938), and *Tinker Boy* (1955). Her own encounters with the tinkers of Cork in the first decade of the twentieth century are vividly described in her autobiography, *A Storyteller's Childhood* (1947), which depicts her early years from a limited child's perspective, in the same straightforward style as her children's fiction. To the settled girl, the Travellers were, above all, a spectacle of disorder: 'Canvas-covered carts with babies hanging over the front and back: tousled women, hidden in ragged shawls, carrying armfuls of shining tins: wild, barefoot boys and girls with blank, staring eyes and tangled hair running alongside: thin, watchful men in tattered clothes, leading horses.'[7] The details of Lynch's childhood meeting with one of these Travellers, 'a tall, dark man' wearing 'a yellow handkerchief ... twisted about his head',[8] were subsequently embellished in her children's stories. According to the autobiographical account, the tinker, who, like his fictional alter ego, remains nameless, one day found young Tricia and a friend 'mitching' from school, and suggested to the terrified children that they might want to join his tribe. On a later occasion, when she had lost her way at a local fair, she asked the same man for assistance, no longer afraid of the now familiar figure. His people fed her and once again asked if she would 'jine us an' be one of Yalla Hankercher's tribe',[9] before delivering her safely to her relatives. Young Tricia later felt compelled to defend the people she had come to regard as 'my tinkers' against accusations that they were 'a bad lot'.[10] Variations on these accounts of 'Yellow Handkerchief' and his inscrutable tribe are recurring features in Patricia Lynch's children's books.

While Lynch has been credited with shaping the fictional characteristics that would come to embody Irish identity for the children of the newly independent Republic for decades to come, tinkers had featured in children's literature produced outside of Ireland well before she began publishing her works in the 1930s. Diana Mulock, for example, who aimed her moral tale of *Two Little Tinkers* (1876) at '[m]y young American readers',[11] focused on the rescue by two Highland ladies of a pair of 'uncivilised' and 'unwomanly'[12] Scottish tinker girls from what is depicted as a life of idle wandering in the inadequate care of their drunk, mad and violent parents. Transformed by their benefactors, with the assistance of reform school discipline, into neat, industrious and church-going members of society, the girls nevertheless face an uncertain future, since the ladies conclude in the end that 'of materials so rough it is difficult to make good domestic servants'.[13]

In *The Black Cats and the Tinker's Wife* (1923), a book for young children by English author Margaret Baker, the focus is on a young tinker couple. The protagonists are used by the author as a tool for teaching children the values of domesticity, a characteristic also associated with Lynch's tinkers, but Baker depicts her Travellers as abstract, fairy-tale figures rather than realistic characters within a recognizable sociocultural context. The book's silhouette illustrations by Mary Baker represent the young tinker couple as ethereal types resembling Peter Pan and Cinderella: the man is wearing a feathered cap, fringed tunic, tights and soft pointed shoes, and the woman is barefoot in a flowing ankle-length dress.[14] While her husband is out mending pots and kettles, the tinker's wife, who can dance 'as lightly as a fairy',[15] tells the local children 'tales of elves and dwarfs and water-sprites'. At the same time, while they are 'as happy as could be', they feel their lives to be incomplete. Their itinerancy is depicted as the result of poverty rather than choice: the wife often looks longingly at the cosy village homes, and the tinker would 'think sadly of how little he could earn – so little that perhaps he would never be able to give her a home at all'. Aided by a little magic, they are eventually rewarded for their kindness and good deeds with their dearest wish: a home of their own, albeit one located in a cave. The association of tinkers with otherworldliness and magic on the one hand, and poverty and homelessness on the other, is commonplace in children's literature, and the didactic aim of the story is revealed when good behaviour is rewarded with the gift of sedentary domestic bliss.

The reverse message, in which the undesirable behaviour of a poor and homeless tinker is used to set a negative example, is evident in a more recent British children's book, *Tinker Jim*, whose whimsical verse and beautiful illustrations by the father-and-daughter team Paul Coltman and Gillian McClure cannot conceal the message that those of Jim's ilk are dirty, lazy and loose-fingered, and should know their place, which is at the bottom of the social ladder. The opening rhyme sets the scene:

> Tinker Jim lived in a chicken house
> by a twist in Dead Mouse lane.
> He squeezed in tight with fleas and mice.
> When his feet got hot
> he popped them out
> and brought them back in for rain.[16]

Although his father 'had taught Jim gypsy jobs', he was 'slack' and 'fussy', refusing to eat 'baked hedgehog' and 'stinging nettle soup'. The rectory hands out charity meals, but Jim does not find the food to his taste, and discovers better fare in the unguarded freezer of the local manor house: soon his 'sooty cooking pot' overflows with 'French fries and oysters, / dumplings and lobsters, / washed down with Lafitte '82'. Jim's notions next take him to the manor's washing line, from where he strolls into town 'in a grey pinstripe, trim and proper', until he finds himself 'face to face with a copper' who puts an end to his grandiose ways with a spell in prison. The end of the tale finds him back where he began:

> Six months later Tinker Jim sat
> at his chicken-house door. He was thinner
> and had learned a bit more
> about this and that.
> But he'd found his pot,
> old clothes, the lot,
> and was cooking a rabbit for dinner.

For most children in contemporary Britain, 'tinkers' may be an abstraction, but for the Travellers who live in the United Kingdom, having to cope with the kind of preconceived notions embedded in the whimsical verse of *Tinker Jim* is a real and unpleasant fact of life.

TINKERS AND THE MYTH OF RURAL IRELAND

Patricia Lynch's rural Ireland of the first half of the twentieth century bears a remarkable resemblance to the Irish country scene, complete with tinkers, as depicted in *The Irish Twins* (1913) by American children's author Lucy Fitch Perkins, the third book in her highly popular 'Twins of the World' series. Encompassing *The Dutch Twins*,

The Japanese Twins, *The Eskimo Twins*, and so on, the series was designed to 'foster mutual respect and understanding between people of different nationalities', particularly those represented by immigrant communities in the United States.[17] *The Irish Twins* explains to its (Irish-) American audience – somewhat anachronistically, since the book is set in the late nineteenth century – why Mr McQueen, exasperated by the prohibitive rent imposed on his neat little Ballymora farm by the English landlord's agent, decides to move his family to the United States.

The rural Ireland of Patricia Lynch's post-independence fiction is still poor, but emigration (despite Lynch's own childhood, which was partly spent in England) is not presented as an option or a necessity, as hard work provides the families in these stories with a modest but decent existence. In *The Turf-Cutter's Donkey*, Eileen and Seamus 'lived in a cabin just beyond the crossroads at the edge of a great bog', where the income from their father's labour provides them with 'a grand little cow from Kerry, an elegant pink pig in a neat, tidy sty ... and any number of hens and chickens, so they didn't do too badly'.[18] The child-hero of *King of the Tinkers*, Miheal Fahy, also lives in a remote cabin, kept tidy by his poor widowed mother, whose knitting provides enough income to buy essentials, and who at night tells her son stories of leprechauns and mythical beings. The boy looks after the potato patch and the turf, and makes clothes pegs for sale in the market.

The stock setting of early twentieth-century children's fiction from and about Ireland is a small rural cottage or farm, kept neat by its occupants' hard work, which also provides them with a frugal but satisfying diet of potatoes and cabbage, and with the warmth of a turf fire. Stories about leprechauns, fairies and mythological figures keep the children entertained and also provide them with a cultural framework that encourages them to be proud of and excited about their Irishness. The tinkers who appear as stock characters in this type of Irish children's fiction fulfil a multiple role: they are a natural and familiar presence in the rural Ireland of the early decades of the twentieth century; their way of life is presented as the opposite of the domestic family routine that these books encourage children to value; and although their elusiveness and otherness is almost invariably juxtaposed with the otherworldliness of fairies and leprechauns, the tinkers do not belong to the mythic realm. As such, their perceived 'homelessness' also leaves them wandering between fictional genres. Children are warned by their mothers of Travelling people, who are portrayed as the enemies of decent settled families, and not as the stuff of wholesome fantasy: Miheal's mother in *King of the Tinkers* 'told him tales of heroes and leprechauns, but she had never told him a single story about the tinkers'.[19] The tinker's role is that of a go-between, a bridging figure between the realism of rural Ireland and the magic of fairy land. Tinkers are introduced as tools to teach the child by negative example: a temporary escape to the world of the tinkers reveals the values and benefits of a settled and domestic routine. Relief from that routine should be found in the imaginary otherworld of Irish heroes and leprechauns; once the lesson has been learned, the actual other world of the Travellers should thenceforth be avoided.

THE TINKERS AS SPECTACLE

The tinkers are the cause of Larry and Eileen McQueen's adventures at the heart of Lucy Fitch Perkins's *The Irish Twins*. On their way home from Grannie Malone's thatched cottage, with her story about leprechauns still lingering in their ears, the children run into a band of tinkers instead of the Little People of whom Grannie had told them to beware. (In a similar plot configuration, Seamus and Eileen's meeting with a leprechaun in Patricia Lynch's *The Turf-Cutter's Donkey* is also preceded by an encounter with tinkers.) *The Irish Twins* may have been conceived to promote 'mutual respect and understanding' between nationalities, but national minorities like the tinkers are clearly excluded from that premise. Travelling people in children's books usually lack individuality and typically have a collective identity. They also act as a group and are usually depicted as travelling in 'bands' or 'tribes', led by a 'king' or 'chief'.[20] Individuals are rarely referred to by name, but are marked by physical characteristics or distinctive items of apparel, as in 'the big dark tinker' or 'Yellow Handkerchief'. In Lynch's *King of the Tinkers*, the Travellers assert their group identity by singing in chorus as they move along, extolling the virtues of Yellow Handkerchief's leadership: 'Right from under yer nose he'll lift all he wants / An he'll dar yez to say him nay!' (p.37). In *Tinker Boy*, they chant, 'We live, and we live without working. / We ask, though no beggars are we. / Refuse and ye'll surely be sorry, / For we are the wild and the free!'[21]

Typically in these books, the tinkers are, at least initially, observed from a safe distance by the sedentary child protagonists. Paul Delaney has pointed out in relation to late nineteenth-century representations of the Travellers that their alterity meant that 'the only way to know them was to observe them unobserved', so that they were 'translated into a dramatic spectacle of cultural Otherness, and their bodies were symbolically inscribed to indicate many of the fears and fantasies of their thoroughly reputable audience'.[22] In *The Turf-Cutter's Donkey*, Eileen and Seamus spy on the tinkers' encampment '[t]hrough a gap in the bushes' (p.3), and observe its occupants going about their business 'while a tall, ragged man, with a bushy black beard and a bright yellow handkerchief twisted about his head, was making a speech. At the end of every sentence he brought down a big stick on the back and sides of a donkey which was fastened to a tree' (p.4). Later, the children study the tinkers indirectly via their reflection in a magical pool: 'As the water became still they saw, very dimly at first, a picture of the tinkers' encampment. Gradually it became so distinct that they almost believed they were looking down upon the camp itself' (p.10). The Irish twins in Perkins's novel also chance upon the tinkers on the bog and peek at them from behind a wall, as if they were studying a pack of wild and dangerous animals: 'The Twins were afraid of Tinkers. Everybody is in Ireland, because the Tinkers wander around over the country without having any homes anywhere. They go from house to house in all the villages mending pots and pans, and often they steal whatever they can lay their hands on.'[23] The noble desire of the twins' father to own his own farm is implicitly contrasted with the frightening rootlessness of the tinkers, which is also the cause of their disregard for private property.

In the course of *The Irish Twins*, one of the tinkers, 'a rough scraggly man with a beard on him like a rick of hay' (pp.61–2), steals the family's geese. Tinkers as a category are depicted in the book as inherently flawed and un-Irish, a quality inscribed in their physical appearance and their culture. When Mrs McQueen wonders where the tinkers got 'the badness in them the way they have' (p.63), her husband cites a familiar folk explanation: it was the result of a curse put on them by St Patrick, Ireland's patron saint, who, having been led astray by the tinkers, condemned them to walking the roads of the world forever. In the inexorable logic of the curse, badness leads to vagrancy, and vagrancy perpetuates badness. Patricia Lynch also presents thieving as an inherent tinker trait. Only one of the Travellers in *King of the Tinkers* is a tinsmith, and he is a pathetic and ragged figure, marginalized even among the tinkers. The 'tinman' works hard at his trade, but Miheal observes that the tinkers are all 'too busy stealing even to sell the tins' (p.150). Considered 'a fool for working' by his fellow Travellers (p.177), the tinman becomes Miheal's ally in retrieving his stolen fiddle from Yellow Handkerchief.

In Patricia Lynch's fiction, tinkers are a spectacle to be watched, but to be observed by the Travellers in turn is a disconcerting experience. Recollecting her own childhood encounter with the tinkers, Lynch mentions the 'blank, staring eyes' of the older children, and the 'dark faces with glittering eyes' of the assembled crowd.[24] These experiences are echoed in *The Turf-Cutter's Donkey*, when Eileen is rescued and fed by the tinkers, but made shy by 'all those bright eyes watching her' (p.80). In *King of the Tinkers*, Miheal Fahy tries to be brave when he is discovered hiding in the tinkers' cart, but 'when the tinkers formed a circle round him and their bright eyes watched unwinkingly, he was terribly afraid' (p.141). Tessa Nolan, the protagonist of *Tinker Boy*, befriends a Traveller mother and son who aspire to a different way of life, but 'the other tinkers ... watched her with their blank, unwinking eyes and she was afraid of them' (p.37). The impenetrable stares of the tinkers suggest both their essential unknowability and otherness, and the threat of being known and mastered by them. In addition to inscrutability, the exotic 'darkness' of the tinkers' eyes also implies moral corruptness and dangerous attractiveness, qualities combined in Yellow Handkerchief when, in *King of the Tinkers*, he arrives with his tribe at the local fair, 'his dark eyes flashing, his white teeth gleaming with amusement at the way he had kept the people occupied while his followers robbed them' (p.100).

RUNNING AWAY WITH THE TINKERS

The 'tinker' figure in Lynch's novels of the 1930s embodies both a threat to the stability of the social and familial order, and the desire on the part of the settled child to be free from the constraints of a world ruled by adults. The 'subaltern' position of children in relation to adults has been a feature of recent academic discourse about children's literature. The general contention that children are the colonized subjects of colonizing adults is forcefully expressed by Roderick McGillis when he argues that 'children continue to be the subaltern and their literature continues to serve as colonizing (socializing, taming, wrecking ...) agent *par excellence*'.[25] Regardless of whether one accepts the colonial metaphor, commentators on children's literature commonly agree that the literary category itself is a myth or a facade, in that there is 'no body of literature which rests so openly on an acknowledged difference, a rupture almost, between writer and addressee';[26] children's literature 'creates a childhood that is controlled, shaped, constructed according to adults' wishes'.[27] However one approaches the notion of difference, then, it is the case that 'children's fiction belongs firmly within the domain of cultural practices which exist for the purpose of socializing their target audience'.[28]

For child characters who are subject to the rules and restrictions imposed on them by adults, the apparently lawless and carefree life of the tinkers cannot but be attractive: 'They had a fine life', Miheal thinks in *King of the Tinkers*: 'Nothing but holidays' (p.37). Once the child has acted on the desire to join the tinkers, however, it soon comes to the realization that home and family, including their hierarchical power structures, are to be preferred to the chaotic alternative. A learning process has brought the child to the point where it willingly accepts that it must be socialized and civilized according to the adult order. In Lynch's later works, particularly in *Tinker Boy*, the adults' socializing and civilizing effort also extends to some of the tinkers, who are thereby placed into the same category as the child characters, and whose culture is therefore, by implication, deemed immature and flawed. Colonized subjects are typically infantilized by their colonizers; in post-colonial Ireland, Travellers are infantilized in much the same way by the settled Irish population, but at the same time often regarded as being beyond 'redemption'. In Irish children's literature, non-Traveller children fear the tinkers (as adults and strangers) but also patronize them (as social inferiors). Tinker children are doubly colonized, but also considered more redeemable than the adult Travellers, precisely by virtue of their child status, while their parents' subaltern status means they need not be consulted about the future planned for their offspring by outsiders.

In *The Turf-Cutter's Donkey*, Eileen learns to appreciate the care and attention she receives at home when she decides to run away and join the Gypsies. It is striking that 'Gypsies' should be her choice, since Romani Travellers were at that time a rare presence in Ireland. Eileen's romantic notion is a variation on a theme with a long pedigree in English literature rather than a choice based on real-life expectations. At least since the eighteenth century, the threat of kidnapping by Gypsies, or sometimes tinkers, has been 'a staple of nursery rhymes, lullabies, and teasing to coax children into proper behavior'.[29] If you are good, a Scottish rhyme suggests, 'The black Tinkler winna na get ye'.[30] Children, on the other hand, have used the fantasy of running away with the Gypsies to cope with and rebel against the strictures of the parental regime. Significantly, Eileen does not decide to run away with the tinkers, because she is overly familiar with their way of life, which consequently does not carry any romantic appeal.

Patricia Lynch uses the literary device of the Gypsies in conjunction with a much more reality-based visit to the Irish tinkers to create a learning experience for Eileen that is highly structured and contrived. Eileen's adventure with the tinkers in many ways resembles Maggie Tulliver's encounter with the Gypsies in George Eliot's *The Mill on the Floss* (1860), but Lynch's Gypsies resemble neither those in Eliot's novel nor the tinkers in her own narrative. In *The Mill on the Floss*, Maggie Tulliver, made uncomfortable by her family's suggestions that her unusually dark skin and hair make her 'like a gypsy, and "half wild"', and peeved by her brother's preference for more delicately feminine companionship, feels compelled to run away so that 'cruel Tom, and the rest of her relations who found fault with her, should never see her any more'.[31] The Gypsies, however, fail to live up to her romantic expectations. An old woman is cooking stew in a kettle, the men look threatening, and a girl snatches her bonnet, so she is glad when she is eventually placed on a donkey and taken back to her father. In *The Turf-Cutter's Donkey*, Eileen is motivated to run away from home, not only by a quarrel with her brother, but also by instances of frustration at her own clumsiness in carrying out domestic tasks. The similarity of these failings to the stereotypical 'tinkerish' flaws of impetuosity and untidiness remains implicit in her identification with the Gypsies, which in any case is only fleeting, since she has already changed her mind and decided to return home before she reaches their camp. Lost in the woods, she stumbles upon the Gypsy caravan by accident.

In stark contrast to the untidy tinkers with whom Eileen is familiar, the Gypsies in *The Turf-Cutter's Donkey* are represented as overly house-proud. Their caravan has a door with a knocker and a brass handle, 'just like the door to a house in the street of a town' (p.69). Inside, a Gypsy woman is maniacally cleaning furnishings, knick-knacks and silverware, and the caravan 'was the cleanest, tidiest place Eileen had ever seen' (p.70). The girl is made to feed the woman's screaming baby twins, while her intimidating hostess sings: 'All day long I scrub and sweep, / While the babies scream and weep. / All day long I clean and shine. / What a busy life is mine!' (p.74). When Eileen is told that more caravans are on the way and she will soon be minding twenty even more unruly babies, she drops the feeding spoon, causing the gypsy to call her a 'dirty, untidy girl' (p.76), before escaping into the woods, where she runs into the Tinker Chief, who takes her to his camp. In its combination of untidiness and gruff hospitality, the camp is both the antithesis of the Gypsy caravan in *The Turf-Cutter's Donkey* and the counterpart of the Gypsy camp in *The Mill on the Floss*: a huge cauldron of stew is being tended to by an old humpbacked woman, surrounded by 'scattered basins, cups without handles, empty tin cans, cracked plates, enamel plates with the enamel chipped off, lids of saucepans, battered spoons' (p.78). Eileen eats while the chief favourably compares the usefulness of the tinkers' tin wares to the brushes and chairs made by the Gypsies, although Eileen is not persuaded, as 'she couldn't see signs of anything at all made by the tinkers' (p.81). A girl steals her tammy, and she begins to fear that 'the tinkers would not let her go' (p.81), so when the chief offers to take her home, Eileen jumps up: 'She was just as eager to escape from the tinkers as she had been to get away from the gipsy caravan' (p.82). The man leads her out of the wood, and when Eileen's people are heard searching for her on the other side of the canal, he leaves her by the bridge to make her own way across before returning to his own world.

The device of running away with the Gypsies has a long history in English literature, but Lynch's familiarity with the tinkers gives it a new and unusual twist in the context of her Irish story. As does George Eliot in *The Mill on the Floss*, Lynch uses the episode to dispossess her girl protagonist of romantic notions about unrestrained freedom; but where Eliot does so by making the ragged and unwashed Gypsies encountered by Maggie Tulliver very unlike the folkloric image of them she carries in her head, Lynch defies Eileen's expectations of liberty by making her Gypsy woman obsessively house-proud. Since it is the familiar Irish tinkers who always embody untidiness in Lynch's work, the unfamiliar and exotic Gypsies come to act as their foil in this highly contrived configuration. The inclusion of the tinkers in the plot of running away with the Gypsies serves to teach a double lesson. A young girl, Lynch appears to say, should not face the demands and responsibilities of womanhood too soon, but neither should she grow up in a lawless and unstructured environment. Home is the golden mean to which Eileen gladly returns: 'The cabin door was wide open. When Eileen saw the glowing fire on the hearth, the shining blue-and-white delph on the dresser, and the table laid for the dinner no one had eaten, she was so glad she could hardly speak' (p.86). The lesson learned, she resolves never to get out of bed on the wrong side again.

In *King of the Tinkers*, it is a boy who temporarily joins the tinkers, and for him the adventure leads to the recovery of his father's legacy. It all begins when Miheal Fahy's magical hens are stolen by Yellow Handkerchief. When the tinker chief returns in the middle of the night to steal his cockerel as well, the boy follows him as if in a dream in which the real world has merged with the mythical world of his mother's stories. Miheal and the tinkers are joined by an otherworldly creature called Red Lanty (who had given Miheal the stones that became the eggs from which the magical chickens hatched), and together they make their way to a place called 'The Secret Valley', which Miheal remembers from his mother's stories as the place where Finn MacCool and the Fianna, the ancient warriors of Ireland, are living in a kind of suspended animation 'until the great days of Ireland would come again' (p.62). Red Lanty is unhappy about the tinkers' presence and urges Miheal to be quick: 'we'll shut them rascals out!' (p.63). The little men in charge of the valley are unsure what to do: 'they didn't want the tinkers in their valley, but they were terrified of being called inhospitable' (p.65). Miheal warns them that the tinkers will 'never leave the valley. They'll turn you out. They'll spoil the valley' (p.66), which prompts the little men to close the mythical place to all comers, including Miheal, who blames the tinkers for the fact that he will not now enter the world of Finn and the heroes of ancient Ireland. The episode seems to imply that the tinkers are a major impediment to Ireland's return to its former heroic greatness: they act as spoilers of the national myth.

Miheal is left in the company of a poor old woman (reminiscent of the *Sean Bhean Bhocht*, a traditional symbol of colonized Ireland, who here, unlike Yeats's Cathleen Ni Houlihan, eventually turns into a gnarled old tree, rather than a young queen); a baby (who later reveals himself to be a changeling); and a little tinker girl called Nora. Of these three 'otherworldly' beings, all capable of transformation, Nora is the only one who can be permanently humanized and domesticated, but for that she must decide never to return to the 'tinkers', who in the book are represented as being without the concepts of home and family: Nora 'was ashamed' that 'she had no home' (p.122), and she later marvels at the idea of belonging to a proper family 'when she had only been one of the tribe' (p.239). As a tinker, Nora resides in a kind of limbo located between the realm of myth and that of settled Irish society. Offered the choice between the 'otherworld' of the Secret Valley, from which return is uncertain, and the world of Irish reality, she eventually chooses the latter, loath as she is to leave behind her new friends, and further persuaded by the candle beckoning in the window of the widow Fahy's cottage. Miheal's mother welcomes her as her own daughter, dresses her in new clothes, and promises to teach her all the domestic skills.[32]

Miheal himself has gone after the tinkers to retrieve his poultry and his father's magical fiddle, which Yellow Handkerchief had stolen years before, and in the course of his adventures increasingly comes to resemble a tinker boy. Yellow Handkerchief asks him, 'Did ye never want to join the tinkers, Miheal Fahy? ... Did ye never want to share our wild, free life?' (p.144), and Miheal admits that he did. Yet very soon he realizes that 'already he was tired of the tinkers and wondered how long he would have to stay with them' (p.153). Fortunately for him, Nora – now committed to a settled existence – has taken it upon herself to rescue him, with the help of the old woman and the changeling. Eventually, the children come face to face: 'He would hardly have known her, she was so clean and neat. But Nora was shocked at his dirty hands and face, his towsled [*sic*] hair and the state of his sheepskin coat' (p.212). While Nora's stay in the Fahys' cottage is experienced by her as liberating and leads to permanent salvation, Miheal's sojourn with the tinkers amounts to a temporary aberration and is felt by him as a confinement.

Nora's meeting with Miheal takes place at the Fairy Fort, where all the tinkers of Ireland have gathered to fight among themselves about whom to crown as their new king. Yellow Handkerchief claims the position by virtue of his cleverness as a thief, and the musical skill he is about to derive from the magical fiddle strings he intends to wrest from Miheal, but he receives competition from the 'thin leader of the poor tinkers' who advocates the choice of a king 'wid brains, that ud larn us how to be respected instead of been druv from piller to post' (pp.197–8). As a former member of the tribe, Nora is handed the King of the Tinkers' crown by the changeling, who is the owner of the Fort, and places it on Miheal's head (implicitly suggesting that his leadership might be what the thin tinker desires, since it would lead to improvements in the tribe's way of life), but the changeling criticizes her choice and explains that Miheal would 'never be happy stravagin the country, takin what he wants and never payin a penny piece for it' (p.234). By acclamation of Yellow Handkerchief's followers, who decide to ignore the thin tinker's advice, the crown is handed to the tinker chief, and even Nora concedes that he is clever and brave, albeit also an incorrigible thief. The election over, Nora and Miheal return home with the widow Fahy.

In *Tinker Boy*, Patricia Lynch also introduces the idea of an outsider as king of the tinkers, who would act as a civilizing force, and there, too, the plan is thwarted by what is presented as the essential waywardness of the tinkers. Mrs MacDara reveals that her late husband (originally a settled carpenter who married into the tinker tribe) failed to become king due to the jealousy of Yellow Handkerchief. Her husband, she claims, 'would have made us all rich!' and 'could have joined us in one tribe and made us respected!' The other tinkers counter that they do not need respect and that the carpenter '[w]anted us to work, he did! Him and his work! Asking dacent tinkers to make baskets. Moyah!' (p.96). Lynch suggests both that tinkers are in need of correction, and that their essential 'tinkerish' qualities stand in the way of their rehabilitation – a catch-22 that legitimizes their marginalization and exclusion from civil society.

EDUCATION AND REHABILITATION

Traveller rehabilitation is a central theme in *Tinker Boy*, Lynch's novel from the mid-1950s. In the opening chapter, 12-year-old Tessa Nolan observes the tinkers unseen from her bedroom window as they are passing by on their way into town, and the spectacle leaves her with conflicting emotions. Her first thought is, 'These aren't the kind of tinkers I like! ... Tinkers are cruel!' (pp.5–6). On reflection, however, she admits to herself that she could like one of the women and her son 'if they were kinder' (p.12), and acknowledges the lure of the exotic: 'She liked everything strange and this tawny-haired woman was very strange' (p.15). As Tessa later passes the tinker camp, the same woman appears from her caravan and asks the girl to accompany her son on his first trip to school. Tessa takes it upon herself to protect Dara from the suspicion he faces from his teacher and fellow pupils.

Tessa likes her new friends the MacDaras, who live in a cosy but untidy caravan that conspicuously sports a bookshelf in one corner, but she cannot reconcile the paradoxical emotions they evoke in her. She envies them the romantic freedom of 'driving into strange towns and out into the country again, of camping by the seashore and hearing the waves all night long' (p.26). If only one could be a tinker without being a tinker: 'She wouldn't want to stay with the other tinkers. If this caravan were hers, she'd take it where the roads were empty and not a soul would know who she was' (p.26). Tessa is impossibly torn between loathing and desire: '"I do wish Dara and his mother weren't tinkers!" thought Tessa, ... "Only they are and, in a way, I'm glad. I almost wish I was one. It must be grand to travel everywhere, to stop where you like, drive all through the night and never be bothered"' (p.38). The MacDaras are not like other tinkers, however, who frighten Tessa and who are not good neighbours. The Wards are singled out as being the worst, and '[n]ot a tinker in the country wished for their company but it wasn't easy to escape them' (p.67). Such statements come close to suggesting that many Travellers do not really want to be who they are, but simply do not know how to stop being tinkers.

In mid-twentieth-century Ireland there was 'a widespread acceptance that a "protected" childhood (characterized by, among other things, sedentary residence and full-time schooling) was a necessary foundation for adult Irish citizenship. Childhoods that deviated from this model, including Traveller childhoods, were easily portrayed as both endangered and dangerous'.[33] In *Tinker Boy*, Dara wishes to learn, but for him to be accepted in school, he must excel and rise above the tinker stereotype: a typical minority predicament. Soon the teacher realizes that Dara 'wasn't the ordinary kind of tinker boy at all' (p.43), since, already able to read and recite poetry, he also picks up the principle of the long division in no time. It is not long before the whole class is full of admiration for him. Dara's mother then reveals to Tessa why she and her son are no 'ordinary' tinkers: her late husband was a carpenter from a sedentary background, 'a good tradesman' (p.28), who was tricked by the tinkers and ended up falling in love with Maura, soon to become Mrs MacDara. His was a civilizing influence, as he taught his wife to read, and she in her turn taught their son. Dara's mother explains that her husband also advocated kindness to animals, a novelty in the tinker camp and news to her son, who immediately begins to treat his horse more humanely. Asked why she had not told him this before, his mother replies, 'Sure, I didn't think! Even if yer father wasn't a true tinker, I am!' (p.63).

Encouraged by his father's memory, Dara vows, 'I won't always be a tinker. ... One day I'll be something grand, mebbe a horse dealer' (p.36). Tessa supports him in his wish, in the face of her brother's belief that tinkers are incapable of change: 'Michael Joe says a tinker has to be a tinker. He's made that way. It's like boys being boys and girls being girls. They can't help it!' (p.76). When a crate of turkeys belonging to Tessa's aunt Bernadette goes missing, the woman accuses Tessa's new friends of stealing them, but the girl decides that '[i]t must be the Wards!' (p.128). As a generic category, all tinkers are held responsible for each others' actions, so the only way for the MacDaras to prove that they are 'good' tinkers is to follow aunt Bernadette's order to 'make the thieves give back my turkeys!' (p.129). With the help of Dara, Tessa and her brothers retrieve the stolen birds from the Wards, but it is not until Dara rescues both his friend Tessa and his enemy Paud Ward from drowning that he definitively proves himself worthy of Tessa's friendship. The act separates him from his tinker origins in the eyes of the law when Garda O'Keeffe (Bernadette's fiancé) praises Dara as 'a hero – that's what Dara MacDara is – a hero!' (p.172). In the Nolans' home, Tessa's heroic 'tinker friend' is welcomed and dressed in her brother's clothes. Dara's mother, also invited to join the family, knows her place and prefers to stay on her humble 'creepy' by the fire, but Dara sits between Tessa's brothers at the table. Garda O'Keeffe offers him a position with his uncle's horse dealership, so that he 'won't always be a tinker' (p.36). Trading in horses is a traditional Traveller occupation, however, so Dara's rise in the world is less defined by what he does than by the context in which he does it: finding sanction and supervision within a sedentary framework is what makes him an ex-tinker. Legitimacy is irreconcilable with the 'wild, free life' of the tinkers, but the 'tinker boy' must not rise too far above his station: while Tessa continues in school, Dara begins his working life in an appropriate trade, and in that context must be subordinate to the policeman's uncle.

In the children's books by Patricia Lynch, the presence of tinkers is used to enhance the Irish quality of the narratives: like the bogs, cottages and fairs, the tinkers are represented as an inalienable part of the national infrastructure. At the same time, tinkers are shown to be 'different' from the Irish protagonists of the novels; the function of that difference, however, is not to challenge the settled cultural norm but rather to emphasize it. Always focalized through the majority culture, the presence of the tinkers is not about 'alterity' but about 'cultural continuity'.[34] Tinkers are generically represented as inferior, although there are 'good tinkers' and 'bad tinkers'. Bad tinkers are violent, work-shy, homeless thieves who spoil the countryside. Good tinkers are passive and non-violent, have romantic traditions, are eager to prove their worth, and some even have the potential to become 'just like us'. Their highest aspiration is to stop being tinkers, and kind settled people are around to help them do the right thing. Patricia Lynch's fiction of the first half of the twentieth century teaches young readers how to behave properly in an Irish context. Being a good Irish citizen, the lesson implies, is incompatible with being a tinker. Today, Irish Traveller organizations are making an effort to dispel that widespread cultural bias, by promoting 'an understanding of Travellers as full and equal citizens of Ireland with their own culture and identity'.[35]

TEENAGE FICTION FROM IRELAND, SCOTLAND AND THE UNITED STATES

A number of novels for teenagers and young adults published in and outside of Ireland in the last twenty-five years depict Travellers as having a distinct culture, yet the aim of these works is less to expose a settled readership to a different ethnicity in order to foster understanding and tolerance, than to use the Travellers' otherness to explore the kind of moral choices and individual decisions the books' young readers themselves might be confronted with on the cusp of adulthood. In *Circle of Fire* (1982) by William H. Hooks, the focus is on a white boy in the American South of the 1930s, whose encounter with Irish tinkers forces him to find a way to respond to the racism and bigotry endemic in his society. Mollie Hunter's *Cat, Herself* (1985) and Kim Ablon Whitney's *See You Down the Road* (2004) are narrated from the first-person perspective of a Traveller girl in, respectively, Scotland and the United States, who faces demands and responsibilities imposed on her by her culture and her family. The implicit question to the young, female and settled readers of these books is, 'What would you do?' Irish writer Mike Scott's trilogy about the friendship of Judith Meredith, a wealthy settled teenage girl, and Sean 'Spider' O'Brien, a young Traveller – *Judith and the Traveller* (1991), *Judith and Spider* (1992), and *Good Enough for Judith* (1994) – addresses similarities and differences between the friends, and questions the extent to which it is possible for them to have a relationship.

Questions of this nature are inevitably based on a comparison between Traveller and sedentary values and practices, and while the characters in these novels seem far removed from the world of Patricia Lynch's fiction, the same issues linger: is being a Traveller acceptable or not, and what determines the answer? Does a Traveller have the choice to cease being a Traveller? 'Being a Traveller', in other words, is problematized even when the author's intentions are sympathetic: it is portrayed as a potentially limiting and anti-modern condition that hampers individual choice. The young Traveller women in these novels are questioners who refuse to be held down by the traditions of their culture. Whether that culture is depicted in a positive light (as in Mollie Hunter's novel) or negatively (as in Kim Whitney's), it must be challenged from within by a teenage rebel whose cause is progress, especially for women. The choices and challenges faced by adolescents are a staple of teenage fiction; however, when a novel written by a settled author for a settled audience depicts a Traveller girl or boy, those choices and challenges have a way of turning into a critique of an entire culture.

RACE RELATIONS IN *CIRCLE OF FIRE*

William H. Hooks grew up on a North Carolina tobacco farm and often played with the children of the fifteen mostly black tenant farmers employed by his father. As Director of Publications of Bank Street College, Hooks was responsible for 'the first "ethnically integrated and urban-oriented" readers for children',[36] and his own children's books also frequently address the problem of race relations in the American South. In *Crossing the Line* (1978), for example, he introduces readers to Harrison Hawkins, a white teenager in rural North Carolina, who confronts racial prejudice in his town. *Circle of Fire* (1982), in which 11-year-old Harrison and his black friends save an encampment of Irish-American Travellers from an attack by the Ku Klux Klan, serves as a prequel to the earlier novel.

In *Circle of Fire*, Harrison's best friend Kitty and the latter's sister Magnolia, otherwise known as Scrap, are 'colored', which the author's note at the end of the book explains 'was the respectable term used by both whites and blacks' at the time.[37] No character in the novel is referred to as 'black': their skin is always described as 'brown'. Harrison would like to ignore the significance of race and cannot understand how skin colour can be a cause for hatred, but he is at times uncomfortably confronted with his friends' poverty and with the pressure of society to discriminate. Though no bigot, his grandmother reminds him that he will soon reach the 'age of accountability' where he will have to find new friends of his 'own kind' (p.21). Meanwhile, Harrison is happy to continue playing 'Eskimo Pie' with Kitty and Scrap, a game that involves shouting 'Eskimo pie' whenever the white boy finds himself flanked by his two black friends. While foregrounding the children's skin colour, the game suggests their dependence on each other at the same time that it reinforces the centrality of the white and the marginality of the black characters.

The Irish tinkers are introduced to complicate the issue of race and racial prejudice. They should have travelled south for the winter, but have been prevented from making their way to Florida by harassment from the Ku Klux Klan, whose hatred encompasses 'thieving Catholic gypsies' (p.69) as well as black people and Jews. Hooks also racializes the tinkers, however, making them dark-complexioned with black hair and blue eyes, so that they appear as a group to combine the predominant racial characteristics of whites and 'coloreds'. When they are attacked by the Klan, the tinkers serve as a symbol of unity around which the two racial groups of the community can gather in a stand against bigotry.

Shortly before Christmas, the three friends run into a strange boy while they are fleeing from their racist neighbour, Klan leader Bud Highsmith. The boy, Liam Cafferty, serves as a means to convey that prejudice is not just a racial issue. When the children identify him as a Gypsy he replies: 'My family is Irish tinkers. Some folks call us gypsies. But my brother says that's because they're ignorant' (p.28). After he has run off, Scrap claims that '[g]ypsies steals children and sells them', and that '[e]verybody knows that' (p.32). Harrison's eccentric friend Little Hattie suggests that perhaps to Irish Travellers, being called Gypsies is like 'us colored folks ... being called niggers. ... Maybe tinkers is what they would like you to call them. Or just their Christian names would do' (p.57). Putting the 'Christian' theory of tolerance and respect into practice is another matter, however, and everyone in the book, including Hattie, persists in referring to the tinkers as Gypsies, although Harrison and Liam eventually call each other by their first names. The focus in fiction for teenagers is often on individual development and relationships rather than social or political structures, and the discrepancy between recognizing and respecting individual identity while ignoring the importance of doing the same in terms of group identity is symptomatic of the limitations of the genre when dealing with ethnic groups, especially those to which the focus readership does not belong.

Hooks makes a point of not overly exoticizing the 'Gypsies', and has Harrison notice that the tinkers are poor, and do not resemble the depictions he has seen in storybooks. The characters are not one-dimensional. At one point Liam tries to steal a crowbar, and justifies this to Harrison by alluding to a legend dating back to the time of Christ which explains why the tinkers have the right 'to take what

[they] need' (p.60), but he is also capable of generosity, and makes Harrison a present of a wood-carved horse. Hooks does provide some romantic touches when he endows the old tinker woman with 'some powers of divination' (p.54), and also gives Liam the gift of foretelling events by consulting Tarot cards. At Christmas, the Travellers decorate their camp with holly and lanterns, and amidst this 'magic scene' (p.111) they perform a mummers' pageant with music and elaborate costumes.[38]

This magical, peaceful Christmas scene is violently disturbed by the Ku Klux Klan.[39] Scrap's childish belief that 'gypsies steals children' has a violent counterpart in the Klan's objection to the mixed marriage of Liam's brother Tom and a settled woman, Kathleen, whose long blond hair Harrison immediately notices as standing out conspicuously among the black Traveller heads: 'They said Tom would never get away with stealing Kathleen from her folks' (p.80). This is not the tinkers' first encounter with the Klan: when Kathleen first became pregnant, the KKK burned a cross in front of their wagon, and punished Liam for trying to tear it down by carving the symbol into his skull, the festering scar of which he still hides underneath his cap. Harrison, Kitty and Scrap overhear Bud Highsmith plotting a Christmas day attack on the Traveller camp and arguing that 'cleaning out that nest of thieving Catholic gypsies would have a healthy effect on uppity niggers and some nigger-loving whites I know around here' (p.69). Ordered to secrecy by his father, but unsure whether the latter is acting on his information and unable to ask Kitty to put his own family in danger, Harrison goes out alone on Christmas Eve to warn the tinkers of the impending attack. At the camp, the Christmas pageant is in progress, and the Klan are already advancing, a day ahead of schedule. Soon a flaming cross lights the scene as men in hoods point guns and demand to see 'the woman and her gypsy violator' (p.119). The tinkers are passive; they do not run or fight, even when Tom is brutally whipped, but stand 'frozen, the way wild animals do at night when they're caught on the highway in the glare of headlights' (p.118). At this moment, Harrison is unexpectedly joined by his black friend Kitty, and together they run to Little Hattie's for help. A brush fire started by her forces the Klan members back to their cars, where they are awaited by the police: Bud Highsmith's own black half-sister (the daughter of his father and the family cook) had provided Harrison's father with the precise details of her brother's plans.

In *Circle of Fire*, the 'dark' and passive tinkers are saved from violent bigotry by the concerted efforts of the black and white members of the community. Their safe passage to Florida is also arranged by Mr Harrison. The Christmas story ends appropriately with the birth of a baby daughter to Tom, the Traveller, and Kathleen, the settled woman, in a stable of sorts: the Hawkins' barn, where the tinker caravan has been parked for shelter. A child of compromise, already halfway between black and white, she enters the world in a place that is an amalgam of the road of her father and the house of her mother. Born on Christmas Day and with a caul, the sign of the veil that will allow the tribe's grandmother to pass on the heavy burden of her gift of divination, the girl represents both salvation and the future vision of a society where race and religion will no longer be a source of conflict.

Circle of Fire extends its message of compromise and understanding even towards the members of the Ku Klux Klan, who are chased across the state line by the sheriff's men, but not arrested. There is no indication that the tinkers are interested in justice or retribution, and they appear unaffected by the brutality recently inflicted on their small community. They are just passing through as a symbolic means of teaching blacks and whites a lesson about race relations and bigotry. Their saviours are not the people most in need of such instruction, however, since they were already respectful of each other to begin with, although Harrison, Kitty and Scrap may have gained a more realistic view of 'Gypsy' life. The only real racists in the novel are the Klansmen, who go unpunished, whose views remain unchanged, and who are likely to return. Harrison's father tells his son that the solution to prejudice lies in human decency, 'a precious thing you have to learn early and keep working at' (p.140). Because the focus of fiction for teenagers and young adults tends to be on individual choice, growth and responsibility (the dilemmas of adolescence), the fate of the society it depicts depends disproportionately on such individual 'decency' rather than on social or political action within a system of law and justice.

GENDER IN *CAT, HERSELF* AND *SEE YOU DOWN THE ROAD*

Both *Cat, Herself* by Scottish author Mollie Hunter, first published as *I Will Go My Own Way* (1985), and *See You Down the Road* (2004) by American author Kim Ablon Whitney, are narrated from the perspective of a Traveller girl. Set in the 1970s, Hunter's novel follows Scottish Traveller Catriona McPhie from age 11 to her marriage at

16. Whitney was inspired to write about contemporary Irish-American Travellers after reading an article about them, around the time when the Toogood case was making headlines in the USA.[40] Her narrator, 16-year-old Bridget Daugherty, also accepts her boyfriend's marriage proposal at the book's conclusion. While *Cat* paints a positive picture of a close-knit family often unfairly treated by the settled world, Whitney's Travellers are scam-artists whose unlawful activities make Bridget increasingly doubtful about her future as a member of the community. When the characters in Whitney's novel are called 'gypsies, con artists, thieves, swindlers, even trailer trash',[41] Bridget feels hurt, but she, too, is troubled by the fact that all the Travellers she knows are indeed perpetrators of scams; in Hunter's novel, on the other hand, common assumptions like '[a]ll tinkers were thieves'[42] are consistently proven wrong by the Travellers' basic decency. Bridget's conflict is that she wants to be 'normal', like 'a Country [settled] girl' (p.28), to the point where she contemplates leaving the Travellers at the risk of being disowned by her family, whereas Cat's struggle is to overcome the limitations traditionally placed on women within Traveller culture.

Although Bridget's dilemma is more pronounced than Cat's, both girls are depicted in a positive light for challenging what are portrayed as undesirable or restrictive practices. *Cat, Herself* pays attention to the wide variety of skilled and unskilled jobs performed by Travellers, ranging from basket weaving, pearl fishing and raspberry picking to trading in vintage cars and antiques. The Travellers in *See You Down the Road* have only two ways of making a living: small scams (like cheating and stealing from individuals and department stores, or painting and tarmacking with inferior materials), and big scams (such as elaborate real estate swindles). Bridget constantly feels ashamed about her involvement in such deceptions, and is sorry for the victims. Since being a Traveller in this novel is defined by these negative practices, her only alternative is to stop being a social anomaly: 'I wanted to do something normal, something everyday, something besides scamming Kmarts or paving driveways. Something a Country girl would do with her Country boyfriend' (p.28). While Bridget is full of misgivings about her culture, Cat is never ashamed of being a Traveller.

In both novels the Traveller characters think a good deal about the essence and origins of their way of life, particularly nomadism, in a self-conscious way that does not ring true but serves as an expository mechanism for the books' settled target audience. Cat wonders how a

Traveller could have 'a home' (p.61), to which her grandmother replies that 'home' for a Traveller means 'being at peace in the one place where – for a while at least – you don't feel the need to journey' (p.62). Bridget argues with her boyfriend that 'we're always far away from home. We don't even have homes', to which he replies that 'home' is 'wherever we all are'. The answer does not satisfy her, for 'home' to her implies social conformation: 'Normal people go to school and have normal jobs' (p.145). According to Cat's grandmother, the Travellers were originally 'just the homeless ones o' this land', but stayed on the road because they had 'something different' in their natures (p.63). Later, she defines that difference as freedom: 'a body should always be free to live as that one wants to live. That's what travellers believe, anyway, Cat. And if you're still wondering what makes us different from other people, *that's* where the difference lies' (p.87). Cat experiences life in a tent as freedom, and considers the 'walled-up lives' of settled people stifling and confining (p.65). For Bridget, by contrast, the trailer is a prison where she can never be herself: 'Even in a parked trailer, somehow I never felt rooted' (p.110). In a rented motel room, however, she can feel that she is 'actually somewhere' (p.111). For Hunter's character, the focus is on Traveller pride and self-confidence; by contrast, Whitney makes Bridget ask herself, 'Why did I think I deserved more?' and wonder, 'What if I wasn't a Traveler?' (p.137). Both Cat and Bridget are acutely aware of their difference from the settled norm, but they respond to those differences in contrasting ways.

Both girls rebel against what their authors present as 'traditional' Traveller ways by advocating women's rights. Cat defends the right of girls to wear trousers, and defiantly believes that Traveller men have no right to beat their wives. Bridget also disapproves of how Traveller wives are often treated by their husbands, and vows her relationship with Patrick will be different: 'I needed us to be best friends – I couldn't settle for less' (p.107). Since Cat is an only child, her father passes on to her his trout-catching and pearl-fishing skills, breaking traditional male-female divisions of labour. His daughter worries about acquiring a reputation as a manly woman, which will affect her chances of finding a husband, but her grandmother, while acknowledging that Traveller men are old-fashioned, assures her that Mr Right will not be put off by her skills. Cat puts aside her worries and becomes a kind of super-Traveller: 'she knew instinctively she could ... never be other than she was then – a traveller, one who had been born to woman's work, but still one who had crossed the barrier that would have stopped her finally having *all* the traveller skills at her command' (p.95). Bridget is an avid reader (of Malcolm X and Anne Frank!) and dreams of college – 'to go to school and study history' (p.169) – but that would mean leaving her family for good, like her estranged older sister, and she is not, in the end, prepared to make that break.

Eventually, both Cat and Bridget settle for marriage within the Traveller community, but only because their partners have revealed themselves as gentle, accommodating males. Cat's boyfriend Charlie, aware of both her nostalgia for the old way of travelling and her advanced views on women's rights, compromises his own future as a car dealer by providing his wife with a pony and cart containing everything they need for their life on the road, including Cat's pearling gear. One of Bridget's objections to Traveller customs with regard to sexuality had been the double standard for boys and girls: 'I didn't see why it was perfectly fine for Patrick to screw anyone he wanted ... – but I was supposed to stay as pure as pure could be until my wedding day' (p.20). When Patrick confesses to Bridget that he has, in fact, 'saved himself' for her, she believes 'he'd be true' to her and accepts his proposal of marriage (p.185). Both *Cat, Herself* and *See You Down the Road* end by emphasizing the importance of family and marriage, traditional prospects made acceptable for each girl by the sensitivity of the young Traveller husband.

The sweeping generalizations about Travellers in both novels are, in a way, the result of the books' focus on the individual growth of their protagonists. In an online forum discussion, Whitney called Bridget 'an Irish traveler and basically they're con artist[s] who steal for a living', in virtually the same breath that she defended her refusal to provide her protagonist with a straightforward solution to her dilemma: 'I found a lot of people wanted my m[ain] c[haracter] to leave her troubled life behind ... to realize the errors of their way of life and change for the better', but she was not prepared to provide such a 'message driven ending'.[43] Mollie Hunter's narrative also emphasizes the personal development of her character while glossing over social issues concerning the Travellers. Both Cat and her mother Ilsa have 'the gift' of foreseeing the future. Ilsa has lost five babies, and when she becomes pregnant again she secretly arranges for the baby to be born in the caravan, with only Cat's help, because a vision has told her that this is the only way to save the child. Cat even goes so far as to disable the car, to make an emergency trip to the hospital impossible, understanding that her mother fears the machines and gadgets of the institution, where women are treated like lumps of meat, especially if they are Travellers. The baby son is delivered safely. In the real world, a high rate of infant mortality is a serious issue for Traveller families; many women lack adequate healthcare during pregnancy and childbirth, and are unable to avail themselves of second sight to bring their babies safely into the world.[44] Hunter's novel, however, nowhere addresses the reason why Ilsa has lost five babies, focusing instead on Cat's lesson in self-confidence: 'you have to trust the gift, Cat, even when you feel you don't want to, even when other people think you're being stupid' (p.213).

Even when *Cat, Herself* does touch upon the issue of social activism, it does not give the Travellers themselves any agency. One of the Travellers' supporters who periodically visits the camp is Dr Ballantyne, an academic who is part of 'an official project that takes an interest in travellers' (p.139). He claims to admire them for their life of resourcefulness and sharing, their determination not to be labelled, and their belief in individuality (pp.261–2). He warns the McPhies about the 'trouble' going on in the nearby town, caused by an English Gypsy named Reevel Faw, who is using the same tactics on behalf of Scottish Travellers that 'he's already used for the so-called benefit of those English gypsies' (p.183) – essentially blackmailing town councils by collecting 'the very worst he can find among the travelling folk', dumping them among 'some decent travellers', whose reputation is blackened as a result, and harassing and threatening the settled people, 'which makes them very hostile, at first, but willing to eventually do anything that'll bring back peace to the town' (pp.183–4). Ballantyne's own organization keeps to the moral high ground by 'pushing away at all the local authorities ... *without* doing any damage to the travellers themselves' (p.185). *Cat, Herself* advocates Traveller passivity: it does not show any Travellers as activists for the improvement of their own living conditions, nor does Dr Ballantyne's 'official' organization appear to include any Travellers.

Both *Circle of Fire* by William Hooks and Mollie Hunter's *Cat, Herself* depict atrocious hate crimes against Travellers, but make a point of asking readers to see the perpetrators of this violence as victims, too. Klan member Bud Highsmith is a vicious bigot, but he escapes punishment. Harrison's father tells his son that 'those high and mighty nightriders are for the most part scared little men hiding under bedsheets who need to have somebody they can bully and look down on. ... There's something in all of us that wants to be top dog, that wants to keep *our kind* in control' (pp.139–40). Dr Ballantyne explains to the McPhies that the young punks who set fire to their camp and killed a baby are actually quite pathetic: having grown up in a town slum, they resembled 'creatures from some kind of hell – a hell of dirt, and ignorance, and violence. And yet they were human beings. Young ones; still young enough to be ashamed of what they'd done' (p.258). For them, the Travellers agree, having to live with the knowledge of what they have done is punishment enough. Good Travellers in these novels are remarkably willing to forgive and forget.

CLASS IN MIKE SCOTT'S *JUDITH AND SPIDER* TRILOGY

The books in the trilogy about Judith Meredith and 'Spider' O'Brien by Mike Scott, a prolific writer who has turned his hand to a variety of genres ranging from folklore and fantasy to science fiction and horror, focus on the friendship between a privileged teenage girl from Killiney and a young Traveller. In *Judith and the Traveller*, the girl, upset at her widowed father's decision to marry her late mother's best friend, runs away from home and encounters Spider, who lives in his van and takes it upon himself to protect her. In *Judith and Spider*, police wrongly suspect the young man of having committed a number of crimes, and Judith runs away with him to help him solve his problems. In *Good Enough for Judith*, Mr Meredith engages Spider's help to rescue his daughter from the detrimental influence of her manipulative, drug-dealing boyfriend.

Judith and the Traveller makes much of the fact that the teenagers are from different backgrounds. The difference between their respective 'worlds' is depicted mostly in terms of externals. Judith is 'tall, blonde-haired, brown-eyed',[45] with perfect teeth and make-up. Spider's skin is 'deeply tanned', his eyes and hair are black, he wears an earring and has a spider tattoo on his hand. Whereas he speaks 'in a strange, almost rural accent' (p.22), Judith's accent is 'posh' (p.21). Material possessions emphatically set the two worlds apart. While Judith dresses in designer clothes, her father wears 'silk pyjamas',[46] and her stepmother's feet slide into 'butter-soft suede slippers' (p.70), Traveller apparel includes 'cheap jeans' (p.26), a 'cheap anorak' (p.46), and a 'cheap digital watch' (p.69). Mr Meredith's Mercedes forms a shrill contrast to the rusty wrecks driven by Travellers: even the Volkswagen stolen by Spider at one point is 'battered' (p.104). The Merediths' house in Killiney is a palace compared to a caravan, and Spider had 'known whole families who lived in spaces smaller than this kitchen' (p.23).

Mike Scott's focus on material possessions and external appearances, combined with his attempt to have his characters transcend such limited perspectives, leads him down paths of tortuous logic. In the first book of the trilogy when Judith initially discovers that Spider is a Traveller, she is surprised because she was under the impression that all Travellers were 'dirty and begged'. Spider, however, does not 'look like an itinerant' but 'like an ordinary person'. Spider explains that he is 'not the usual traveller', since his parents 'settled' just after he was born, to give him 'a chance' (p.44). At a halting site, Judith meets a more 'usual' Traveller in the person of Kathleen Ryan, a teenager with designs on Spider; she has 'bad teeth', and her 'clothes were cheap, threadbare in places, and her swollen feet had burst through the sides of her low-heeled shoes' (p.50). After living with Spider in his van for only a few days, Judith realizes she herself is beginning to smell and look dirty: 'she looked like a traveller' (p.9). People driving by look at her in disgust. The nurse in the casualty department where Judith takes Spider after he has been beaten up by Kathleen's brothers 'immediately tagged them as travellers' because of their looks, as she remembers the drunken Travellers who had come to the hospital the previous weekend: 'the four of them had caused absolute chaos in the busy Casualty Department' (p.89). On the one hand, then, Spider does not look like a Traveller because his parents raised him in a house; on the other hand, the settled rich girl is soon mistaken for a Traveller because she looks dirty. Twisted logic aside, the bottom line appears to be that Travellers are not clean and do not live in houses.

In *Judith and the Traveller*, Spider makes a point of explaining to Judith that Travellers are often dirty because they do not have access to facilities, and criticizes her for lumping all Travellers together: 'like settled people, there are different sorts of travellers – good and bad' (p.45). That dichotomy is starkly depicted through the Ryan family. While police unfairly suspect Spider of committing robberies and of kidnapping Judith in *Judith and Spider*, the Ryans actually burgle for a living and end up abducting Judith for her involvement with Spider. While Kathleen is holding Judith captive, she wonders what had attracted Spider to the settled girl: 'Was it her blond hair, or maybe her flawless skin, her snow-white teeth or her puppy-dog eyes? Kathleen Ryan's hair was red and coarse, her skin was speckled with blackheads and she had a rash of pimples across her forehead, her teeth were yellow and uneven' (p.123). Kathleen's accusation – 'You've had hot water every day of your life' – combines hatred with self-disgust, and when she touches Judith's cheek and comments on her 'soft skin', comparing it to the 'coarse, rough, texture' of her own, Judith knows she is 'going to cut her with the knife, scar her face' (p.124). In a pre-emptive strike with a chisel, Judith cuts Kathleen's chin instead and is able to escape. What characters do in Mike Scott's trilogy is always less important than what motivates them.

If Spider and Kathleen represent good Travellers and bad Travellers respectively, the difference between them lies less in how they behave and more in how they relate to the settled world. According to the gardaí, Spider has been 'living rough on Dublin's streets, stealing and begging what he can' (p.59). When Judith is with him, he steals bread and milk for breakfast, as well as a car, so that they can follow the Ryans and find out which warehouse they are going to rob. Judith is initially shocked at the theft, but Spider has 'encountered similar reactions before from settled people', and explains why there was no alternative: 'We needed the car. ... Judith, when you're living on the streets, you'll often end up doing things not because you want to, but because you have to. You'll steal food to survive: is that so wrong?' (p.97). Convinced by his argument that this is the way of the Travellers, Judith later confronts Kathleen by telling her, 'you're no traveller. You're nothing but a thief', whereas Spider had stolen 'to survive. ... He's not a thief' (p.119). When the Ryans are caught, Judith's father predicts they will get 'fifteen years apiece' for burglary and kidnapping; Mr Meredith's 'money and contacts', however – 'this man was a personal friend of the Taoiseach and the Commissioner of Police' (p.59) – are able to keep Spider 'from joining them in jail' (p.127).

'Being a Traveller' in Mike Scott's trilogy is depicted mostly in terms of poverty, dirt and living 'on the streets'. Why the Travelling community is so disadvantaged is not addressed directly, and Scott sends out mixed signals about Spider's life as a 'Traveller'. His parents gave up life on the road to give him 'the chance of a way of life they had never known' (*Judith and Spider*, p.29), but their nostalgic stories of the past made their son 'determined to have his own adventures and to escape the routine boredom of school and home' (p.29), to try and 'relive the life they had wandering the roads of Ireland' (*Judith and the Traveller*, p.45). Running away from home and living on the streets with junks and down-and-outs is consistently referred to by Spider as 'travelling'. He tells Judith: 'I love travelling, always have. It's in my blood you see, but I always loved coming home ... having someone to come home to. I could always go home to my mother. It was my safety net. When things got too bad, when I couldn't stand the streets any more, she was always there' (pp.111–12). Spider claims that Travellers on the road never make friends because 'those friendships will be broken' (p.127), and Judith realizes that his is 'a cold, friendless, often dangerous world' (p.130).

Spider cannot read, and in *Judith and the Traveller* he explains that for people who are moving from place to place, simply trying to survive, schooling does not 'seem so important' (p.101). When Judith points out that his parents were settled, however, he tells her, 'There never seemed to be enough time. I hated school. I didn't want to learn' (p.102). Judith also worries about her friend's alcohol use, and while he tells her that he resisted the pressure to drink or use drugs from 'friends' he made on the streets, who 'weren't real friends', he does drink because '[l]ots of travellers drink. ... All the problems that surround you, that are part of your life when you're a traveller, cease to exist' (pp.110–11). The sociological explanations of Traveller habits are juxtaposed with Spider's individual choices, but in each instance the underlying cause of Spider's undesirable behaviour is being a Traveller: Spider drinks because he is a Traveller; and while he left school because he was bored, that boredom was the result of travelling being 'in his blood'.

Travellers are depicted as society's losers because they are not like settled people. Spider tells Judith that they cannot love each other because Travellers have no future: 'You have a future, Judith; you can read and write, you know what you're going to be. You'll have a career, a house of your own, a husband and children if you want them. I don't have a future. I can neither read nor write. I'll probably never have a place of my own that doesn't have wheels' (p.112). Being a Traveller also means that he has no chance of finding a job. Once Judith is back home, and Spider has disappeared to avoid being questioned by police about crashing the Ryans' van into their roadblock – and they will not catch him, Judith says, because '[h]e's a traveller' (p.143) – she tells her stepmother that 'he had seen so much of life; he had done so many things ... and yet, because of who he is and what he is, there's no future for him and the others like him'. She wonders 'what he'd be able to do if he had the opportunities that I have' (p.142). She thereby ignores the fact that Spider's parents had left the road to give him some of those 'opportunities', but that he preferred the 'adventure' of living in an abandoned building and serving as a bodyguard for a heroin addict. As a Traveller, Spider may be a loser, but his friendship with the settled girl makes him 'good', and the settled gaze can faultlessly distinguish the difference. The Ryan brothers in *Judith and Spider* are brainless thugs, and Kathleen is a bully with a 'fiery temper' (p.27), but when Judith's father finally meets Spider he is impressed, even though the boy is fighting with Mr Meredith's hired protectors at the time: 'the young man facing him was darkly handsome and obviously intelligent'. Meredith also admires his 'extraordinary courage' and his self-control (p.107). The endorsement from the wealthy non-Traveller is Spider's saving grace.

Although Mike Scott's trilogy makes much of the 'two worlds' to which Judith and Spider belong, their friendship is more about personal growth than gaining a real understanding of the workings of those separate worlds. When Judith falls in love with Spider in the first book, she learns that love 'makes you look at things in a different light' (p.142): she realizes that her father and stepmother love each other, and that her reaction to the marriage had been selfish and caused by jealousy. In the second book, Spider learns from Judith that his preference for the 'freedom of travelling ..., of being responsible to no-one but himself' had been 'aimless' and 'selfish' (p.30), and he thanks her for encouraging him to face Kathleen: without Judith, he would 'still be running. Now, you've given me the chance' (p.89). Judith's father learns to listen to his wife's opinion, and to accept that Spider is not a bad person. Spider does not stick around after his street smarts, combined with Mr Meredith's wealth and influence, have saved Judith from the Ryans: 'He wanted to do some travelling before he settled down' (p.127). At the end of the trilogy's final instalment, *Good Enough for Judith*, Spider definitively walks away from Judith, and from a job offered him by her father, towards an uncertain future on a building site in England: 'There was nothing for him in London ... but was there any more of a future for him in Ireland?'[47] Judith remains behind as the loser who, like Pegeen Mike in Synge's *Playboy*, only belatedly realizes the extent of her loss; but unlike Christy Mahon, Spider, likely gaffer though he may be, is unlikely to go romancing through a romping lifetime. By being born a Traveller, he has drawn the short straw in the lottery of life, and is therefore destined to be an outcast forever.

The Irish children's fiction of the first half of the twentieth century represented Travellers as acceptable only if they were passive and non-violent, possessed of romantic traditions, and potentially ready and willing to fit into the sedentary way of life. Fifty years or so down the road, the books for young adults discussed above sometimes present the Travellers in more nuanced language, but otherwise not much has changed. In *See You Down the Road*, Kim Whitney has written what Lara Zeises calls 'an engaging novel about a little-known ethnic minority of Irish nomads called the Travelers',[48] but one in which 'Traveller life' equals a life of crime. Travellers may be an 'ethnic minority', but their whiteness may partly explain why their fictional treatment often lacks the sensitivity accorded to racial minorities. To a question in an online forum about the importance of racism as a topic in young adult fiction, Whitney replied that it is 'very important but I think in our pc world people might be wary of it', and, ironically perhaps, could not think of any authors who write well about race.[49] Two online reviews of her novel by members of the book's target audience are revealing in this regard. One reviewer wrote that Bridget 'wonders what it would be like to live in a real house and go to school like a real kid', and concludes: 'I heard about "gypsies" before, but I didn't know the scams they pulled to make money. I wouldn't want to live like that and sympathize with Bridget, who is a tough and strong person.'[50] According to another reader, Bridget asks herself 'whether she should stay a Traveler (they've also been called gypsies and grifters) ... and try out life in the "regular" world'.[51] Travellers or 'Gypsies', then, are not perceived as 'real', 'regular' or 'normal' people, and once their novelty wears off they can be dismissed: 'You don't have to know anything about the Traveler lifestyle to appreciate Bridget's struggles. The search for self is universal and poignantly played out here.'[52] The young adult is central in young adult fiction; the Travellers just happen to be passing by.

NOTES

1. Margaret Burke, 'The Development of Patricia Lynch's Writing in the Light of an Exploration of New Archival Material', in Celia Keenan and Mary Shine Thompson (eds), *Studies in Children's Literature, 1500–2000* (Dublin: Four Courts Press, 2004), p.99.
2. Nancy Watson, 'A Revealing and Exciting Experience: Three of Patricia Lynch's Children's Novels', *The Lion and the Unicorn*, 21, 3 (1999), p.345.
3. 'Patricia Lynch (Mrs Richard M. Fox).' Accessed 20 January 2005: http://catholicauthors.com/lynch.html
4. Ciara Ní Bhroin, 'Forging National Identity: the Adventure Stories of Eilís Dillon', in Keenan and Thompson, *Studies in Children's Literature*, pp.112–13.
5. Margaret Burke, 'The Development of Patricia Lynch's Writing', p.98.
6. 'Patricia Lynch'.
7. Patricia Lynch, *A Storyteller's Childhood* (1947; New York: W.W. Norton, 1962), p.3.
8. Ibid., p.24.
9. Ibid., p.80.
10. Ibid., p.83.
11. Diana Mulock, *Two Little Tinkers*, p.237.
12. Ibid., p.241.
13. Ibid., p.287.
14. The illustrations in Patricia Lynch's fiction – by Jack B. Yeats in *The Turf-Cutter's Donkey*, by Katharine C. Lloyd in *King of the Tinkers*, and by Harry Kernoff in *Tinker Boy* – all rep-

resent the tinkers as women in shawls and men in battered hats, driving horse-drawn barrel-top wagons.

15. Margaret Baker, *The Black Cats and the Tinker's Wife* (1923; New York: Dodd, Mead and Co., 1938), no pagination. All subsequent quotations in the text are from this edition.
16. Gillian McClure and Paul Coltman, *Tinker Jim* (New York: Farrar Straus Giroux, 1992), no pagination. All subsequent quotations in the text are from this edition.
17. Rita Smith, 'Lucy Fitch Perkins.' Accessed 25 February 2005: http://www.recess.ufl.edu/transcripts/2004/1021.shtml
18. Patricia Lynch, *The Turf-Cutter's Donkey* (London: J.M. Dent, 1934), p.1. All subsequent page references in the text are to this edition.
19. Patricia Lynch, *King of the Tinkers* (New York: E.P. Dutton, 1938), p.180. All subsequent page references in the text are to this edition.
20. According to George Gmelch, 'although Tinkers sometimes claimed to settled Irish that they were divided into "tribes" and elected their own "kings", these were only public fictions probably intended to enhance the Traveller mystique' (qtd. in Hayes, *Irish Travellers*, p.205).
21. Patricia Lynch, *Tinker Boy* (1955; London: J.M. Dent, 1960), p.121. All subsequent page references in the text are to this edition.
22. Delaney, 'Representations of the Travellers', p.55.
23. Lucy Fitch Perkins, *The Irish Twins* (Boston and New York: Houghton Mifflin, 1913), p.47. All subsequent page references in the text are to this edition.
24. Lynch, *A Storyteller's Childhood*, p.81.
25. Roderick McGillis (ed.), *Voices of the Other: Children's Literature and the Postcolonial Context* (New York and London: Garland, 2000), p.224.
26. Jacqueline Rose, quoted in Sebastien Chapleau, 'A Theory without a Centre: Developing Childist Criticism', in Keenan and Thompson, *Studies in Children's Literature*, p.130.
27. Rose, quoted in ibid., p.132.
28. John Stephens, *Language and Ideology in Children's Fiction* (London and New York: Longman, 1992), p.8.
29. Nord, *Gypsies and the British Imagination*, p.24.
30. Ibid., p.11.
31. George Eliot, *The Mill on the Floss* (1860; Edinburgh and London: William Blackwood and Sons, n.d.), p.92.
32. In terms of plot and characters, Bríd Mahon's *The Search for the Tinker Chief* (Dublin: Allen Figgis and Co., 1968) is virtually identical to Lynch's *King of the Tinkers*. Surrounded by an entourage including leprechauns, witch or grandmother figures, and a changeling, a boy from a bogside cottage and a tinker girl pursue a tinker chief (who is 'dark and handsome' and wears a yellow handkerchief around his neck) to retrieve a gold bracelet belonging to Aengus of the fairies, who needs it back to lift the spell of enchantment from the Children of Lir.
33. Helleiner, *Irish Travellers*, p.70.
34. Stephens, *Language and Ideology*, p.207.
35. Cathleen McDonagh, 'Preface', in Erica Sheehan (ed.), *Travellers: Citizens of Ireland* (Dublin: The Parish of the Travelling People, 2000), p.10.
36. Zena Harvley-Felder, 'Author Profile: William H. Hooks', *Library Media Connection*, 21, 5 (2003), p.48.
37. William H. Hooks, *Circle of Fire* (New York: Atheneum, 1982), p.147. All subsequent page references in the text are to this edition.
38. This interest in pageantry may be explained by the fact that Hooks was at one time a choreographer.
39. In his autobiography *The Candlelight Painter* (2004), Irish Traveller William Cauley compares a night-time attack by Oranmore farmers on his family's tent camp during his childhood to 'a scene from one of those films you see about the Ku Klux Klan and the way they used to attack the black people in America in times gone by' (p.27).
40. Irish American Travellers were in the news in 2002, when Madelyne Gorman Toogood, a Traveller from Texas, was videotaped beating her daughter in a department store parking lot. Much was made in the media of alleged criminal activity by the 'reclusive' Travellers, as in Lynne Duke's article, 'Unwelcome Stares at Quiet Clan', in the *Washington Post* of 20 October 2002: 'Some of them have a reputation, backed by arrests and convictions, for

being relentless con artists. Like grifters, they move around the country running home improvement swindles. And the women run shoplifting scams, police say' (p.F1).

41. Kim Ablon Whitney, *See You Down the Road* (New York: Alfred A. Knopf, 2004), p.77. All subsequent page references in the text are to this edition.
42. Mollie Hunter, *Cat, Herself* (New York: Harper and Row, 1985), p.4. All subsequent page references in the text are to this edition.
43. Lara Zeises, 'Y[oung] A[dults] Authors Café, Chat Log 14 September 2004: How Far Is Too Far?' Accessed 20 October 2006: http://mysite.verizon.net/selimsa803/9-14.html
44. An Irish Department of Justice report issued in June 2006 noted that 'the differential in sudden infant deaths between Traveller families and the settled community has increased to 12 times the national figure'. Kitty Holland, 'Traveller Cot Death Rate 12 Times the Average', *Irish Times*, 1 June 2006. Accessed 15 June 2006: http://www.ireland.com/newspaper/ archive.
45. Mike Scott, *Judith and the Traveller* (Dublin: Wolfhound Press, 1991), p.13. All subsequent page references in the text are to this edition.
46. Mike Scott, *Judith and Spider* (Dublin: Wolfhound Press, 1992), p.32. All subsequent page references in the text are to this edition.
47. Mike Scott, *Good Enough for Judith* (Dublin: Wolfhound Press, 1994), p.143.
48. Zeises, 'Y[oung[A[dults] Authors Café'.
49. Ibid.
50. 'Grace', 'Interesting Way of Life', review of *See You Down the Road* by Kim Ablon Whitney. Accessed 20 October 2006: http://www.yabookscentral.com/ archive.
51. Kimberly Pauley, 'What Kind of Life Would You Choose?', review of *See You Down the Road* by Kim Ablon Whitney. Accessed 20 October 2006: http://www.yabookscentral.com/ archive.
52. Ibid.

CHAPTER 4

Mid-Century Anxiety: Modernity and the Return of the Repressed

The old days are changing you cannot deny
The day of the traveller is over
There's nowhere to go and there's nowhere to bide
So farewell to the life of the rover.
Ewan MacColl, 'Thirty Foot Trailer'
From *The Travelling People*, a Radio Ballad (1964)

Historically, Angus Bancroft tells us, Travelling people have been more explicitly targeted as outsiders in periods 'associated with major developments in the emergence and consolidation of the modern, centralized bureaucratic nation-state'.[1] As attested by the literature of the Revival period, the rise of Irish cultural nationalism at the end of the nineteenth century made the Travellers a source of great interest, whereas their presence had been largely taken for granted in earlier decades. The creation of the Free State in 1922 not only intensified the attention focused on this internal minority group, but also gave it an increasingly negative turn. Defining modernity as 'a set of systems and sub-systems such as the nation-state based on specific forms of time-spatial order and control', Bancroft argues that Gypsy-Travellers in (late) modern Europe 'have been subject to a variety of regulatory surveillance techniques and structures produced by various institutions of modernity'.[2] Within settled European identity, '[t]he work ethic, the morality of property, and civility, were set off against the vagrant, the vagabond and the wandering Gypsy'.[3] Within modern Irish borders, too, 'tinkers' were increasingly portrayed as 'a "dirty people", not entitled to participation in, or protection from, the institutions that constituted the material and moral structures of the modern nation-state'. The rise of bourgeois nationalism went hand in hand with anti-Traveller racism, as the Travellers' way of life 'was viewed as a political embarrassment, an obstacle to progress and a barrier to rural modernisation'.[4]

If one accepts Zygmunt Bauman's argument that 'a part of the project of modernity is to impose an order on disorder, to organise chaos through the process of naming, organising, [and] categorising',[5] it becomes apparent why the Travellers were seen as such a threat to this project. In the bourgeois, settled imaginary, the 'tinker' does not acknowledge boundaries, be they those associated with labour, property or even the nation itself. Many of the bourgeois concerns about the Travellers' perceived transgressions were enumerated in two articles by Seán MacGrath about 'The Tinkers of Ireland', published in the *Irish Times* of November 1955. Tinkers, MacGrath claims, 'worry little about the Road Traffic Act', many follow 'no fixed trade' or 'are expert beggars', most are illiterate, and 'every man jack of them seems to possess a constant thirst'. Tinkers fight mostly among themselves, 'but at times they tend to injure public property – particularly plate-glass windows'. Houses 'were never meant to hold them', and neither borders nor religious affiliations 'prevent them from a 32-county realm'. In warfare 'they proved to be experts in guerrilla tactics', a skill the author associates with 'the manner in which farmers' produce disappears'.[6] MacGrath also reiterates the popular belief that the tinkers were 'doomed to everlasting wandering' by some ancient offence against property or decency,[7] a view that portrays nomadism 'as punishment for unethical practices associated with their particular way of making a living'.[8]

The categories and classifications created by the institutions of modernity lead to an emphasis on stereotypes to exclude groups of people from mainstream society. Stereotypes not only 'map out the boundaries of acceptable and legitimate behaviour, they also insist on boundaries exactly at those points where in reality there are none'.[9] In *Transgressing the Modern*, John Jervis contends that exclusions and repressions are central to the modern sense of identity: that modernity can be seen as a consciousness set against an unacceptable Other. Central to the development of the modern West has been imperialism, 'which has always sought to validate itself through an encounter with those it can define as "primitive", thereby confirming the superiority of its essential attributes of "civilization" and "rationality"'.[10] To be 'modern' is 'to be capable of self-representation, ... hence be capable of self-government. The other hence lacks these attributes', and must be forced to self-recognition in the images produced of them by the colonizer.[11] Colonization thus becomes a regime of representation.

There are, of course, numerous examples of British representations of the Irish as feckless, dirty, animalistic and irrational, and consequently incapable of self-rule. The simian faces of Irishmen in nineteenth-century *Punch* cartoons are the most striking visual example of such 'Othering' depictions. Within such discourse, even the Great Famine could be explained from a British perspective by referring to the intellectual and moral shortcomings of the Irish. The popular theory prevalent in the late twentieth century, that the Travellers originated in people who 'dropped out' of settled society during the Famine, therefore not only portrays them as economic failures but also, implicitly, associates them with this narrative of immorality and indolence.

Modern identity is constructed and validated through the construction of the Other as 'primitive', which confirms the superiority of the modern Self's essential attributes of 'civilization' and 'rationality', while unacceptable facets of the Self are often projected onto the Other, and denounced.[12] The scapegoating of the Travellers in post-independence Ireland was a way of transferring the tensions of the 'imagined community' of the Free State and the subsequent Irish Republic – imagined as sedentary and middle class – to a pathologized group of outsiders. Such scapegoating of minorities like the 'tinkers' is often justified on the basis of Oedipal claims that they are guilty of taboo acts like incest, wife-swapping or other transgressive sexual behaviour, but 'it does not successfully resolve tensions around sexuality, gender, class and so on. It is a means of controlling and repressing – but not transcending – these different tensions.'[13] Because modern 'civilization' is negatively constructed through the projection of 'primitive' urges onto a demonized minority, the primitive necessarily comes to stand for 'the other that is past, yet ever-present', representing both the threat of regression and the temptation of nostalgic longing.[14]

As primitive Others, the colonized Irish had been both a source of danger and of great fascination to the colonizing British. A late literary example of this can be found in *Lady Chatterley's Lover* (1928), where D.H. Lawrence describes the young Irish writer Michaelis, 'a down-at-heel Dublin street-rat',[15] as 'obviously' not an Englishman, 'in spite of all the tailors, hatters, barbers, booters of the very best quarter of London',[16] because of 'something old, old and acquiescent in the race. Aeons of acquiescence in race destiny, instead of our individual resistance'.[17] English civilization in this view is a matter of 'individual' resistance to the primitive urges to which the Irish as a race are 'destined' to succumb, which nevertheless always remain a temptation. For Lady Chatterley, Michaelis 'had a certain fascination', but she can only allow herself to give in to the attraction because the Irishman knows his place, 'the same old place outside, where the born outsiders are',[18] and because she remains separate and in control of their sexual relationship as she actively achieves 'her own orgasmic satisfaction from his hard, erect passivity'.[19] It is interesting to note that, while D.H. Lawrence does not hesitate to essentialize foreign (Irish) colonial subjects as primitive, in his novella *The Virgin and the Gypsy* (1930) he deliberately debunks similarly stereotypical notions about the domestic Gypsy by giving Joe Boswell an identity and suggesting that he is just an ordinary Englishman: 'the story's naming of Boswell seems a deliberate redress of the notion of the iconic Gypsy, the Gypsy who is less than human, the Gypsy who lacks individuation'.[20]

As Paul Delaney has shown, the British fascination with the 'primitive' Other manifested itself at the end of the nineteenth century in the creation of organizations like the Gypsy Lore Society, which was established in 1888 with the purpose of preserving information about the Roma people that 'might otherwise perish'.[21] Much like the Irish within the British colonial perspective, Gypsies in Europe had for centuries been stereotyped as dishonest and dirty, but the purpose of the Gypsy Lore Society was rather 'the romantic representation and positive identification of the "genuine Gypsy"'.[22] Operating within the parameters of Social Darwinism, it sought to define the racially 'pure' Gypsy before that breed became extinct – another combination of the modern fascination with the primitive and the belief 'that the passing of the primitive is an inevitable consequence of the forces of modernity and history'.[23] The fetishization of the Roma 'prompted the lorists to delineate between the "true" Gypsy and the "false" nomad. In part, their delineation was effected by reference to the Irish Travellers.'[24]

THE 'TINKER' BENEATH THE SKIN

In the early years of the Irish Free State, as nationalists struggled to live up to the expectations they had created for themselves in the period leading up to the signing of the Treaty, writers often seemed unsure whether the tinkers should be regarded as degenerate throwbacks to a less civilized time, or wholesome survivors of a more benign age. The nation's collective anxiety about failing to live up to its new, modern image was projected upon the Travellers, who came to represent the possibility of regression to an earlier primitivism; yet in the face of some of the less palatable manifestations of modernity, the past, reflected in the 'uncomplicated' life of the Travellers, sometimes took on a rosy glow. Such nostalgia is expressed, for example, by the writer Paddy Joe in Maurice Walsh's novel *The Road to Nowhere* (1934). Paddy greatly admires his tinker friends, even though their hard life means that 'the tinker's clan is a dwindling one':[25]

> 'if I had my way ... I would go and live a year or two years with Jamesy Coffey, and write one book worth while. But even if I got the chance I don't suppose I could stick the life for a year. I am getting past my toughness, and, to be a man of the road, a traveling man, an enemy of all settled life and settled men, calls on the best qualities of a man – and sometimes the worst. A great and cleansing life – for good or ill'. (p.110)

The Listowel writer Bryan MacMahon – the author of the play *The Honey Spike* and the novel of the same title (1967), both of which tell a rather sentimental tale of birth and death featuring Traveller characters – took an interest in learning Travellers' Cant, and mastered it by 'joining crowded campfires and pretending that [he] was a tinker who had made good by "flogging waxy" (selling linoleum)'.[26] The pretend-tinker, in real life a schoolmaster, compared his own testing of 'the edges of consciousness and sanity' in his writing with the tinkers' testing of 'the edge of physical living', but gave the edge, so to speak, to the tinkers:

> Mankind has as many layers as an onion, and when all these layers are peeled off, the core is tinker or gypsy; the traveler is in me, in you, in everyman. Yet, compared with the tinker we are lapdogs by the parlor fireside quivering in commingled fear and ecstasy when, through the sound of the gusting storm outside, we hear the baying of wild dogs running free by the light of the moon.[27]

It has been noted before that the idea that beneath the civilized exterior of every modern Irish citizen there lies a 'tinker' core runs through much of Irish literature in the twentieth century, but the sense of wistfulness and nostalgia with which this notion is initially often expressed shifts over time to an attitude of acute anxiety. The sequence of poems in Sigerson Clifford's collection *Travelling Tinkers* (1951) broadly reflects the way in which the settled world's perception of its own position *vis-à-vis* the Travellers evolved during the first half of the century. The narrator of the collection's opening invocation invites a 'tinker-man' to stop 'footing fast', and instead sit down and 'swop tales of the tinker-men:[28] from a real presence on the roads, the Traveller is therefore encouraged to become, instead, a figure in a story. The underlying assumption, that the tinkers are a dying breed, is reinforced by the poem that follows, 'The Ballad of the Tinker's Wake', which depicts the Traveller's corpse 'stiff on the bed' in a cottage belonging to settled people (p.2). Other tinkers arrive to pay their respects to the dead man, as 'we', the cottage owners, give 'them' porter, tobacco and snuff, but 'they could not wake the dead' (p.3). The dead man is unaware that his fellow tinkers kneel, pray and depart 'through the open door', nor does he know 'when the day crept in' (p.4). There is no new dawn for him in the great outdoors.

The three subsequent poems move from a depiction of the romanticized, unencumbered life of the old-time Traveller, via the problematization and repression of that depiction after the foundation of the Irish Free State, to the 'return of the repressed' in the modern, bourgeois nation-state. In 'The Ballad of the Tinker's Wife', the daughter of a strong farmer is seduced by the exotic charms of 'a travelling tinker man' and runs away with him to learn 'the lore of tinkers' (pp.6–7). That the relationship has no future is represented by the couple's childlessness; for the wife, this 'emptiness' is obsessively reflected in the landscape and the weather, as the memory of the 'fine home of her father' comes to preoccupy her mind before she gives up and dies 'within her shawl' (p.9). Her tinker husband, by contrast, takes his childlessness as it comes ('no blame at all') and her death as given ('she is happier now'), as he 'turned his face to life, / And hit the road to Puck Fair / To get another wife' (p.10).

The romantic and carefree tinker of the earlier generation literally meets his demise in the next poem, 'The Tinker's Son', at the very moment when the modern Irish Republic is born. In the opening stanza of the poem, the settled first-person narrator recalls the day in school, long ago, when 'the tinker came / With his wild eyes like a frightened hare's / And his head with its thatch of flame' (p.12). As the boys strike up a cautious friendship, the tinker boy queries the usefulness of school knowledge for his outdoor existence, and after he returns to his life on the road, the narrator envies him his freedom as he himself goes on to a job where he is 'chained ... to an office stool' (p.14). A share of that 'freedom' becomes his own, however, in the natural environment of 'the mountains and the rain', when he finds himself 'up in the hills with the fighting men' during the War of Independence; one of those 'fighting men' is the tinker's son, with whom he again becomes close. But upon the arrival of another kind of 'freedom', in the form of the Irish Free State, the narrator finds himself forced to end his friend's life: 'The tinker's son should be back again / With the roads and the life he knew, / But I put a bullet through his brain / In nineteen twenty two' (p.15). The tinker's 'wildness' may be appropriate for a guerrilla campaign against the colonial oppressor, but has no place within the boundaries of the independent nation. At the same time, the context of the Irish Civil War suggests that, when the narrator shoots the tinker's son, he also ends up eradicating part of himself and his cultural heritage.

That last sentiment is foregrounded in the final poem of the collection, 'The Ballad of the Tinker's Daughter', whose events echo the mythical plot of the tale of the death of Cuchulainn's only son (adapted half a century earlier by W.B. Yeats in his short play *On Baile's Strand*). A farmer on his way to tend to his cattle is struck by the vision of a girl 'like some fairy queen', and, enchanted by her beauty and 'magic', steals her 'from her tinker clan' (p.19) and marries her. From the confinement of his house, she watches the seasons change until, one night, she flees 'the fields that tied her down' (p.20) and returns to her people, among whom she dies giving birth to a son. As the years pass, the angry farmer, armed with dog and gun, walks his fields which are now 'weedful' because he 'made the tinkers travel on' (p.21). One day, those fields are crossed by 'a barefoot tinker-lad / With red, red hair and laughing eyes'. Shot by the farmer, he 'told his name and died' (p.21). Recognizing that his obsession with land and property has led him to kill his own son, the farmer hangs himself. As father and son are buried, the spirit of the tinker's daughter hovers over the graves, but 'when the mound was patted down / The tinker-maid was gone' (p.22). By eradicating its past in the form of the wandering tinkers, the bourgeois nation-state also kills part of its own future – the spiritual, carefree part. 'That is how the story goes' (p.22), the narrator ends the poem. The tinker is dead: long live his story.

Rumours of the tinker's death in the newly emerging nation, however, turned out to be greatly exaggerated, as the Travellers simply would not go away. For Irish writers, the resilient (or resistant) cluster of survivors of an older way of life in the midst of the developing fabric of modern economic and social institutions became the focus of the expectations and anxieties associated with the transition from a traditional rural society to a modern bourgeois state. For those who were wary of the new developments, the Travellers represented a living museum of values and mores about to be lost for ever; for those who embraced modernity, the tinkers served as a reminder that the bad old ways die hard and must therefore be repressed with force.

NOSTALGIA AND THE BACKWARD GLANCE

A typical example of the nostalgic school of thought is *The Road to Nowhere* by Maurice Walsh. The opening scene of the novel presages the fate of the Travellers in modern, capitalist Ireland through the image of tourists camping in the countryside – modern 'travellers' who emulate the life of the 'tinkers' they both romanticize and come to displace. Two friends, Scottish-American Alistair MacIan and Irishman Paddy Joe Long, are camping in a shabby tent on land belonging to a mansion recently bought by Elspeth Conroy, an Irish-American woman married to the son of a retired British proconsul. While their tent is being minded for them by their new acquaintance Rogan Stuart, who is 'tramping' around the country in an attempt to forget his wife's adulterous love affair and her subsequent accidental death, Elspeth arrives and orders him off her property for camping without a permit. Modernity is here, as well as elsewhere in Irish fiction of the period, represented by the insistence on rules and the boundaries of property, and by the presence of imported foreign – predominantly American – wealth, taste and attitudes. From Rogan's perspective, the natural Irish landscape clashes badly with Elspeth's modern house: 'what Fomorian had raised those red turrets? Some foreign man coming into these Irish glens and aping baronial architecture in red brick!' (p.18). Later he learns from Paddy Joe that the house was built by a Northern Irishman, 'one of these here famous business magnates who scrape their wealth in the brutal places of the earth' (p.35). Rogan is bemused by the Stetson-wearing American woman on her cow-pony: 'Perhaps all this countryside was being turned into some sort of rodeo film, some soul-destroying unreal reality where the native, himself included, was a mere aborigine sitting stoically on his hunkers' (p.20). In the event, however, it is the 'native' tinkers who save the souls of both Rogan and Elspeth from the perils of inauthenticity and despair.

When Elspeth's degenerate husband is found killed, and Rogan discovers that the same man who had seduced his late wife now also has designs on Elspeth, Paddy Joe decides that Rogan may come under suspicion for murder and needs to disappear for a while. He arranges for him to spend a year with the tinker Jamesy Coffey, in the guise of Rogue McCoy, 'tinker's curate'. Rogan takes to travelling like a duck to water: 'A tinker's life was a cleaner life, where passion was brutal but not complex, where life set stark but simple problems. A tinker! That's what he was' (p.164). When he coincidentally meets Elspeth again, and explains why he had needed to hide even though he was not guilty of murder, she shows herself surprisingly understanding of the demands and attractions of the travelling life: 'I have wrangled and ridden my own horse from Wyoming to the Staked Plain, cooked grub – and sometimes shot it ... I wish I could go back to those clean days in the wind and the sun. They were finer and rougher than any tinker's life' (p.170). The affinity of the American woman for Rogan and the tinkers goes back to the shared nobility of their ancient Irish roots, for Jamesy Coffey is the 'king of the tinkers' (p.104), and his wife Maag Carty boasts, in Paddy Joe's words, 'the blood of MacCarthy More, Prince of South Desmond, mixed with the older blood of a gypsy king. As a matter of fact, some authorities hold that tinkers are descended withershin from the bards and romancers of royal houses' (pp.105–6). Perhaps those bards entertained Elspeth's ancestors, for she also has a penchant for Gaelic music, which surprises Rogan until he realizes that 'she was a Conroy – daughter of kings – and laments like that were her heritage' (p.72). The truth eventually emerges that it was Elspeth herself who had caused the accidental death of her husband, and it is therefore only natural that she, too, is given temporary sanctuary among the tinkers when she feels that she must 'get away from that ugly house' (p.312).

While Elspeth is finding her Irish roots and transforming herself into 'Ailish' Conroy in Jamesy Coffey's caravan, Rogan returns to Dublin to try and resume his role of 'respectable man of business', only to find that he 'no longer fitted inside that skin' (p.291), having been permanently altered by the tinker's life. Instead, he is 'Rogue McCoy, the tinker, the traveling man, firm on his own feet, wary in life, wise in experience, clear-eyed to good fortune or mishap, no longer vulnerable to an abasing despair' (p.292). The tinker's life also has a healing effect on Ailish: 'She would give this life a fair trial, and, if it did pall, and go on palling, it would at least have given her a sane outlook by the time she returned to her normal existence' (p.348). It is Jamesy who succeeds in tying Rogue and Ailish together in a bond with each other and with the tinkers, while at the same time clearing their way back to a 'normal existence', by insisting that they 'obey [his] law' by jumping the budget: 'Any other marriage ye can make or not make as ye like when mine is bound' (pp.373–4). By performing this ritual, 'as ancient as fire worship ... in a Gaelic of many obsolete words' (p.369), Ailish and Rogan are able to face the modern world with a tinker's age-old wisdom that paradoxically gives them 'a fresh slant, a new orientation, a different outlook' (p.292).

MODERNITY AND THE FORCES OF LAW AND ORDER

Whereas Walsh's nostalgic narrative places the emphasis on the material aspects of modernity and their detrimental moral and sociocultural effects, other writers address modernity in terms of the establishment of a system of law and order that comes to replace a more volatile and less regulated mode of existence. Both Liam O'Flaherty's short story 'The Stolen Ass' (1926) and Sean O'Faolain's 'The Squinty Tinker and the Black Powlraddy' (1937) present tinker characters on trial in a court of law, a regulated environment where their incoherence and lack of restraint cause both bewilderment and amusement. The accused in 'The Stolen Ass' is 'a very disreputable young tinker with red hair and a pointed chin'.[29] In his statement to the judge, the tinker claims that when his own black she-ass went lame on the road, he swapped her for a jackass he happened to find in a field, with the intention of retrieving his own animal on the return journey. Further on his way, he swapped asses again, before being caught in the attempt of making a fourth exchange. The old ass in his possession at the time of his arrest was put in the pound, where it died, leaving him 'no ass to put instead of my own ass at Ballyfarnagaoran'.[30] Thoroughly confused by the story and annoyed by the laughter in the courtroom, the judge concludes that the tinker never had an ass to begin with, and that 'all these stories about asses are deliberately concocted to misdirect the court'. He imposes a sentence of fourteen days' hard labour, a verdict brushed aside by the tinker, however, who is still trying to make his point about 'me own ass'.[31] In the case of O'Faolain's story, the judge interrupts the 'squinty' tinker's rambling narrative about drunkenness and theft and dismisses the charges, showing, in Paul Delaney's words, that the presence of the tinkers 'has become little more than an irritant and an anachronism in the

Free State, as they fail to provoke either the interest or the rigour of the law'.[32]

Upon the creation of the Irish Free State, the Royal Irish Constabulary was replaced by the Civic Guard, which was renamed the Garda Síochána in 1923. Members of the new force did not carry guns; in fact, Michael Staines, the first Garda Commissioner, argued that the new national police service would 'succeed not by force of arms or numbers, but on their moral authority as servants of the people'.[33] Walter Macken focuses on this transitional period of Irish history in 'Battle', a story written in the 1940s, by pitting Sean Martin, an idealistic young guard, against the atavistic force of the Galway tinkers.

Although he realizes that it will take time for 'the good people' of Ireland to get to like and trust their policemen,[34] Sean's hope is that they 'will begin to look on the police as their guardians instead of men to be defeated in every possible way through lying and trickery' (p.11), and that they will accept 'the fact that the bad days were gone and that law and order once more roamed the land and should be encouraged' (p.12). When Sean talks back to his Sergeant, whom he considers 'a throw-back to the old peelers. Brute strength personified' (p.13), the veteran responds to the rookie's act of insubordination by sending him to patrol the town square by himself, without his baton, knowing that the day is Tinkers' Thursday, when 'all the tinkers of Ireland came to sell their horses' (p.19). Everybody in town except Sean knows that 'a good drunk and a good fight was the epitome of a successful fair' (p.22), and as if on cue, Big Peadar, a tinker, swings his stick at a farmer, whereupon 'the whole crowd around him became a vortex of fighting' (p.25). Sean is forced to call upon all the violence he can muster, but the tinker is too strong. Just when Sean thinks, 'If I had the baton now ... I would beat him into a clot of blood' (p.26), the Sergeant appears and makes short work of Peadar, allowing Sean to administer the final blows. Afterwards, the Sergeant sums up the lesson learned: 'Things are not as rosy yet as you think. And they won't be for a long time. ... You think maybe that many things can be settled with peaceful means. That may be true of the future' (pp.28–9). Sean apologizes for his earlier insubordination and concedes that 'there are occasions on which it is essential to use force' (p.29). The tinkers in this story represent the pre-modern forces of chaos and anarchy that are still inherently part of the Irish people, even if the country now 'belongs to them and they belong to it' (p.16).

In *No Resting Place* (1948), Scottish writer Ian Niall (pseudonym of John McNeillie) deals with the subject of law and order in a more balanced way, by juxtaposing the tinkers' sense of injustice and fair play with the official forces of the law represented by the police and the justice system; the clash of the two incompatible approaches to justice inevitably leads to a tragic outcome. An Irish treatment of the novel was filmed by Paul Rotha in County Wicklow, with a cast of Abbey Players, and released in 1952; although the film was nominated for two BAFTA awards, it never went into general distribution. According to Niall's son Andrew McNeillie, a showing of the film in 2001 at the Irish Film Centre in Dublin 'drew a considerable audience, among them representatives of traveller communities, for whom the film gives the first ever unsentimental cinematic account of their way of life, told from their side of the story'.[35]

The plot of *No Resting Place* revolves around the Kyle brothers and their families. As the tinkers are travelling to a farm where they will be employed thinning turnips, Tam Kyle gets into an argument with a gamekeeper over a dead rabbit, the man fires a warning shot, and Tam kicks out at him before moving on. When Alec, who is coming up behind Tam, draws level with the keeper, the enraged man shoots at him (in the film version the pellets strike Alec's son in the leg), and the tinker, in an equal fury, starts beating the keeper with a rock until he is dead. Knowing that, as tinkers, they can never hope to explain the complex circumstances surrounding the death to the inherently hostile authorities, the brothers hide the body, but the comings and goings of the tinkers arouse the suspicion of a local constable. Although the gamekeeper's corpse is soon discovered, there is no proof to back up the inspector's speculation that poachers, gypsies, or tinkers are most likely the culprits. Remembering the brothers' behaviour, constable Claybody makes it his business to keep pressure on the Kyles to get them to confess to the murder. One night, drunk and harassed, the Kyles cause havoc in a public house and end up in a fight with police, during which Alec hits Claybody over the head with a bottle, injuring him severely. The brothers are arrested and sentenced to several months' hard labour.

Whereas the film version depicts Alec's relationship with his wife and son as very loving, and tells us nothing about the gamekeeper's domestic situation, in Niall's novel, the tinker, the gamekeeper and the constable are all unlovable characters, flawed in similar ways. Alec Kyle is an ugly man with a withered arm; he also suffers from irrational bouts of violent rage, which his own brothers can only keep in check by beating him unconscious. At such moments, his wife 'wished she had never seen him; wished he and she had never been born'.[36]

Behind Alec's back, the townspeople in the local pub say that he is 'the worst monkey o' the lot' and '[q]ueer in the head' (p.83); to them, the Kyles are self-evidently 'thieving good-for-nothing trash! ... Only the scum of the town could speak to tinkers and vagabonds like the Kyles' (p.85). The gamekeeper of the Big House is a more respectable figure, although his wife, too, has few illusions about his character: 'Ted Ross was aloof and distinguished, just like his master, but Ted Ross had distinction in hired clothes and his aloofness was vacancy' (p.31). Considering his lack of humour and his wooden mind, his wife 'wondered why she had ever been foolish enough to marry the gamekeeper' (p.30). Constable Claybody's wife is more supportive of her husband, but resentful of the fact that he was never promoted and 'had been held back and never appreciated' (p.146). While he is still recovering from the head injury inflicted by the bottle, she encourages him in his resolve to prove Alec guilty of the gamekeeper's murder by following him until he is 'sorry he was born' (p.151). Claybody's superior, however, finds the constable's behaviour 'not quite normal', and regards his obsession with the Kyles as 'bordering on madness' (p.152). Just as the locals had questioned Alec's mental state, Alec himself comments on Claybody's psychological condition from a local bar stool: 'Took queer again. ... I think I'll complain t' the inspector an' get'm locked up in a mad-house' (p.217).

No Resting Place provides an even-handed account of the mutually dependent relationship between the Travellers and the farmers who hire them to work in their fields. One injured farmer considers the arrival of Alec and his family a blessing, and when the police come asking questions about the tinker, the grateful farmer's wife is only too eager to assume that it concerns 'some wee odd thing' and to stonewall them: 'I don't like to get anybody in bother', she tells the tinker (p.129). The Craigs, who had hired the Kyle families earlier to thin their turnips, express more mixed emotions, considering the tinkers a 'wild lot' even if they 'work hard' (pp.26–7). On balance, they are inclined to think the worst of them, and when the police arrive to ask questions, Mrs Craig's preconceptions are given free rein: 'We'll be in some scandal o' some kind afore the summer's past. They a' sleep together like animals, young and old, male and female. Like as not there's somethin' comin' to them. We'd better get rid o' them when the thinnin's done. Let them take their barrows and their thievin' somewhere else' (p.65). With the Kyle brothers on the run after their fight with the police, their families are left on the farm, and when Craig refuses to pay them for their work an escalating stand-off ensues, in the course of which Craig fires his gun and the tinkers pelt him with stones. Perplexed by a situation for which he has no remedy, the police sergeant advises the Travellers to move on. Later, the tinkers return to the farm and pull up the turnip plants, 'feeling the savage satisfaction of having righted a wrong in a crude way' (pp.115–16). They, too, however, argue about the nature of justice; when Tam refuses to shift to evade the police, arguing that the Kyles 'has been in this country since afore the poliss come. ... We've a right here', his brother Hugh counters, 'Them that's done murder has no rights' (pp.114–15).

After his release from prison, Alec lives in a dilapidated cottage and makes an honest living selling firewood. Shortly after the death of his wife, who received indifferent care from a doctor with a dismissive attitude towards tinkers, Alec and his children are evicted from their home for endangering 'the health of those living nearby' (p.199). Secretly housing his family in a hut in an abandoned quarry, Alec continues to do the rounds on his barrow, and receives a measure of sympathy from the townspeople. Claybody's obsessive surveillance of the tinker, by contrast, is beginning to turn the town against him, leading him to observe bitterly that '[t]he goodwill of the public was never on the side of the police' even as Alec Kyle 'had all the beer servers in the place on his side' (p.216). Justice and injustice appear equally haphazard processes as Alec's fate is finally determined by an accident that echoes the accidental killing of the gamekeeper in the narrative's opening scenes. When Alec's small son chokes on a piece of chalk, the father desperately tries to rub the lethal object from the child's throat, bruising him in the process. The ever-present Claybody watches as the child dies with his father's hands around his neck. Arrested for the murder of his son, Alec Kyle hangs himself in his police cell.

The different ending of the film version is consistent with its depiction of Alec's family as close and loving. As Alec and his son are driving on the country road where the keeper was killed, the tinker stops for a minute to relieve himself in the bushes. The son keeps talking in a loud voice, wanting to know about the incident and the reason for the attack, and Alec shouts back that he killed the keeper because the man was threatening his family. Meanwhile, the obsessive policeman has cycled up behind the tinker's cart. When Alec reappears he realizes he has just confessed to a crime, and quietly gives himself up.

The troubled picture of law, order and justice that emerges in *No Resting Place* left at least one contemporary film reviewer confused. Writing in the *New York Times*, Bosley Crowther considered the film's theme to be the 'tragic lot of the tinkers who roam the byways of Ireland, warily tolerated by good people and the police', but wondered 'what purpose is meant to be served by this illustrative excursion into Ireland's rural lower depths'.[37] The 'moral values', after all, are clear:

> Although one may feel very sorry for the poor wretched tinker who kills the man, especially since the victim is a gamekeeper who has injured the other's little boy, one cannot concede that the tinker should get away with it. And although one may not like the policeman who hounds the poor tinker, his wife and child, one has to allow it is his duty. Where is the irony in this?

For Crowther, the 'velvet beauty of the Irish countryside' is the film's best feature, 'no matter what else it contains': 'one certainly must get from it a knowledge and an envy of what an Irish tinker is privileged to see'. The reviewer's discourse is that of modernity, which seeks to regulate the 'wretched' Travellers as remnants of a less civilized era, and only allows the rural past to be acknowledged within the nostalgic confines of the tourist's gaze.

THE 'TINKER ECONOMY' VERSUS THE BOURGEOIS NATION-STATE

Within the discourse of modernity and its economic parameters, the 'tinker' is essentially given two options: conform to the strictures of the bourgeois work ethic, or be forever a pariah. Maurice Walsh's story 'Son of a Tinker' (1951) presents the former scenario, in which 'a tinker born and bred, ... an outcast by race amongst settled men',[38] remakes himself into a successful businessman. Having initially fallen so low 'as to take to plain peddling, the tinker-woman's trade' (p.8), Owen Oge O'Callaghan decides not to yield to 'a slow and inevitable degradation' (p.9) but instead hires himself out to Murnahan's store as 'a commercial agent on foot' (p.14), using the people skills he acquired as a tinker to his advantage, and gradually becoming 'civilised altogether' (p.17). Given that there is little difference between his *modus operandi* as a 'commercial agent' and as a pedlar, it is clear that 'civilization' has less to do with what he does, and more with the context in which he does it. When Owen begins courting Murnahan's daughter, it is her brother who reacts in an uncivilized manner by trying to kill the tinker; the latter, acting from a new-found bourgeois spirit, takes his case to a lawyer but eventually settles with Murnahan for 500 pounds – the very sum the latter had demanded for 'talk[ing] matchmaking' with him, 'tinker's son or no tinker's son' (p.20). Initially a drop-out, the tinker's son drops back in with a vengeance. With a share in the family business and married to the boss's daughter, whose bidding he must now do – 'Whatever you say, Mrs O'Callaghan, ma'am' (p.34) – Owen's story is one of success, as he finds himself thoroughly integrated into the national and domestic economy.

Written in the same year as Walsh's 'Son of a Tinker', which focuses on the 'rehabilitation' of one individual Traveller, Donagh MacDonagh's ballad opera *God's Gentry* (1951) presents the 'class' of tinkers as intrinsic opponents of the virtues of capitalism, law and order, and the democratic rights and obligations inherent in the nation-state. The 'tinker', according to an opinion expressed by MacDonagh in a later article in which he discussed the genesis of his ballad play, 'sees himself as the victim and the policeman or the farmer as the harrying vigilant'. Forming an unregulated 'nation within a nation', tinkers 'live among, and largely on, the settled members of the community', and when one of them gets in trouble with the law they 'exhibit the solidarity of the non-working class, and, if necessary, ... put up bail in cash, frequently in hundreds of pounds'. The origin of that money is anybody's guess, although tinkers 'believe that they are entitled to take anything that is not nailed down'. When MacDonagh was 'seeking a theme for satirising totalitarian governments and the welfare state', he conceived the idea 'of making the tinkers the rulers of Ireland with the aid of the old Irish god, Balor of the Evil Eye'.[39] This idea he developed into the ballad play *God's Gentry*.

In *God's Gentry*, once the pagan tinker's republic is established, its members 'dance a ballet of tinker domination over landlord and tenant, over merchant and lawyer, over priest and policeman'.[40] They eat, drink and are merry, served by members of the former bourgeoisie:

> I've been a tinker all my life
> I'll die a tinker laddie O,
> Unwashed, uncombed and carefree as
> My hundred year old daddy O.
> And just like him, I'll have ten wives,
> Or twenty if they're willing O,
> I will dance and sing and have my fling
> As long as there's a shilling O. ...
> The lawyer, doctor, priest invest

Their cash in stocks so risky O
The tinker wiser than the rest
Invests it all in whiskey O! (p.43/60)

Eventually, when 'The cellars are all empty, / The food has all been eaten', and Balor confesses that 'The miracle bank is bankrupt' (p.50/60), the tinkers' rule meets its untimely demise: 'This is the end of their constitution, / Now for the counter revolution' (p.51/60). The tinkers' leader, 'Marks' Mongan, having already been jilted by the shopkeeper's daughter who had been temporarily stricken with romantic notions about him, is further derided by his fellow Travellers when he proposes that they 'Work not for ourselves alone, but work / For Ireland's good' (p.56/60), now that the supply of free food and drink has dried up. Their refusal spells the end of the 'tinker's republic', but before he departs, 'President' Balor leaves his constituents a gift: 'All property of whatsoever type, manner of description ... / Shall belong, if not nailed safely to the living earth, / To the tinker who can take them and carry them away in his cart. / And this act ... / Shall be known as the Tinkers Property Protection Act' (p.58/60). From that day on, 'no tinker need work, think or grieve', and the play concludes with the tinkers singing, 'Oh, who wouldn't be a tinker when he's free' (p.60/60).

GENDER, MARRIAGE, AND SEXUAL RELATIONS

The process of rural embourgeoisement that began in Ireland in the 1880s was accompanied by a system 'of late and arranged marriages centred upon impartible male inheritance and female dowries', and in the moral climate that developed around these practices, 'the young marriages of the "tinkers" represented sexuality loosened from economic considerations of landed-class reproduction and Church regulations'. Anxiety about the transgressive mores of the Travellers among the sedentary population 'was apparent in the preoccupation with the possibility of inappropriate liaisons with them', which expressed both the seductive power of the primitive Other and the fear of reverting to the 'tinker' the middle classes had repressed within themselves.[41]

By the middle of the twentieth century, when the Republic's family-values-based constitution and the dominance of the Catholic Church had conspired to create a climate of sexual repression, anxiety about the 'tinkers' translated itself into a fear of contamination, literally by the tinkers' 'dirt', and metaphorically by their immorality.

In literary texts of the period, particularly those by male authors, such anxieties are often projected upon an attractive but dirty female tinker figure, who lures a settled male character towards a life of dissolution by releasing his irrational, primitive (read: sexual) urges. In his poem 'Tinkers Tune', for example, Ulick O'Connor, who elsewhere refers to the 'tinkers' as 'chancers and tramps' who would 'lift the froth off your pint if you didn't keep your nose well in over the edge of the glass',[42] acknowledges the transgressive nature of the attraction by linking the forbidden sexual temptation to the certain knowledge of immediate punishment:

> A blowsy-haired tinker girl,
> As I passed, showed me a blue eye,
> There was a welcome in her brown face,
> If I stopped by.
>
> That her dark man might be lurking near
> By Heavens, I knew;
> Skinning rabbits, or poaching fish,
> And he'd skin me too.
>
> Then she'd throw back her tawny head
> And laugh at the batin' I'd get;
> I tell you that's why I scorned
> The blue eye that beckons me yet.[43]

If O'Connor's male persona is prevented from acting on his own primal urges by the fear of male primal violence, irrational physical brutality is precisely what often attracts the modern female character to the male tinker figure. In Walter Macken's story 'The Eyes of the Cat', a young, well-off, sophisticated woman witnesses a fight between three tinker men. She has her eyes glued on the winner as he approaches her: 'It's a coarse face, she thought then. It is a coarse, rather brutal face after all. She was afraid. Because she wanted to step out of the car and go close to him and feel the heavy arms around her.'[44] Later, the tinker discusses the woman with his mother: 'I felt strings out of her.'[45] The old woman quotes an ancient saying: 'Its origin breaks through the eyes of the cat', explaining that the girl's father 'was of us', although he 'calls the police now if a gypsy puts a foot over his fence. Own cousin of me own well back. But well back. ... Very powerful the Man is.' Her son laughs and recalls the woman's expression: 'Frightened she looked and then her eyes open and you see the green fields in them.'[46]

He decides he wants to 'look into the eyes of the cat', and disappears inside the farm's big iron gates. The repressed past is about to sneak up on the modern present, unstoppable by the fences thrown in its path by the power and money of the bourgeoisie.

Una Troy's novel *The Benefactors* (1969), written around the same time as Macken's story, suggests that for some women writers, who had to deal more directly than their male counterparts with the limitations imposed on female sexuality by Church and state, a sexual liaison between a settled woman and a male Traveller was not necessarily a trope for regression into pre-modern primitivism, but rather for physical and psychological liberation. In the opening chapter of *The Benefactors*, an extended family of Travellers arrives in Cloona, a locality known for its harassment of tinkers. Eleanor Moore, the Anglo-Irish owner of the local Big House, invites the tired group to spend the night within the walls of the estate where she lives with her grandniece, Rose Sinclair. Rose has withdrawn from life, traumatized by a facial scar resulting from a car accident and botched plastic surgery, while Mrs Moore is old and tired, and afraid of slowly declining into death. Moore Park is a typical emblem of the declining Ascendancy, 'a poverty-stricken tumbledown old mansion with two women rattling around in it like dried peas in a withered pod'.[47] As the tinkers, who are 'as unattractive as any of their ilk' (p.23), extend their stay over the winter months, both groups of residents, especially the women – marginalized as they all are, because of their class and gender, in the modern Irish Republic – draw closer together, gain insights about themselves and each other, and readjust their lives accordingly.

The practical and rather cold-hearted Mrs Moore opens up emotionally in the course of her friendship with Granny Fogarty, the Travellers' matriarch. The initial reasons she gives Rose for allowing the tinkers to stay on her property reflect her stoic attitude:

> I have no sentimental notions about any of these tinkers. I would not choose their company if I had an alternative. As it is, I give them shelter; in return, they allow me to occupy myself with the physical well-being of themselves and their animals. I find it agreeable to have my days filled in this manner. They tolerate just that amount of interference. (p.136)

In a moment of crisis, however, Mrs Moore and Granny Fogarty grip each others' hands, 'each of them getting and giving comfort from one to the other' (p.216). Symbolic of their bond, the old Traveller woman bestows on Mrs Moore her treasured image of the Sacred Heart. When the Travellers depart, Mrs Moore tacitly acknowledges that the symbol is no substitute for the genuine article:

> I must put it away; Mrs Fogarty would be hurt to find it still lying there as if it were of no account. Put away the Heart and then call back Mrs Fogarty. For there is something I omitted to say, for I did not realise it until now. I said: I am your friend, Mrs Fogarty. But I did not say: You are my friend. (p.232)

The realization is more important than its execution, but it also comes too late for this representative of a dying class. In rushing down the stairs to carry out her intentions, as Granny Fogarty embarks on her travels, Mrs Moore stumbles and falls to her death.

Eleanor Moore's grandniece Rose Sinclair is a physically scarred and emotionally frustrated, reclusive virgin until she is 'cured' by the tinkers. Living too much in her head, she is both attracted and repelled by the physicality of Mike Casey, the Traveller who comes to mend a broken shutter in the dilapidated house:

> He was very strong. He had a good waist. He had narrow hips. She watched him while he grunted and heaved and pushed. At last the bar was grindingly forced into place and he turned around triumphantly. It was a pity he hadn't a more attractive face. Apart from the snub nose and the foxy lashes and brows, it had that indefinable something that was pure tinker. It was a pity, too, that he had that unwashed sickly-sweet tinker smell. (p.29)

Later, she fantasizes about him as if he were an abstraction: 'Back in bed, she spent ten minutes repelling his impassioned advances before falling asleep. His face had become blurred and he didn't smell' (p.33). In his conversation with her, Mike is quick to correct her romantic notions about the travelling life: when she warbles, 'it must be absolutely fascinating to be so free and untramelled compared with the rest of us stick-in the-muds', he replies, 'I don't think as how you'd care for it all that much, somehow' (pp.30–1). While Rose is assuming that Mike is in awe of her sophisticated charm, the Traveller keeps his real opinion, that a tinker woman who behaved like Rose would be considered a slut, to himself, until one night he drunkenly takes out on Rose his anger at the villagers' dismissive attitude towards him: 'you're as bad as the rest, you hoor! Having your fun with me like as if I wasn't a man at all. ... Nor maybe I won't mind doing it proper for you neither after all, pettie' (p.142). If, in the discourse of modernity, the primitive 'Other' represents 'the threat that one's boundaries will be defiled and hence violated, and that one will be corrupted or "unclean" as a result',[48] the literal violation of the fragrant and upper-class Rose by the smelly tinker in Una Troy's *The Benefactors* results, in fact, in the restoration of her sanity. After Mike has humbly apologized for raping her, and she has had a good cry, '[t]hey were friendly and comfortable with each other from then on', and after that he visits her bedroom on a regular basis, to their mutual satisfaction. No longer faceless himself in her presence, Mike also restores Rose's personality: she pins back her hair 'as if she didn't give a damn how much of her face was seen', and Mike realizes that 'you could look straight at the bad side easy and never give it a thought' (p.153).

Mike's interest in Rose is not entirely altruistic, since he has designs on two fields belonging to Mrs Moore which would allow him to settle down on a farm and 'live down his travelling origins' (p.75) by keeping the place so neat that 'the Casey family of Cloona would hold their own with any in the parish' (p.77). When Mrs Moore agrees to sell him the fields, Mike goes down to view his future property, only to be confronted by Jim Cullen, an angry neighbour, who also covets the land. In the ensuing confrontation, Mike is killed by a blow from Jim's blackthorn stick. The 'tinker' literally and metaphorically dies at the moment he enters into the bourgeois, sedentary world of land ownership, at the same time that his 'primitive' presence there releases his murderer from impotence into manhood. Just as Mike's rape of Rose had been an impulsive act brought on by impotent rage at being slighted and belittled in the village, so Jim's attack on Mike is the outcome of bottled-up resentment at being treated like a child by his mother: 'I'll tell you why I killed that tinker. I killed him because he'd bought the Madam's fields that you wouldn't let me buy and because he flung it in my face that I'm nothing but a penny boy around the Quinlan farm' (p.218). Just as Rose was (passively) liberated into womanhood by an invasive act of sexual violence, so Jim Cullen's masculinity and his relationship with his wife and mother are (actively) rescued by his violent and irrational attack on Mike. His wife acknowledges: 'What's wrong with us is that we've been so considerate of one another's feelings that we've been concealing our own. ... I think it's time we started speaking openly, even if it hurts at first' (p.219).

Whereas Mike Casey's 'tinkerish' impetuosity inadvertently has a liberating effect on Rose and Jim, his bourgeois farming aspirations, which include the need for a wife to look after their 'little houseen' (p.41), strike Sibby, the young Traveller woman who is the object of his marital intentions, as limiting well before Mike meets his demise:

'To be stuck there for ever, like one of them trees, would be even worse than travelling the roads constant to nowhere' (p.82). She wonders why 'so many people were silly enough to tie themselves to ways where they could see step by step ahead until they stepped into their coffins' (p.185). Sibby's secret destination is the city, where she intends to 'rise above being a tinker woman' (p.83) and live in luxury. This economic independence is to be gained through the free use of her sexuality, since, unbeknownst to anyone close to her, Sibby has been prostituting herself to sailors for money. She finds liberation by placing herself outside the domestic boundaries of family and marriage within which the Irish constitution sought to confine female sexuality, and eventually by leaving Ireland altogether. At Christmastime, she agrees to sell her sexual favours to a resident of a Cloona boarding house, Tim Doonican, although he resents having to pay for what he assumes tinkers habitually give away 'for free in every ditch in Ireland' (p.121). Having stolen her incapacitated client's money, Sibby sets out from the boarding house to catch the boat to England; as she is leaving she encounters another resident, the kindly schoolmaster Andrew Hogan, and kisses him farewell. The embrace is witnessed, and causes Hogan, who is already in trouble with the Parish Priest for supporting the Travellers, to lose his job and his fiancee. Since he had already come to regard both as something of an encumbrance, not much harm is done, except to his pride: 'Poetic justice, perhaps. ... Cloona's done the right thing by me even if it's for the wrong reasons' (p.227). As for Doonican, he cannot indict Sibby without revealing the reason for her presence in his bedroom. Rose and Sibby may be 'hoors' in the eyes of respectable villagers, but unlike them, they live guilt-free lives on their own terms. Rose acknowledges her affinity with the independent Traveller girl: 'However ineptly, she had gone after her mirage. As I, thought Rose, shall later go after my own mundane and quite achievable aims. At least we are sisters under the skin in that we both know what we want' (p.233).

THE RETURN OF THE REPRESSED TINKER

Whereas in Una Troy's *The Benefactors*, the female members of the Anglo-Irish Ascendancy and the Traveller community discover that they have more similarities than differences between them, which to some degree separate them positively from the general Irish population represented by the villagers of Cloona, in both Francis MacManus's *Watergate* (1942) and Brian Moore's *The Mangan Inheritance* (1979), the tinkers serve as a profoundly negative anti-modern force. In both novels, a comparatively sophisticated Irish-American character is placed alongside a dissolute Irish female character who is a 'tinker' not by birth but by association. By the mid-twentieth century, 'genuine' tinkers (who, in earlier decades, had already been relegated to the status of second-rate Gypsies by entities like the Gypsy Lore Society) were frequently portrayed as a dying breed. Folklore collector Seán MacGrath, in particular, made a point of challenging the authenticity of contemporary Travellers by claiming that outrages perpetrated by bogus Travellers were marring 'the rating of the real traveller', who, in any case, was fast disappearing: 'Despite the apparent increase in the tinker population, the older type steadily seems to disappear ... there are vagrants on the Irish roads today, and they are a shame and a disgrace to the genuine tinkers of the country'.[49] In such arguments, as Paul Delaney points out, 'the authenticity of the Travellers as a discrete cultural group [is] at once declared and disavowed',[50] as the 'genuine' article is consistently pushed further and further back into a distant past. The preoccupation of sedentary people at this time with bogus Travellers was also an expression of their deep-rooted anxiety that regression from a civilized (settled) state to pre-modern (itinerant) primitivism was not just a hypothetical possibility.

In the novels by Francis MacManus and Brian Moore, an Irish-American character (Alice Lennon in *Watergate*, Jamie Mangan in *The Mangan Inheritance*) returns to Ireland in search of a homecoming experience, and becomes inextricably involved with a female, Irish, inauthentic 'tinker' figure (Ruby Butts and Kathleen Mangan, respectively), who carries associations with mental instability or retardation, dirt and moral irresponsibility. John Jervis argues that, within 'the deep structure of the characteristic modern experience of otherness, ... notions of gender, nature and reason are superimposed and interlocked in powerful ways, via binary distinctions'.[51] Itinerancy also figures into this construction, as 'the mad were often incarcerated indiscriminately with vagrants, the poor, and criminals, all seen as manifestations of ... "want of reason"'.[52] In *The Mangan Inheritance*, Jamie's sexual attraction to Kathleen, despite, or because of, her unwashed appearance, is the cause of his deterioration; in *Watergate*, Ruby's slovenliness gradually rubs off on Alice. Physical dirt and cleanliness have strong overtones of moral and sexual defilement and purity. The 'erotic power of dirt' hinges on the idea of pollution, 'the threat that one's boundaries will be defiled and hence violated, and that one will be corrupted or "unclean" as a result.' Dirt thus represents 'both a threat to the "civilizing process," and a manifestation of it,' particularly in the home, 'the sacred arena of domesticity'.[53]

The idea of home is central to both novels, just as each plot suggests the underlying trope of woman and house as nation. The farmhouse called Watergate in MacManus's novel represents de Valera's Irish Republic in the way that the Big House formerly stood for Ascendancy Ireland. It is the ancestral home to which Alice Lennon returns after twenty-nine years in the United States. The house is now occupied by her sister Catherine and her husband Martin Brunton; their brother John lives close by. The Bruntons are poor stewards of the home: Martin drinks too much and has a tendency to violence, while Catherine is sickly and unable to run the house. For the past eight years they have employed a housekeeper, Ruby Butts, a woman who used to travel the roads with a tinker. Under her 'care', Watergate has a neglected appearance: 'There were hens rooting under the unclipped hedges, and hens in the ruined flowerbeds, cluttered with old cabbage stalks, skins and peelings and old tins, before the porch door.'[54] John describes it as 'not a Christian's house at all' (p.30). Alice strongly disapproves of Ruby and a battle of wills ensues for domination of the house.

The ancestral residence in *The Mangan Inheritance,* a house called 'Gorteen', is in a bad state of disrepair, and its rightful owners, Kathleen Mangan and her brother Con, live in a 'dirty yellow-colored caravan trailer' in a nearby field.[55] The connection of the house with the nation is reinforced by the name of Jamie's 'tinker' lover, Kathleen – a traditional designation for Ireland – and Jamie's association of her with Mangan's poem 'Dark Rosaleen', another symbolic representation of the nation. Both Alice in *Watergate* and Jamie in *The Mangan Inheritance* represent the end of their line: Alice's husband and only child are dead, and the son Jamie had with his ex-wife was still-born. With the future thus cut off, the Irish-American character's return to the ancestral nation, now symbolically ruled by 'tinkers', amounts to a double regression to a past state of being.

While, in these novels, Ireland as a nation is associated with the unwashed backwardness of the feminized tinker figure, America represents modernity and cleanliness. Alice sings the praises of American civilization to her brother: 'electric light, bathroom installations (the word made John lift his eyebrows!), refrigerators, central heating' (p.38), while in the opening scene of Brian Moore's novel, Jamie is having some 'bathroom trouble' fixed in his expensive Manhattan apartment (p.8). The obsession of the modern individual with bathrooms and sanitation reflects a fear of contamination that results from a repressed awareness that 'civilization' itself can be seen as 'a mechanism for the production and proscription of increasing amounts of dirt'.[56] The young woman in D.H. Lawrence's novella *The Virgin and the Gypsy* who fetishizes Joe Boswell also projects her feelings of desire and loathing on indoor plumbing, which 'becomes emblematic of both psychic putrefaction and hypocrisy':[57] 'She loathed these houses with their indoor sanitation and their bathrooms, and their extraordinary repulsiveness. ... The whole stagnant, sewerage sort of life. ... If gypsies had no bathrooms, at least they had no sewerage. There was fresh air.'[58] In this regard it is significant that New Age Travellers, whose lifestyle 'represents an attempt at turning a critique of modernity into a way of life', often reject modern conveniences: 'their refusal to acquiesce in the contemporary fetish of the *bathroom* is an implicit rejection of the modern obsession with sanitation'.[59] In making 'a vocation, a lifestyle, out of living off the excess of modernity',[60] New Age Travellers frequently antagonize representatives of 'traditional' Travellers, who are engaged in campaigns to demand better facilities for their halting sites. Traditional Travellers resent that their New Age counterparts actively seek to embrace the ugly stereotypes – so vividly portrayed in *Watergate* and *The Mangan Inheritance* – from which they are attempting to extricate themselves. The trope of the returned American who is contaminated and corrupted by the Irish 'tinker's' moral and physical dirt reveals the post-colonial anxiety at the heart of the mid-twentieth-century Irish identity construct: the projection of filth and irrationality onto the primitive Other both disavows and acknowledges the fear that underneath the civilized, Americanized exterior of the modern Irish person there (still) lurks a dirty, irrational 'tinker'.[61]

In *Watergate*, the schoolmaster explains to Alice that Ruby Butts first came to the attention of the local police some eight years ago, when 'this family of tramps or tinkers' arrived in their caravan, 'though they didn't belong to any of the clans' (p.56). Ruby was married to Crick Butts, a man with a scarred face which he likely got in a fight 'with real tinkers, who are decent people' (p.56). The guards were suspicious of Butts 'going around with a woman that seemed to have some breeding in her' (p.57), and when Ruby complained to them about her husband, the ensuing row between the couple led to a suspicious fire that burned down the caravan. Ruby, who was pregnant, was saved in the nick of time, but the girl she gave birth to shortly afterwards turned out to be mentally impaired. Butts was killed soon afterwards in a road accident.

The contrast between Alice and Ruby is presented quite starkly to begin with. Alice is smartly dressed and refers to herself, with her bleached hair, as a 'blonde' (p.31), while Ruby wears an ill-fitting 'dirty cotton overall' (p.21) and has 'jet-black' hair (p.20). Alice is determined to work hard and clean up Watergate, while Ruby is a late riser and idles her time away chatting to a Travelling woman at the gate. John recalls that Alice always was 'a torment for neatness' (p.37); by contrast, Mrs Butts sleeps in 'unwashed sheets' (p.42). MacManus thus creates a set of binary distinctions: clean versus dirty, hard-working versus lazy, light versus dark, Christian versus pagan, and settled versus itinerant. Another binary that pervades the novel places Irish in opposition to foreign, with the foreign (often Eastern) element always depicted as negative, and often equated with the Otherness of the Traveller, as when Ruby is said to look like a 'Spaniard' (p.102). When John muses that he would have inherited Watergate if he had not married so young, his wife Sally berates him, 'You needn't blame me, you Turk' (p.27), and when their children make too much noise, she complains that they sound like 'Red Indians' (p.28). John calls swimming in the local river 'a most unChristian habit', the kind only indulged in by 'those Eastern peoples' (pp.131–2). The novel's first-person narrator, Peter Walsh, asks John whether Alice was ever married, to which her brother reluctantly replies in the affirmative: 'Some class of foreigner he was. A Swede', with a job 'that took him here and there every week of the year'. The narrator concurs that '[t]hat was no life for a woman like her. ... She's the kind that like to settle in the one place.' Moreover, the foreigner 'had no religion either and left her in the end' (p.41).

Ruby Butts, with her sallow skin, black hair, dirty clothes and retarded offspring, also represents unacceptable alterity; at the same time, because she disregards the authoritative commands of her employers, she threatens to displace them as the dominant occupant of the house. The first time Alice sees the housekeeper, Ruby stands 'immobile on the threshold' of Watergate (p.32). The 'tinker' woman represents the threat of contamination and pollution by her disorder and irrationality. Her invasion of Watergate, the domestic space and the emblem of the nation, reveals the novel's fundamental anxiety about Ireland's newly found status as a modern, independent state.

Indeed, Alice herself draws attention to the precariousness of the nation's ability to live up to its new responsibilities when she compares Ireland unfavourably to the United States and asks, 'What kind of laws are we making in this country since we got our own government?' (p.47). A priest she met on the train just after her return home had ominously remarked that America is 'a civilized place to spend a life-time', but as for Ireland: 'the wildness is in us yet' (p.12).

While Ruby is the irrational force who must be expelled if modern 'civilization' is to prevail, she is also Alice's mirror image, the person Alice is perpetually on the verge of becoming. Alice's eyes seem 'peculiarly black' beneath her bleached hair (p.31), and soon the roots begin to grow out 'dull and discoloured' (p.48). In the local shop she looks for 'spices of some sort, curry-powder, chillies and peppercorns' (p.47), and has her sister complaining about the 'queer hot dish' she gives them for dinner (p.69). Her voice grows harsh and she begins to smoke and drink a lot, to the point where her public loudness and inappropriate clothes begin to embarrass her brother John. While she refers to Ruby as 'that dirty thing out there' (p.106), her own appearance begins to show signs of neglect, and a night of drinking leaves her with a feeling as if she 'never washed' (p.117). By the end of the book, Alice 'looked oddly like a respectable housekeeper dressed up in borrowed things' (p.160). Jervis contends that 'what disgusts the racist is ... difference that threatens to become the same, the hint of kinship, of shared identity, beneath the hated signifiers of racial otherness'.[62] That hint of kinship is also the reason why Alice feels compelled to represent the tinker woman as a 'filthy old moll' (p.44): the more she comes to resemble Ruby, the more hostile she becomes to her.

When Alice takes her sister and brother-in-law on a three-week holiday, she deliberately leaves the house in Ruby's care to expose the tinker woman's inadequacies. The narrator describes the effect on Watergate:

> However indifferent to the house and however detached from its affairs you might consider yourself, you could not help feeling a little sick with fear of the wildness that could return so easily, and creep like covering grass and weeds and stone-shattering thorn into every corner and crevice that had been fashioned for human usage; with the flies buzzing as they might, in a damp cattle-dunged ruin. It was the wildness of people who had never possessed anything stable and so never had been bred to the habit of cherishing. You could smell it. (pp.172–3)

As soon as Alice returns, she evicts Ruby Butts along with her retarded daughter. Watergate has been saved from the tinker, but 'the wildness is in us yet' and cannot be so easily dispelled. After Ruby's departure, Alice 'readied the fire and tidied the kitchen as if it were an ordinary evening; but all at once, as she began to sweep the floor, she felt she could not stay in the house and she ran out to wander around the yard in the dark and to take shelter, in the end, under the haybarn' (p.195). Afterwards, she represses the episode, putting it from her 'like some of her time in America' (p.196), and invests all her energy in cleaning the house and garden.

Brian Moore's *The Mangan Inheritance* – a Gothic extravaganza generally considered a seriously flawed novel – shares many of *Watergate*'s themes. James Mangan is an unsuccessful Irish-Canadian writer who lives in New York City; he and his wife Beatrice, a well-known actress, have just separated. Mangan is his father's only son, 'continuance in a line which stretched back to Ireland and their grandfather's claim to be descended from the poet Mangan himself' (pp.18–19). While spending the Christmas vacation at his father's house in Montreal, Jamie receives the news that Beatrice has been killed in a car crash. With his mind in turmoil about his identity, broken marriage and failing writing career, he decides to go to Ireland to find his roots, armed with a daguerreotype of an ancestor believed to be the poet James Clarence Mangan, to whom he bears a striking resemblance.

In Bantry, Jamie meets two families of Mangans: Dinny and his mother, and Dinny's first cousins, Con and Kathleen. Both families have come down in the world, but while Dinny and his mother cling to respectability and cleanliness, Con and Kathleen have embraced their new status and revel in it. Con tells Jamie that Kathleen spent two years on the road 'with a tinker that already had a wife', and that 'when she came back from hooring around with that tinker in his caravan ... no decent person would speak to her' (p.161). Jamie recalls seeing a group of shabby Travellers on the road on his first day in Ireland, and the gas station attendant telling him these were not Gypsies, but Irish people:

> They wander up and down the country, itinerants, as you might say. Mind you, the County Council has houses provided for them, but they will not bide in them. Always in trouble, that lot. You'd have to watch your belongings if some of them are around. ... God help them, there's some say the tinkers is people left over from another time, from the famine days when half of Ireland walked the roads without a home. (p.164)

Con, Kathleen and the caravan in which they live are filthy. Jamie's response to the much younger Kathleen, who soon becomes his lover, initially takes the form of lust: 'despite her dirty clothes and slum pallor, he felt an overwhelming attraction toward her'. This is immediately counterbalanced by a sense of disgust: 'But then she walked past him to pour the tea and the acrid smell of her body came into his nostrils, filling him with distaste. So these were the Irish Mangans, dirty, semiliterate gypsies. And yet, despite his distaste, the attraction remained' (pp.106–7). Almost from the beginning, Jamie is dimly aware that the signifiers of difference conceal a shared identity: 'they may be my relatives', he muses, 'but they're very different from me. They're dirty and wild. ... I said they're different from me, but supposing they're not?' (p.132). And if Con and Kathleen live like 'tinkers', Jamie realizes that his association with them makes him one, too:

> Tinkers. But come to think of it, what difference was there in that life and the life she now lived in a caravan with her drunken, ne'er-do-well brother? ... [Were they] descendants of the poet, or simply people left over from another time, their speech debased, their lives mean and pointless as that of cur dogs snuffling around a trash heap? And don't I fit in, too? Walking down a road now, carrying two bottles of gin in a plastic bag, waiting for an eighteen-year-old tinker's whore to come to my bed. A cur dog engaged in a pointless sniffing out of unknown ancestors, living off the scraps of his dead wife's fortune (p.165).

After two men beat him up in the toilet of a public house, Jamie also comes to look the part of the stereotypical 'tinker'. Left with a cut and swollen face and a missing tooth, he notices people's reactions to his rough appearance: '[h]is bruised face and swollen lip ... acted as his passport into that tinker world, stamping him as dangerous, drunken, a man you would not cross' (p.202).

Jamie's sexual attraction to Kathleen is also part of his 'fitting in', but at the same time he guiltily experiences their relationship as a transgression. The fact that Kathleen is prone to bouts of frightened madness while they are together is part of his unease. His altered appearance – his 'tinker' identity – acts as the signifier of that guilt, for while his beaten-up face makes him look even more like the double of the man in the photograph, who has a missing tooth as well, his face in the mirror also foreshadows his encounter with another, as yet unknown presence:

> He stared in terror at the face ... glaring at him, ghostly pale, eyes glittering with the steely hysteria of an insane person, the features frighteningly bruised, lip swollen, missing front tooth: himself. And in that moment he knew why this house resisted him. *I am the ghost that haunts it*. I am come back to these rooms where whatever bloody deed that frightened Kathleen once took place. ... And then he put his hand in his pocket and for the first time in days drew out that other face in a frame. ... It was as if the daguerreotype was now a document sentencing him to some future doom. (p.213)

The ghost face Jamie senses behind his own turns out to belong to Michael Mangan, Dinny's father. Years earlier, in a lurid Gothic scenario, Michael had used his wife's bouts of insanity as an excuse to begin sleeping with his daughter Maeve; when Michael began bothering 12-year-old Kathleen as well, Maeve decided to protect her by castrating her father with a kitchen knife. Since then, Michael has lived a withdrawn existence in a ruined Norman tower, where, unrepentant, he spends his days writing unpublished poetry and deludedly nursing his unrecognized genius. Jamie is horrified when he visits him, and finds himself 'filled with a premonition that he was looking at what he himself might one day become' (p.259); before he can digest the implications of his discovery, however, he is called back to Canada to be with his dying father. He leaves the Irish Mangans behind, but carries the 'tinker' with him to Canada beneath his own skin: 'Through his father ... the uncanny facial resemblance, the poetry, the wild blood had been transferred across the Atlantic Ocean to this cold winter land' (p.284). Before he left Ireland, moreover, he had given Kathleen a large cheque for a plane ticket to the United States, thereby leaving open the possibility of releasing the 'wild blood' yet again.

Variations on the theme of the liaison between a male Irish-American character and a female Irish Traveller continue to be written. In *Fork in the Road* (2000), a sprawling novel by New York-based journalist Denis Hamill, an Irish-American film maker visiting Dublin to conduct research for his new movie becomes amorously involved with the beautiful, promiscuous Traveller woman whom he catches in the act of picking his pocket on his first day in Ireland. Driven to distraction and near bankruptcy by Gina Furey's erratic ways, and by the rapacious and destructive behaviour of her numerous relatives, Colin Coyne is nevertheless bound by a deathbed promise to his mother to stand by the son he fathers with Gina, and to take care of the child she has from a former relationship. In this novel's configuration, the relationship with the Irish 'tinker' ultimately serves to rescue Colin from the initial directionlessness of his life (his 'inner tinker'), rather than sucking him into a moral morass. Gina's criminal habits eventually cause her death when she is stabbed in a scuffle with a potential robbery victim. After her funeral, Colin settles down as a responsible breadwinner and father of two. In this millennial perspective, in which the threat of the 'tinker' is successfully dispelled, the anxiety about modern identity that can be perceived in texts from earlier decades is replaced by the imperative to embrace its moral order and structures. One constant that informs novels of this configuration throughout the twentieth century, however, is the depiction of the Traveller as a profoundly anti-modern force of irrationality and disorder.

NOTES

1. Angus Bancroft, *Roma and Gypsy-Travellers in Europe: Modernity, Race, Space and Exclusion* (Aldershot and Burlington, VT: Ashgate, 2005), p.1.
2. Ibid., p.2.
3. Ibid., p.18.
4. Jim MacLaughlin, 'The Evolution of Anti-Traveller Racism in Ireland', *Race and Class*, 37, 3 (1996), p.48.
5. Quoted in Carmen Kuhling, 'New Age Travellers on *Cool* Mountain', in Michel Peillon and Eamonn Slater (eds), *Encounters with Modern Ireland: A Sociological Chronicle 1995–1996* (Dublin: IPA, 1998), p.149.
6. Seán MacGrath, 'The Tinkers of Ireland', I, *Irish Times*, 15 November 1955, p.5.
7. Seán MacGrath, 'The Tinkers of Ireland', II, *Irish Times*, 16 November 1955, p.5.
8. Helleiner, *Irish Travellers*, p.44.
9. Richard Dyer, *The Matter of Images: Essays on Representation* (London and New York: Routledge, 1993), p.16.
10. John Jervis, *Transgressing the Modern: Explorations in the Western Experience of Otherness* (Oxford: Blackwell, 1999), p.58.
11. Ibid., p.73.
12. Ibid., p.58.
13. Robbie McVeigh, 'The Specificity of Irish Racism', *Race and Class*, 33, 4 (1992), p.42.
14. Jervis, *Transgressing the Modern*, p.6.
15. D.H. Lawrence, *Lady Chatterley's Lover*, in *Seven Novels by D.H. Lawrence* (London: Heinemann/Octopus, 1976), p.773.
16. Ibid., p.774.
17. Ibid., p.775.
18. Ibid., p.778.
19. Ibid., p.779.
20. Nord, *Gypsies and the British Imagination*, pp.166–7.
21. Delaney, 'Migrancy and Cultural Disappearance', p.174.
22. Ibid., p.175.
23. Ibid., p.171.
24. Ibid., p.176.
25. Maurice Walsh, *The Road to Nowhere* (New York: Frederick A. Stokes, 1934), p.105. All subsequent page references in the text are to this edition.
26. Bryan MacMahon, 'A Portrait of Tinkers', *Natural History*, 80, 10 (1971), p.33.
27. Ibid., p.109.
28. Sigerson Clifford, *Travelling Tinkers* (Dublin: Dolmen Press, 1951), n.p. All subsequent

page references in the text are to this edition.
29. Liam O'Flaherty, 'The Stolen Ass', in *The Tent*, p.225.
30. Ibid., p.229.
31. Ibid., p.230.
32. Delaney, '"A Marginal Footnote"', p.162.
33. Patrick J. Egan, 'Garda Síochána (Guardians of the Peace)', in Lelia Ruckenstein and James A. O'Malley (eds), *Everything Irish: The History, Literature, Art, Music, People, and Places of Ireland from A-Z* (New York: Ballantine, 2003), p. 162.
34. Walter Macken, 'Battle', in *City of the Tribes* (Dingle: Brandon, 2001), p.13. All subsequent page references in the text are to this edition.
35. Andrew McNeillie, 'John McNeillie 1916–2002'. Accessed 27 December 2006: http://www.clutagpress.com
36. Ian Niall, *No Resting Place* (1948; London: Readers Union/Heinemann, 1950), p.10. All subsequent page references in the text are to this edition.
37. Bosley Crowther, review of *No Resting Place*, dir. Paul Rotha, *New York Times*, 5 May 1952. Accessed 27 December 2006: http:/www.nytimes.com archive.
38. Maurice Walsh, 'Son of a Tinker', in *Son of a Tinker and Other Tales* (London and Edinburgh: W. and R. Chambers, 1951), p.7. All subsequent page references in the text are to this edition.
39. Donagh MacDonagh, 'God's Gentry'. *The Word: A Catholic Pictorial Magazine*, February 1964, no pagination.
40. Donagh MacDonagh, *God's Gentry*. 60 pp., no pagination. Accessed 20 November 2004: http://members.tripod.com/IrishBornMan/Gods_Gentry.htm. All quotations in the text are from this edition.
41. Helleiner, *Irish Travellers*, p.45.
42. Quoted in Brendan Lehane, *Dublin* (Amsterdam: Time-Life International, 1978), p.9.
43. Ulick O'Connor, *Travels with Ulick* (Cork: Mercier Press, 1967), p.16.
44. Walter Macken, 'The Eyes of the Cat', in *The Coll Doll* (London: Macmillan, 1969), p.115.
45. Ibid., p.116.
46. Ibid., p.117.
47. Una Troy, *The Benefactors* (London: Robert Hale, 1969), p.22. All subsequent page references in the text are to this edition.
48. Jervis, *Transgressing the Modern*, p.159.
49. Qtd. in Helleiner, *Irish Travellers*, p.49.
50. Delaney, 'Representations of the Travellers', p.53.
51. Jervis, *Transgressing the Modern*, p.6.
52. Ibid., p.98.
53. Ibid., p.159.
54. Francis MacManus, *Watergate* (1942; Swords, Co. Dublin: Poolbeg Press, 1980), p.20. All subsequent page references in the text are to this edition.
55. Brian Moore, *The Mangan Inheritance* (1979; London: Corgi, 1981), p.105. All subsequent page references in the text are to this edition.
56. Jervis, *Transgressing the Modern*, p.159.
57. Nord, *Gypsies and the British Imagination*, pp.163–4.
58. Lawrence, *The Virgin and the Gipsy*, p.723.
59. Kuhling, 'New Age Travellers', p.150.
60. Ibid., p.152.
61. Many of these themes come together in John B. Keane's play *The Field* (1965; Cork: Mercier Press, 1991), which focuses on 'Bull' McCabe's forty-year obsession with land in the form of 'a sweet little field, ... an independent little field that wants eatin'' (p.26). Bull's wife has not slept with or spoken to him in eighteen years, ever since he battered her for allowing a tinker's pony to graze in the field, despite his attempts to placate her: 'I put in electric light and bought the television. I built that godamned bathroom ... *for her* ... all over a tinker's nag, a dirty one-eyed pony' (p.55).
62. Jervis, *Transgressing the Modern*, p.70.

CHAPTER 5

Beyond This World: Fantasy and Myth

I have begged from time to time,
I have drunk the golden wine,
I've fought men and I've done my share of lovin',
I've met wise men, I've met fools,
But I've always known the rules:
A tinker man must always be a movin'.
Gemma Hasson, 'Dan Malone'

'The Irish Travelers Dwell in a Mysterious Parallel Universe', a headline in *Time* magazine claimed in October 2002.[1] Fictional texts written from a sedentary perspective also frequently represent the Travellers as living, literally, in another world. Often such fiction associates them with figures from – mostly Celtic – mythology and legend to underline both their otherworldliness and their separation from the settled cultural and societal norm. The mythical impulse, with its basic purpose of expressing and affirming group identity, is a fundamental one in all cultures. One way for societies to access what Paul Ricoeur has termed their mythical 'nucleus' is to express their most deep-rooted fears and desires by translating core questions about origins and ends – Where do we come from? Where do we go? – into fantastic, fabulistic or utopian narratives. Ricoeur suggests that 'cultures create themselves by telling stories of their own past', but warns that the symbols of a community can readily become 'fixed and fetishised' to serve a monopolistic elite at the expense of submerged or marginalized groups.[2] This tends to be especially the case when the consensus-based identity of an imagined community is felt to be under pressure (for example in times of war or economic crisis, or as the result of an influx of immigrants with rival identities). In a discussion with Irish philosopher Richard Kearney about the resurgence of nationalism in the Baltic states, Ricoeur confessed to having 'underestimated the fragility of each identity which feels threatened by another. People must be very unsure to feel threatened by the otherness of the other.'[3] In light of the prevalence of such human insecurity, he argues that myth cannot be approached at the level of *naïveté*: we must always 'critically assess the content of each myth and the basic intentions which animate it'.[4]

The mythical dimensions of the 'tinkers' and 'Gypsies' who are a staple of popular Irish and Anglo-American fantasy fiction, and who feature particularly in quest narratives based loosely upon Arthurian or northern European legend, must therefore be scrutinized with Ricoeur's words of caution in mind. The fantastic aspects of such works allow the creators of alternative or parallel worlds to fashion the tinkers according to the imaginative needs of their narratives, but at the same time the stereotypical traits that are most associated with the tinker 'type' are often enhanced. The almost obligatory inclusion of tinkers in fantasy literature inspired by Celtic mythology reveals the extent to which Travellers are perceived as belonging to a different world than 'ours'. Even when the tinkers' way of life is used positively to express a utopian longing for change (for example, when Traveller culture is presented as an alternative to industrialization, materialism, and so on), this call for change focuses on a revival of the hegemonic culture by means of an idealized version of a minority culture, rather than on a utopian alternative for the real-world problems of the minority culture itself. In fantasy literature, Katie Trumpener has argued, Travelling people such as Gypsies act as figures 'whose prophecies break through historical time into myth, or conversely, who bring historical perspectives or innovations with them into the mythic time of a closed community'.[5]

An example of Travellers whose sole function is to help save the hegemonic culture of the story from its own worst excesses can be found in *The Golden Compass* (1995) by British writer Philip Pullman, the first book in his fantasy trilogy entitled *His Dark Materials*. Pullman depicts Gypsies as aides in a young girl's complex quest that eventually leads to the genesis of an alternative creation myth without original sin. Set partly in the 'Oxford' and 'London' of a world parallel to the one with which its readers are familiar, the novel follows the adventures of Lyra, a young girl who is rescued from the forces of evil by the 'gyptians' of Oxford led by a 'king' named John Faa.[6] Lyra's own story is a dark variation on the family romance: born from a liaison between Lord Asriel and a married woman, Mrs Coulter – both dangerously ambitious scholars – she was nursed by a gyptian woman before her father took her away to be raised within the walls of an Oxford college. When Lyra runs away to save the children kidnapped by Mrs Coulter from being used in her soul-destroying experiments, the gyptians are able to help her evade the officials because they themselves are elusive and have 'little standing in the law'.[7] They make it clear to Lyra that she is not like them: 'You might pass for gyptian with practice, but there's more to us than gyptian language. We're water people all through, and you en't, you're a fire person.'[8] This sentiment echoes statements by contemporary Irish Travellers: that they are 'out-and-out travellers'[9] and 'a different people',[10] who are looking for a mutually understanding relationship with the settled population while resisting assimilation by them.

While the 'gyptians' in *The Golden Compass* predominantly embody elusiveness and freedom, other fantasy narratives associate 'tinkers' more narrowly with myth and magic. In *The Star-Glass* (2004) by Canadian writer Duncan Thornton, designed to appeal to younger children, the tinkers, who speak a kind of Irish 'brogue' and live underground in a world populated by elves, trolls and monsters, provide a safe haven for the book's child protagonists. The world of internet gaming is also fond of the tinkers. In *Ultima*, a series of computer role-playing games set in a vaguely Arthurian fantasy realm called Britannia, the tinkers are a class of character. Their characteristics vary from game to game, but various internet sites describe tinkers as warriors suspicious of magical armour but well-versed in the use of all weapons, especially the double-bladed battle-axe. Highly skilled artisans and excellent fighters, the tinkers in some game versions are also capable of opportunistically draining the magical power of other characters for their own use.

Some fantasies make a direct connection between the 'tinkers' and the otherworldly beings of Irish mythology known as the *Aes Sídhe* (the people of the fairy mounds) or the *Tuatha Dé Danann* (usually translated as 'the tribes of the goddess Dana'), who are inhabitants of a parallel universe often imagined as being located underground. This mythical connection gives the travellers a spiritual and magical dimension that renders them doubly 'otherworldly'. In *The Wheel of Time*, a series of fantasy novels by South Carolina native Robert Jordan, the tinkers are a nomadic people known for their singing and dancing. They travel through the world looking for 'the Song', although it is not clear what its significance may be. Long before the time in which the series is set, the tinkers split from a people known as the Aiel, a race physically reminiscent of the Celts with a culture similar to that of the Native Americans, because the Aiel assisted the Aes Sedai, 'servants of all', some of whose members had gone over to the dark side, although they had at one time used their channelling abilities for the benefit of all mankind. The tinkers are regarded as outcasts by the other Aiel, who call them the 'Lost Ones', but in the series they are also known as the Travelling People or the Tuatha'an. The tinkers believe in the 'Way of the Leaf', a philosophy of non-violence and acceptance of whatever happens in life, but they have an undeserved reputation as thieves and kidnappers.[11]

A similar association between the tinkers and the otherworldly beings of Irish mythology is made by Charles de Lint, a Canadian author and Celtic folk musician, in his fantasy for young adults, *The Harp of the Grey Rose* (2004). De Lint's primary characters, Tess and Finan Kelledy, are 'tinkers from Lillowen originally', although Tess is now settled and 'played the part of witch-wife to the folk of Wran Cheaping'.[12] Her brother still travels and makes 'tinker blades' or small swords, and practices the old religion: 'Ballan, the god of the tinkers, was of the Tuathan, but he rarely meddled in their affairs.' Tess, however, 'turned more to the Moon-goddess Arn for her prayers, she who was the Mother of the World'.[13]

Tinkers also present an alternative way of life in *Rebel Sutra* (2000) by American writer Shariann Lewitt, a science-fiction narrative with spiritual overtones taken mostly from Indian sources, as the book's title indicates. In this work, the people on the isolated colony planet Maya are ruled by an aristocratic group of genetically enhanced humans known as the Changed. Della, a rebellious young Changed woman, escapes from the domed city of Xanadu where her people live: 'I ran away with the Tinkers when I was twelve. I was on the Eastern Gate ... and saw the motley caravan with stars and moons painted on the candy-colored vehicles.'[14] The tinkers in this narrative represent wisdom and knowledge. During the two years she spends with them, Della discovers that they 'know who we are and they have not forgotten. They are a strange tribe, scientists trained in disciplines that we have deliberately ignored, cutting ourselves off from the rest of the civilized empire.'[15] The tinkers themselves, however, are also displaced, and many are addicted to drugs: 'So many of them were unhappy, homesick for the comforts of civilization, for the refinement and elegance that they had once taken for granted. Now they were exiles.'[16] Both the spiritual and the scientific side of the tinkers is represented by their female leader, Suu-Suu, who 'had the uncanny sense of a Pythoness, even an Oracle',[17] and who had worked as a 'genetic Tinker' for the Imperial Genetics Laboratories of the Empire to which the planet Maya belongs, a name given to the scientists because they 'tinker with the workings of the Imperial genotype'.[18] In the world as we know it, scientists and engineers commonly describe the way they work on advancing complex problems as 'tinkering', and in her science fiction story, Lewitt has seamlessly merged the scientific tinkerer with the travelling tinker.

Fantasies of the type discussed above reveal the extent to which the Travellers are associated in the popular imagination with the mythic past, with magic and mystery, but above all, with separation from a given norm. Even within the otherworldliness of the fantastic realms created in these narratives, the tinkers represent both alienation from mainstream society and the possibility of escape to another world: for Lyra in *The Golden Compass*, the children in *The Star-Glass*, and Della in *Rebel Sutra*, the Travellers provide a safe haven away from the authorities and the law. Theirs is a secret world within an otherworld, albeit a benign, even pacifist one. Several fantasies suggest that the tinkers embrace matriarchal principles both in their leadership and their religion, a trait also found in forms of more 'serious' literature that associate the Travellers with myth, as examples discussed hereafter will demonstrate. In so far as the use of myth represents 'a tendency to align Travellers with an earlier moment in the settled past',[19] that return to the past 'is coded in terms of a return to maternal origins, perhaps suggesting a culturally specific investment in "myths of motherland"'.[20]

Questions of how imagined communities (worlds, 'motherlands') are defined, how they relate to each other, and who is included in them, are fundamental to mythology. Myths are, in essence, narratives that explain origins and consolidate the status quo (of the world, a people, a nation, a culture, etc.), which is one of the reasons why the mythic imagination has played such an important role in the rhetoric of Irish nationalism. Writing about the collision of myth and reality in the discourses of Irish poetry and politics, Irish philosopher Richard Kearney follows his French counterpart Paul Ricoeur in concluding that 'myth is a two-way street' that can incarcerate (that is, lead to bigotry and racism) as well as emancipate (in the sense of projecting genuine utopias of universal liberation).[21] Ricoeur warns that '[t]o the extent that myth is seen as the foundation of a particular community to the absolute exclusion of all others, the possibilities of perversion – chauvinistic nationalism, racism, etc . – are already present',[22] and suggests that a distinction should be made between different layers of myth: the 'chronicle dimension', which addresses the foundations of a culture or nation, and a 'wisdom dimension', which 'makes up a body of truths valid for all mankind'.[23] The question is whether the Travellers, as both Irish and Other, can ever be truly included as equals within the 'chronicle dimension' of the myth of Irishness.

Myths are narratives about origins, about how certain people and circumstances came into existence, and the scarcity of documented evidence relating to the 'origins' of the Irish Travellers, as well as the fact that the Travellers have not maintained a strong sense of their own collective history, means that mythic speculation about that subject is rife among both Travellers and non-Travellers. The idea that Travellers are a remnant of people made homeless and destitute by the Famine has been rejected by its opponents as a 'myth', but the world of Celtic mythology has been embraced by those who choose to believe that today's Travellers are descendants of the wandering smiths and bards described in the most ancient legends of Ireland. Such a notion was pursued in the first decades of the twentieth century by Eóin MacNeill, professor of early Irish history at University College, Dublin. His mytho-historic approach to Traveller origins led him to speculate that the mysterious Fir Bolg mentioned in early Irish texts were one of the 'industrial castes of ancient Ireland', and subsequently to surmise that '[t]he tinker clans of recent times in Ireland and Scotland may well be survivals of some of these ancient industrial communities'.[24] This notion still has considerable popular appeal. Fox News in the USA referred to the Irish Travellers as a 'secretive, nomadic group' whose 'origins are mysterious, though theories link them to pre-Celtic inhabitants of Ireland or European Gypsies'.[25] In 2005, a headline in the British newspaper the *Independent* claimed, 'Academics Suggest Irish Travellers Are Remnant of Pre-Celtic Culture', only to reveal in the following article that the claim was made by a single academic at a symposium 'on the travellers' mysterious past'.[26]

Some Traveller activists have supported the theory that links the Travellers with the mythic, pre-Milesian people of Ireland, because such an origin provides them with aboriginal roots in Irish soil. Gypsy and Traveller activist Grattan Puxon, for example, put forward such a notion in a pamphlet of the mid-1960s:

> Thousands of years ago a free travelling people lived on the island today called Ireland. They roamed as they wished, seeking the best grazing land for their animals. They spoke their own language, which we call the gammon or shelta, and lived in the same kind of tents that many families on the road still use, covering their wattle frames with skins instead of canvas.
>
> The travelling people were never big in number and when other peoples, with different ways of life, arrived on the island they began to take over the land, plant crops and settle down. As years passed, it became harder for the travelling people to live. Houses and fences went up in more and more places and the travelling [people] had to leave the open land and began following the new roads that led from one village to another.[27]

In a more recent publication, Michael McDonagh, himself a Traveller, modified this version of Traveller origins as follows:

> We, as a community, have existed for a long time. Even when you read the more famous stories particularly the Tain Bo Cooley, you will come across these landless people who are not accepted by either Maeve's army or Cu Culainn's. Yet they would fight for any side. These people would always be the best hunters, their tents would be up first, others were frightened of them and didn't want them with them. There are lots of stories in Irish mythology that mention the existence of people who had a diverse identity and culture from mainstream society.
>
> Whether you accept everything I have said or not, you must at least agree that our origins go back a long way and may indeed be 'lost in the mists of time'.[28]

As Mary Burke and others have argued, pre-Celtic origin theories are a double-edged sword: on the one hand, they have the disadvantage of configuring the minority as 'an eternally vanquished people', but on the other, they emphasize the Travellers' ethnicity and long-standing presence in Ireland and refute 'those who ... would construct the Travellers as descendants of recent sedentary "drop-outs"'.[29] Michael McDonagh also discusses alternative origin theories and does not wholeheartedly endorse the idea of mythical beginnings; his main concern is not 'to prove the exact origins of Travellers in Irish society, but to disprove any theories that suggest that we only came about as a result of some disaster in Irish history'.[30]

In the rhetoric of late nineteenth- and early twentieth-century Irish nationalism, a utopian vision of the future was contingent on the mythical construct of a unified, heroic past – an idealized and exclusionary prehistory of the Irish 'race'. Foundational national myths, such as those based upon the heroic defiance of Cuchulainn, or the renewal of the nation through blood sacrifice, or the rootedness of the peasant in the land, or the genuine Gaelic nature of the west, which originated as efforts to emancipate the Irish from their colonial inferiority complex, inevitably, to use Richard Kearney's term, draw a magic circle around the definition of Irish identity, often to the exclusion of a dialogue with any group or set of individuals that did not fall within its bounds. A minority group within Ireland such as the Travellers occupied a problematic position within these narratives of national identity and unity, and their representation had to be carefully 'managed'. Revival writers uneasily tiptoed between including the 'tinkers' in their projects about Irish folk life (as Lady Gregory did, for example, in her *Poets and Dreamers*), and rejecting the depiction of a way of life that, in its wildness, might reinforce ingrained British preconceptions about the drunken and unruly Irish (which was a factor when the Abbey Theatre refused to stage Synge's play *The Tinker's Wedding*, although anticlericalism was cited as the primary concern).

When the Irish Free State came into existence in 1922, the mythic projections of the Revivalists of a decade or two earlier quickly lost their appeal, since the reality of the 1920s and 1930s showed little sign of living up to the heroic model. After the creation of the nation-state, Celtic mythology was essentially abandoned as a vehicle for defining Irishness, and adopted by satirists like Darrell Figgis and Eimar O'Duffy to reveal the gap between heroic idealism and all too human reality.[31] As discussed previously, the children's fiction of Patricia Lynch of the early decades of Irish independence appeared to answer the unspoken question, 'Where did we go wrong?' by inserting the Travellers into the national myth in a telling way. In *King of the Tinkers*, the reputation of the Travelling people for creating trouble bars them from entering the mythic-heroic world of the Secret Valley, which holds the ancient heroes of Ireland in suspended animation until some future time when they can awaken and restore the nation to its former greatness. The tinkers' behaviour prevents not only them, but also the book's boy protagonist (who represents the nation's future) from coming face to face with Finn and the Fianna, the once-and-future saviours of Ireland. In Lynch's fiction, the Travellers function as bridging figures between the realism of rural Ireland and the magic of fairy land, without having a sanctioned place in either world.

TINKER GODDESSES IN THE NOVELS OF OLIVIA ROBERTSON

Olivia Robertson's strange fictions of the mid-twentieth century are also critical of the new state, and mount an almost Yeatsian critique of the modern, capitalist tendencies of the rising Irish middle class, while simultaneously configuring a utopian Irish future that centres around the matriarchal principles of the triple goddess, rather than the heroic figure of Cuchulainn. In these feminized revisions of the national myth, the tinkers' way of life is presented in an idealized form as an antidote to both the patriarchy and capitalism – as both a remnant of the past, and a signpost to a more spiritually balanced future world. The tone of sustained whimsy of Robertson's fictions is not easy to gauge. Mary Burke reads *Field of the Stranger* as a comic novel that satirizes 'the creation of a distant, tragic Traveller past as a folly of romantic patriots and nationalists';[32] she sees the views on the archaic nature of tinker origins held by the 'Vallanceyesque' amateur archaeologist Titus Melrose as a satire of 'both the discourse of the tinker as fallen gentry or inverted aristocrat, and the draw of the tinker figure for the Irish Protestant writers of the Revival'.[33] Read in isolation from Robertson's other works, *Field of the Stranger* does indeed appear to present a send-up of some of the more exotic theories about Traveller origins that had been advanced by scholars before her time. Read in the context of some of her other works, however, and with the knowledge that Robertson is a self-styled priestess in the Fellowship of Isis, an alternative religion she founded in 1976 with her brother Lawrence, the ideas about Traveller origins expressed by her characters may have to be taken with fewer grains of salt than might initially be assumed.

A member of an Anglo-Irish family, Robertson was born in London in 1917 and educated in England and Dublin. In the early 1940s she worked as a children's playground attendant in a disadvantaged area of north Dublin. She recorded her observations of Irish life in general, and her experiences with the women and children of the tenements in particular, in several works, including *Field of the Stranger* (1948) and *Dublin Phoenix* (1957). In addition, she wrote two novels, *The Golden Eye* (1949) and *Miranda Speaks* (1950), in which she fictionalized certain aspects of the experiences recorded in her other books. In a chapter of *Field of the Stranger* entitled 'Progress and the Tinkers', Titus Melrose answers his friend Olivia's question, 'Why ... are tinkers so fascinating?' by referring to the fact that they are not bourgeois and have an ancient presence in Ireland: 'The tinkers are the rightful owners of Ireland', being 'the original inhabitants who fashioned the magnificent gold ornaments and were conquered and overcome by the Gaels'.[34] In addition to a love of horses, a disrespect for respectability, and a love of travel, they share with the Anglo-Irish aristocracy an ability to 'survive in their habitat' even though they are pushed aside by the 'Progress' of the upwardly mobile (p.195). While Titus's views are extreme – he would like the Irish to return to speaking 'the genuine Irish language, the tinkers' Shelta' (p.213) as well as reintroduce an agricultural calendar based on the phases of the moon – the Olivia character is sympathetic to many of his ideas. Titus acknowledges that a world entirely composed of tinkers 'might put an end to organised government and to civilisation; but the tinkers I look upon as an essential antidote to the organised state, as Diogenes in his tub was a fitting contrast to Alexander the Great' (p.196). What the tinkers have above all else is vitality, and Titus correctly predicts that tinkers such as Olivia's friends the 'Almonds' (actually Ormondes) will provide an antidote to 'death-loving' forms of modern art, of which the play written by their pretentious friend Cornelius, entitled *Oedipus O'Hara*, is an example. Hubert Almond later disrupts its performance with a lusty rendition of 'The Charladies' Ball'.

In *Field of the Stranger*, Olivia recognizes that several of her friends have different visions of the future of Ireland: one version of the new nation is 'to be governed by a committee of biologists, the other to be influenced by tinkers', and a third is 'to be ruled by women' (p.228). In her two novels, Robertson integrates these different ideas into a playful spiritual fantasy that presages her decades-long commitment to the Fellowship of Isis.[35] The protagonist of *The Golden Eye* is 22-year-old Eva Tracey – rumoured to be the illegitimate offspring of the late Major Gubty Blair – who arrives in the 'Golden Eye' art shop of her uncle and aunt, members of the rising middle class, to pursue a career as an art dealer and, under the name of 'Seeta', to work as a part-time fortune-teller. In pursuit of a painting of Aphrodite, Eva meets its owners, the Traceys of Napper Tandy Street, who are her distant relatives. The novel creates an effective contrast between the 'otherworld' of these courteous, cheerful but penniless Northside Traceys and their money-conscious Southside counterparts. Throughout the novel Eva also experiences a more metaphysical 'otherworld' of dreams and visions. Eventually, she contracts tuberculosis, and *The Golden Eye* ends with her realization that she is about to die and become part of the otherworld of her dreams.

Cornelius Blair, the protagonist of *Miranda Speaks*, is a middle-aged Anglo-Irish playwright and a distant relative of Major Gubty Blair. Cornelius is writing a play from the perspective of Shakespeare's Miranda, which is to be staged in the Golden Eye theatre, formerly the art shop of the earlier novel; Miranda herself appears to him in dreams to provide clues for the play, which Cornelius struggles to interpret. Convinced of the reality of his character, Cornelius searches for her in the 'otherworld' of Dublin's Northside, which to him, like his dreams, comes more and more to represent the real world. Eventually he meets Miranda's physical counterpart in his cousin Anthea, whom he marries, and her spiritual counterpart in an old tramp, Singing Molly, a friend of the Almond tinker family. The dream-Miranda, meanwhile, takes on a more and more fluid personality. Eventually the Napper Tandy Street Traceys are able to link Miranda with Eva Tracey, who had died three years earlier of tuberculosis. In Miranda's final dream appearance she explains to Cornelius that, now that he has been sufficiently transformed by his 'otherworldly' quest, she will move on to a new task. Cornelius foresees that Miranda will be reborn as his own daughter.

In his initial dreams, before he goes on his otherworldly quest, Cornelius keeps seeing Miranda as a tinker woman. At first, his reaction is negative: 'She has a look of some of those smarmy tinker girls who come round selling things at the back door and "God blessing" you.'[36] For his play, he visualizes Miranda 'as a tinker woman in a shawl, light, witty, and passionless' (p.36), and attempts to interpret her appearances metaphorically: artists like himself were meant to 'live in dreams and beauty, ... yet they had to behave like tinkers offering to tell fortunes or mend cars' (p.37). Or perhaps 'the mental image of his Miranda begging, a borrowed baby in her arms', was meant to convey 'the feeling that in begging one set at nought the world, the flesh, the devil, and respectability itself?' (p.38). In a subsequent appearance, Miranda, 'looking peculiarly low-class and tinkerish' (p.42), provides Cornelius with more clues about her mission: 'there're hundreds of me all over the world. But you must find me in the right place' (p.44). Cornelius thinks of Dublin's Northside and its tenement women, and 'remembered the story of Etain, the mortal woman in love with the shining Irish God Midir with the red hair' before rousing himself from his dream. He is not ready yet for the message and 'cried out at Miranda with the voice used by householders to begging tinkers' (p.44).

In his search for the perfect girl to play Miranda on stage, Cornelius finds himself entering Dublin's Northside: 'The feeling that he had come into another world came over Cornelius as he made his way over Butt Bridge towards the Majestic Theatre on the North Bank of the Liffey' (p.58). He realizes that, even though his plays had featured 'tinkers, drunkards, workmen and old IRA men' before, they had been acted 'according to classic Irish formulae', and he had never visited their 'habitat' (p.59). He therefore makes his way through a narrow archway to Napper Tandy Street. Soon it dawns on him that he may have misinterpreted Miranda's message about tinkers: 'Heretofore he had imagined that Miranda had told him to go to the very poor people on the North side to find others like her and then, from compassion, to help them. Now in a flash the reverse idea struck him. ... To find Miranda in such surroundings might be a help for himself' (p.65). Subsequent visits to Napper Tandy Street leave him enchanted by the 'gaudy gaiety of the population', especially the children: 'The little Royal children of old days were equally ornate with bracelets and rings and necklaces. He also noticed the bows and jewelled slides in the girls' hair – and such hair! Black and chestnut and flaxen and above all the glorious fuzzy tinker vermillion and ginger. Cornelius felt extraordinarily elated' (p.86). In *Dublin Phoenix*, Robertson also emphasizes the striking redness of the tinkers' 'elf-locks',[37] and the fact that the general population 'are not proud of hair the colour of the setting sun, the "red-gold" of legend. It suggests defeat, poverty, tinkers – the lack of respectability.'[38]

Cornelius in *Miranda Speaks* is learning to let go of respectability. The singing games of the Northside children bring to his mind ancient myths and rituals, and their mysterious symbolism makes him determined 'to seek Miranda, not because of any fantasy in his own mind but because she stood for beauty, a beauty not his own' (p.94). It is the beauty of the Goddess, whether she be Sycorax, Dana, Psyche, Sita or Isis, and her presence is eternal: Cornelius 'felt that past, present and future were really one' (pp.170–1). His personal life reflects his new-found wisdom, for it now includes the 'happy-go-lucky' Singing Molly, an old woman tramp rejected by her own middle-class children and only cared for by the tinkers, but now taken into his home by Cornelius; his marriage partner Anthea, who is the biological counterpart of Miranda; and the dream woman, whose spiritual presence completes the matriarchal trinity that enables Cornelius's artistic and spiritual rebirth and the return of Miranda herself.

To Olivia Robertson, the otherworld of the tinkers and the North Dublin slums retains vestiges of an ancient, matriarchal culture now lost in middle-class Ireland, but of vital importance for its survival and health. Even in the women's world of Napper Tandy Street, matriarchal principles are under threat, as the Traceys have social aspirations and look down upon inferior relatives like Twisty Nellie Tracey, who makes a living as a beggar and fortune-teller. In *The Golden Eye*, Eva has a vision of Twisty Nellie in her first dream after her visit to the tenements: '"She has sprung from the Dublin slums", thought Eva, "and there she stands in the moonlight, a thorn in the side of the respectable, wrapped in a dirty black shawl".' Yet when Eva asks dream-Nellie to remove the shawl, a mystery is revealed, as in the unveiling of Isis: '"She is a Queen", thought Eva. "She is very powerful and can move beautifully as if she could balance on anything".'[39] Afterwards, Eva thinks of 'the half-savage yet courteous slum dwellers and tinkers and peasants, who seemed another race, who had produced no intelligentsia, and who had preserved faint vestiges of an older culture' (p.103). In the Golden Eye art shop, Eva compares the intellectual, sophisticated Chinese figurines, which she likens to the Irish middle class and finds 'more British somehow' (p.106), with the 'ebullient, sensuous' Indian deities, preferring the latter because they are 'just like the Napper Tandy Traceys!' (p.105). They 'are curiously reminiscent of the Irish tinkers even in appearance. I mean like the fierce "wild Irish". ... Like those O'Flahertys and those tinkers from the West' (p.106). Indeed, she imagines that 'these Indian figures are about to dance like tinkers' (p.107).

In Olivia Robertson's novels, the red-haired, feminized tinkers with their roots in ancient, mystical Ireland, form a conduit through which the goddess announces a new era for Ireland in which the balance between mind and body, between masculine and feminine principles, is redressed. To this day, the Fellowship of Isis dedicates itself to similar principles: 'It is to the ancient myth we must return, for integrity. ... For the dark powers of the Mothers are not to be feared: but they are to be respected.'[40] Based in a castle in County Wexford, and led by Robertson, now Lady Olivia, the 'multi-religious, multi-racial, and multi-cultural' Fellowship claims to be 'dedicated to honoring the religion of all the Goddesses and pantheons throughout the planet. ... The Gods are also venerated.'[41] Lady Olivia has also unearthed her own links to the Goddess: 'The Priesthood of the

Fellowship of Isis is hereditary in source, traced through the Robertsons of Strathloch. The priestly line comes to Lawrence and Olivia Robertson from the Egyptian Princess Scota, who was the daughter of the Pharaoh Cincris. Scota was hereditary Daughter of Isis through her descent from Isis and Osiris, Queen and King of Egypt.'[42] Such a venerable lineage makes the tinkers' roots in ancient Ireland pale by comparison. No 'tinkers' are mentioned in the Fellowship's promotional materials, and none appear to be involved in its activities.

THE MATERNAL SUPERNATURAL IN *INTO THE WEST*

As Joe Cleary has argued in his essay, 'Into Which West? Irish Modernity and the Maternal Supernatural', the 1993 film *Into the West*, scripted by Jim Sheridan and directed by Mike Newell, 'will also lend itself to a "feminist" reading as a fable about the need to renew contact with some feminine principle perceived as exiled from a patriarchal world'.[43] In the film, two young Traveller boys, Tito and Ossie Riley, travel on a beautiful white horse from the concrete jungle of North Dublin, associated with their dead-beat father, to the west of Ireland, the land of their dead mother and their 'origins', a location which at least since the Revival has been depicted as retaining an 'authentic' Celtic quality deemed to have been erased by British influences elsewhere. Ossie and Tito's adventures are plotted upon the myth of Oisín in Tír na nÓg (the Land of Eternal Youth), in which the hero travels to the otherworld to marry a beautiful princess, only to discover that he cannot return to the real world because too much time has passed and he has, effectively, died there. In the film, Ossie is granted a vision of the dead mother he never knew – the beautiful princess – in a near-death experience, before he is rescued from drowning in the nick of time. Indeed, his shanachie grandfather, who still lives the old-style travelling life with a horse-drawn barreltop wagon, had promised him that, unlike Oisín, he would not die once he stepped off the magical white horse (dubbed Tír na nÓg by Ossie). But Ossie's salvation can only happen because the world to which he returns from near-death is not the modern, capitalist world of Dublin, but the magical, pre-industrial world of the Travellers in the west. Ossie, Tito and their now reformed father return to the 'traditional' Traveller way of life and will never go back to living in Dublin. The script implies that the move into the city has victimized Travellers, and has severed their connection with the 'pure' Traveller traditions of the past.

Traveller activist Michael McDonagh identifies flexibility as a core characteristic of the Traveller economy: 'There is always change happening. When one way of earning a living is gone another will take its place. Travellers adapt to survive and respond to what is needed in mainstream society at any given time.'[44] However, rather than acknowledge that Travellers move with the times, like everybody else, *Into the West* fixes the 'true' Traveller in an immovable romantic past or 'Tír na nÓg'. As Oisín discovered in the myth, a return from the land of eternal youth to the real world is impossible and leads only to death. For all its sympathetic intentions, the movie denies Travellers a place in the modern world by implying that they cannot survive there: they can only 'live' happily ever after in a mythical location. Joe Cleary therefore argues that *Into the West* is not a work of social realism, and is not in any real sense about the Travelling community. We are not meant to ask, for example, how the 'unfallen' Travellers in the west maintain their idyllic lifestyle economically. Rather, the Travellers are a metaphor in that they 'function for the audience as an object of utopian longing for a form of extended family or clan or communal collectivity of the type that is systematically dissolved within the world of advanced capitalism'.[45]

Cleary identifies three 'wests' in the film: the 'Celtic' west of Ireland, the modern industrial 'West' and the 'Wild West' of the cowboy movies so beloved by Tito and Ossie. 'Are we the cowboys or the Indians?' they wonder at one point, and as Irish citizens who also belong to a minority group, they have a right to be confused. The utopian ending of *Into the West* can be likened to a Western movie in which the Indians outwit and defeat the cowboys in order to re-establish their idyllic way of life of the pre-cowboy era – albeit within the confines of a mythical reservation. As Cleary points out, the pre-lapsarian Traveller community in *Into the West* is imagined as a matriarchate and presided over by a 'Spirit-Mother' in the person of Kathleen, 'the living surrogate of the spirit mother who really presides over the journey',[46] whose name also evokes Cathleen Ni Houlihan, the goddess figure whose transformation from crone into young queen symbolizes the rejuvenation of Ireland as a nation. Because the prospect of an actual journey into the past is unlikely to appeal to contemporary Irish women, the film presents the mother only 'as a supernatural presence: as a vague signifier of some previous state that is never named'.[47]

Maeve Connolly considers Irish movies featuring Traveller characters, including *Into the West*, *Traveller* (1981), *The Field* (1990), *This Is My Father* (1998) and *Country* (2000), as typical examples of 'heritage cinema' in that they engage with themes like 'emigration, repressive social norms, and traumatic memory'[48] – in other words, they deal with 'the loss and recovery of a cultural identity and familial stability through recourse to a rural, preindustrial past' by, typically, displacing this post-modern crisis onto a community of Travellers.[49] Jack Murphy in *Country*, for example, a timid boy often beaten by his widowed father, befriends a Traveller boy named Michael who teaches him to stand up for himself. Jack's adult brother Con is in love with Sarah Clifford, whose parents disapprove of the relationship. When her lecherous and bigoted uncle Mick is defeated in a fight he has picked with Michael's father, he drunkenly reasserts his manhood by raping his niece, telling Con afterwards that Sarah had been attacked by 'knackers'. Together, Mick and Con set fire to the Travellers' site, but Mick is killed by Michael's father, and Con runs away when he discovers that Jack has witnessed the entire event. In the end, the Travellers move on, but Jack is reconciled with his father, who has meanwhile been forced to confront his own guilty past, in which his drunkenness had led to the accidental killing of his wife. Maeve Connolly identifies 'the recurrent emphasis on Traveller society as inherently, and ideally, maternal' as a key issue, and notes that '[t]he coding of the settled past (and by extension Traveller culture) in this way would seem to have particular implications for women, and this invites further analysis'.[50]

FATE AND 'TINKER BLOOD' IN TWO PLAYS BY MARINA CARR

In her plays *Portia Coughlan* (1996) and *By the Bog of Cats* (1998), Marina Carr places her female characters, Portia Coughlan and Hester Swane, in an aggressively materialistic contemporary world of property and commodities, at the same time that each plot is carefully staged against a backdrop of myth and otherworldliness. Both characters have 'tinker' heritage. The tension between the material 'here' and the mythical 'elsewhere' is also represented by the plays' location in the Irish Midlands, which Carr has described as 'a metaphor for the crossroads between the worlds'.[51] Caught on this faultline, Portia and Hester struggle with questions of identity, fate and self-determination. In Mary King's reading of *By the Bog of Cats*, the play's plot 'mockingly interrogates neo-bourgeois, post-nationalist Irish pretensions to and prevarications about identity' in its concern with 'narratives of heredity, legitimacy, inheritance and descent'.[52] As in the films discussed previously, these contemporary concerns are displaced onto the Travellers and focused through an obsession of the settled characters with 'a tinker/peasant past, regarded by social climbers as a mésalliance'.[53] Each play depicts a family tragedy, in which a dark curse has repeated itself over several generations, until the female protagonist breaks the cycle by taking her own life. The question remains whether and to what extent the inherited mythical 'curse' destroys the characters, or to what extent they are guilty of creating a wilfully self-destructive, self-fulfilling prophecy.

In each case, the protagonist's fate is tied up with a specific location in the Irish Midlands, a myth associated with the place that is of significance to the character, a personal loss that took place there, and an inherent genetic ('tinker') quality that marks the character as tainted or unnatural. Portia Coughlan cannot leave the Belmont river because her twin brother Gabriel, with whom she claims to have had an incestuous love relationship, took his own life there. The river derives its name from the god Bel, who allegedly rescued a girl from that location where she had been impaled on a stake by the people around her because she was 'different', as Portia sees it, or evil, as another character claims. Hester Swane in *By the Bog of Cats* is haunted by the loss of her mother, who disappeared when she was 7 years old, more than three decades ago; she cannot leave the bog in case her mother returns. Her fate is tied to that of the black swan that lives on the bog, since her mother declared when she was born that the child would not outlive the bird. Both Portia and Hester are also loosely based on Euripides' tragic heroine Medea, who, within the context of the Greek tragedy, represents otherness (as a foreigner), female rage at perceived injustice, and lack of moderation. Haunted by a sense of incompleteness, Portia and Hester construct a myth of the self that is bound up with external, archetypal myths that justify but also perpetuate their despair.

Clare Wallace has remarked that the primary importance of the Midlands as a location in these plays is derived from 'its metaphorical dimensions, as a no-man's land, a claustrophobic zone of entrapment, a state of mind, and ultimately as a dystopia'.[54] The Irish and Greek myths in the plays function in much the same way, to entrap the characters in a predetermined plot from which they feel unable (and unwilling) to escape. 'There's ways round curses', Catwoman tells Hester: 'Curses only have the power ya allow them';[55] but the curse of social and cultural rejection is not so easily discarded. Mary King suggests that Hester's tragedy is that of 'doomed resistance to estrangement from a reified Self, brought about by being brutally cast as the inferior, inauthentic other, the outcast black swan in a cold white world'.[56] Wallace notes another metaphor of destiny in the subplot of incest in *Portia Coughlan* – Portia is unnaturally close to her brother Gabriel, she is the child of parents who are half-brother and sister, and her grandmother Blaize is accused by her daughter-in-law of being her own brother's child – which 'serves to heighten the sense of claustrophobia, violence and predeterminacy which dominate the characters' fates'.[57] The inescapable nature of this destiny is revealed by Maggie, who argues that, even if Portia does not consciously know that her parents were brother and sister, 'her blood do'.[58]

Another common determining factor for the fatedness of Portia and Hester is that they both have 'tinker blood', which is the accusation thrown at the women by several of the other characters. Portia's mother, a Joyce, is accused by her mother-in-law of being a 'tinker': 'We don't know where ye came from, the histories of yeer blood. ... There's a devil in that Joyce blood, was in Gabriel, and it's in Portia too. God protect us from that black-eyed gypsy tribe with their black blood and their black souls!' (p.31). Later she reiterates that the Joyces were '[f]uckin' tinkers' with their '[d]irty ignorant blood the likes of Belmont never seen before' (p.45). Hester in *By the Bog of Cats* is also a 'tinker', who is accused by her ex-lover's mother of having 'lazy shiftless blood' (p.54). Only too aware of what people say about her 'tinker blood' (p.16), Hester defiantly claims to be proud of her heritage, and eventually uses it to explain why she burned down the house built for her by her lover Carthage because he wanted her to see 'how normal people lived' (p.73): 'That's what the tinkers do, ... burn everythin' after them' (p.63)

In an interview, Marina Carr told Eileen Battersby that she chose to make Hester a 'tinker' because 'travellers are our national outsiders aren't they?'[59] Like the Midlands locations and the myths associated with them, 'tinkerishness' is used in these plays as a trope for unnaturalness, psychological alienation and abjection. Even if one sees Hester's 'totemic cutting out of her own tormented heart' as a rebuke to the inhumanity of a 'discontented, dysfunctional, settled community' seeking to 'extirpate the internalised, expropriated, feminized other from the epistemic "we"', as Mary King does,[60] such a metaphoric *j'accuse* that cuts short Hester's own life as well as the future represented by her daughter can hardly be seen as a victory. The relegation of the Travellers to this abstract position within a mythic pattern is itself a move that fixes and predetermines Traveller identity. The move towards abstraction, as Vic Merriman has argued, ignores questions of class and entitlement and 'results in the unproblematic ascription of fatedness to the poorest and most vulnerable in the social order'.[61]

ANIMALISM, ATAVISM AND TABOO IN *THE NATURE OF WATER AND AIR*

Regina McBride's novel *The Nature of Water and Air* also intertwines the world of the Travellers with the otherworld of Celtic legend and the theme of incest. McBride, a third generation Irish-American writer of popular fiction sometimes characterized as 'Gothic romance', whose parents romanticized the country of origin they had never visited, writes, like Marina Carr, about mothers and daughters who do not feel 'at home' in the world. The tinkers in this book are associated with nature, animality and freedom from convention and taboo (in that they have no sexual inhibitions), but their 'animal nature'[62] is also a kind of atavistic force – tinkers are described as 'a relic of the Iron Age' (p.144) – which expresses itself in a primitive impulse that enslaves the individuals subject to it. Agatha, the mother of the book's main character, Clodagh, was a tinker. As a teenager, she appeared 'from nowhere' (p.14) and was taken in by the dying occupant of the local Big House, who married her because of an animalistic quality that stirred something 'vital' in him. Soon after, a tinker man approached her as she was sitting on the beach, and asked her if she was a selkie. As a child, Clodagh believes that her mother is indeed a mythical sea creature (a seal in the ocean but a human being on land), brought to shore against her will to be the wife of a land dweller. Clodagh resents her mother's 'incomplete humanity' and wishes she would either run away with her secret tinker lover – who has given her a sealskin dress for their trysts, 'silvery, speckled in places, fitted to her body' (pp.92–3) – or go back to the sea. When the mother drowns herself, Clodagh tells the housekeeper that her mother has 'gone after the tinkers' (p.111). Throughout, Agatha's identities as a selkie and a tinker are intertwined: she is like a wild and free animal imprisoned in a house, and more properly at home in an 'other' world.

A tinker man Clodagh meets on a bus, 'a giant of deep grace and feeling', arouses 'a reckless yearning' in her (pp.122–3). As the sealskin dress keeps haunting her, she in turn haunts the tinker, whose name is Angus Kilheen; presenting herself as a friend of Clodagh's, she tells him she is called Mare (the name of her dead twin sister), and expresses the belief that she and he 'are tied together by destiny' (p.167). Eventually he becomes her lover. She discovers more selkie lore, according to which a man gains control over the seal woman by hiding her skin; but some men forge the skin into a dress in order to domesticate the wife, as 'an attempt to balance the animal with the human' (p.199). By now Clodagh no longer literally believes her mother was a selkie: 'If she was like an animal it was in the way a girl raised outside of houses was like an animal. ... Not magical' (p.202). Yet the mythical element keeps returning. A friend tells Clodagh that the Travellers are 'a true relic of ancient Ireland', who some people said 'came from the sea' (p.216), and selkies, too, 'are living relics of an older time' (p.219). Although Angus berates Clodagh for romanticizing him and his way of life, she feels that being with him makes her 'darker, more elemental' (p.238). She is also told that having a dead twin means she has 'one foot already among the dead. ... You surely must have eyes that penetrate the layers of this world' (p.220). Angus may have similar eyes; Clodagh's false identity makes her feel that Angus loves Mare, not her, and that she is an 'imposter in two worlds' (p.233).

When Angus gives Clodagh the sealskin dress that belonged to Agatha, she realizes that he was her mother's lover. She does not disclose her true identity, however, even after he reveals that he was the father of Agatha's twins, telling herself that such a thing as their relationship was unspeakable 'in the other world. ... But maybe not here' (p.264). When Angus eventually discovers the truth, Clodagh is already pregnant. He tells her she must henceforth 'make a home in the wold of houses' (p.302) and leaves her with her aunt in the Big House. Earlier, he had told her the legend of Finvarra, a fairy king who carried off a beautiful woman to the Land of the Dead, using it in part to illustrate the fact that he and she 'live in two different worlds' (p.205). When Clodagh gives birth to a son, she calls him Finvarra, but by then the magic has waned and the sealskin dress is just 'a relic of Agatha and Angus, of their private story' (p.310). Although she tells her aunt that she is 'more tinker than you know' (p.297), in the same way that her own mother had 'moved between worlds, no home in either' (p.302), she follows Angus's advice and decides to follow her son 'back to the realm of air and civilization' (p.310).

If Agatha was not a selkie, and Clodagh's fear of permanence and longing for a more 'aboriginal' world is not determined by mythical origins, then – or so the implication goes – it must be inherent in her tinker roots. Unlike Marina Carr's characters, however, McBride's Clodagh learns that, in spite of her restlessness, she can 'make a home in the world of houses' and move into the realm of 'civilization' because, as an old Travelling woman tells her, '[p]atience conquers destiny' (p.310). Myths are magical stories people tell to 'soften the hardness of the world' (p.308), but a tinker heritage is merely human, a deficiency that can be overcome with effort. The notion in *The Nature of Water and Air* that Travellers are excluded from the world of magic and only acceptable in the real world if they make an effort to overcome their 'animalistic' tinker urges is ultimately not far removed from the position adopted in the children's books written by Patricia Lynch more than half a century earlier.

MYTHIC PREDETERMINATION IN *TROJAN EDDIE*

The 'other worlds' of Celtic myth and the Travellers also overlap in Billy Roche's screenplay for the film *Trojan Eddie*, directed by Gillies MacKinnon in 1996. Roche's intention, according to the introduction to the published script, was to write a genuinely Irish film scenario, a quality he sought to capture by basing his plot on the myth of Diarmuid and Grania, in which the old king, Finn MacCool, loses Grania, his young bride, to her handsome lover Diarmuid. Roche transposed the otherworldly plot to what he called 'the strange world of the Irish Traveller – at once uniquely Irish and strangely other. At times I felt like I was treading on foreign soil in my own homeland and simple wisdom was everywhere'.[63] Roche decided to make the Travellers the insiders of his story, given that they are usually portrayed 'as "victims" or as "outsiders" or worse again as the "shunned"' (p.vi), and to make Eddie, the settled character, the outsider. John Power, the character based on Finn (played in the film by Richard Harris), is a settled Traveller and a well-off antiques dealer. In an interview with Stephen Rea, who played Eddie, Luke Gibbons praised the film for not primitivizing the Travellers, and for integrating them 'into the modern world, into the black economy, into electronic culture'.[64] On the surface, then, the film manages to associate the Travellers with modernity while also placing them within an Irish mythical paradigm.

Trojan Eddie does indeed provide a more realistic representation of the different aspects of Traveller culture than is generally the case in literary texts, but it nevertheless does not quite do what Billy Roche says he intended. Although Eddie is an 'outsider' in the Traveller community, the narrative is focalized through him. Eddie's point of view is dominant, and both the film's title and its plot development suggest that Eddie is the hero of the story. This is clearly how Gillies MacKinnon, the film's director, interpreted the script and the characters when he summarized the action as follows: Eddie 'works for him [John Power] and is under his thumb. The question is – will he ever get free and get the better of him in the end? He does of course.'[65]

John Power, an older man and a Traveller 'king', becomes enchanted with the much younger Kathleen (Grania), and offers to marry her. Although she is in love with Power's nephew Dermot (Diarmuid), Kathleen accepts, because she dislikes life on the road and the squalor of the halting site, from which marriage to John (who is settled and rich) provides an escape. For Power, conversely, Kathleen represents 'a link back to the old life that he has forsaken' (p.vi): she reminds him of his late wife, Kitty, and of his youth and vitality. He woos her by reminiscing about the old life in the barrel-topped wagon on the bank of a river where he learned to swim: 'we were fine and snug here' (p.20). Kathleen responds by going for a swim herself, in the nude, which makes him feel 'a little ashamed and a little frightened' (p.23). John Power, the successful dealer in antiques, is associated with the backward glance, with nostalgia for the past, his lost 'place in the tribe' (p.vi). Forward-looking Kathleen clearly does not represent the idyllic Traveller past John longs to recapture, and backward-looking John does not represent the beautiful, non-Traveller future Kathleen craves; as in the mythic plot of Finn and Grania, their scenario is clearly doomed from the beginning.

Eddie, the 'outsider' both to the Traveller world and to the mythic subtext in which he has, significantly, no part, acts as a go-between for both John and Dermot, without committing himself to either. In the end, it is he who walks away with what the other characters desire. He finally cuts his emotional ties with his no-good ex-wife Shirley, leaving him a way forward with his loving partner Betty and his two children. His treacherous former business associate Raymie is killed by John Power's son Ginger (who ends up in jail), leaving Eddie, very coincidentally, in possession of £11,000 – dowry money belonging technically to John but taken by Dermot and subsequently appropriated by Raymie, in whose room Eddie eventually discovers it – which enables him to set up his own trading business. Kathleen is soon deserted by Dermot, and returns to John Power, as Grania returned to Finn. The closing scene of *Trojan Eddie* shows John and Kathleen in a movie theatre. Kathleen is heavily pregnant with, presumably, Dermot's child. John is slightly paranoid, afraid people are laughing at his predicament. An advertisement appears on the cinema screen, in which Eddie is promoting his new bargain warehouse, with a phrase that appears to be addressing John Power directly: 'What you want, I got' (p.82). Trojan Eddie is the winner on all fronts: he moves forward, while the Traveller characters are trapped in the mythic plot. Billy Roche's version of the myth of Diarmuid and Grania may integrate the Travellers into the modern world, but it still portrays them as has-beens and losers.

PROBLEMATIZING THE MYTHICAL PARADIGM

Some writers have dealt more consciously with the potential problems and limitations of placing characters within a mythical paradigm. In the story 'Summer Pudding', from her 1997 collection *The Inland Ice*, Eilís Ní Dhuibhne creates a connection between a tinker character and the mythical plot of Deirdre and Naoise (a variation on the plot of Diarmuid and Grania from a different Irish mythological cycle), but she uses a variety of intertextual devices to explore the psychological function of myth-making as survival mechanism, and to problematize the notion of individual and group identity within a mythical and historical framework. 'Summer Pudding' takes place during the Potato Famine. The unnamed first-person narrator (the 'Deirdre' figure) is a young woman who has emigrated to Wales with her sister Mary, the only other surviving member of her family. At the docks in Holyhead, the destitute sisters fall in with a group of Irish tinkers, who have survival skills they lack. The narrator loves the itinerant life, and is also attracted to a young married tinker man named Naoise, but Mary hates the tinkers, and eventually secures scullery maid positions for both girls in the house of two Anglo-Irish women known as the Ladies of Llangollen, where they spend the winter. In the spring, Naoise reappears, and the narrator goes 'out with him on the road'.[66]

Broadly speaking, the references to the tinkers and the Ladies of Llangollen in 'Summer Pudding' were taken by Ní Dhuibhne from the account by George Borrow of his journey through Wales in 1854, published in 1862 under the title *Wild Wales*. By then, Borrow had already written *Lavengro* (1851), a pseudo-autobiographical account in which he depicted his alter ego living among tinkers and Gypsies;

all Borrow's works, however, fudge the line between fact and fiction, leading Ian Duncan to describe his creations as 'a shifty ... mixture of genres: fiction, memoir, travelogue, ethnography, and natural history'.[67] Ní Dhuibhne's selective and creative use of Borrow's material introduces a similarly ambiguous note into her story, which simultaneously anchors itself in historical fact and reveals itself as a mythical construct.

The narrator, her sister Mary, and Naoise, each put their faith in an Irish saviour figure who owes more to the imagination than to reality. Each of the characters wilfully clings to her or his chosen myth as a survival mechanism that arguably entraps them rather than sets them free. Naoise may lead the 'free' life of a tinker, but he is cramped in his style by his superstitions: he refuses to leave Wales before he has received a blessing for the journey back to Ireland from the only Irish priest in Wales, Father Toban. The narrator is sceptical: 'Father Toban. Who is he? ... Maybe he is an old *piseog*, like the banshee' (p.45). But Naoise insists he recognizes a passer-by as Father Toban: 'I know him by the cut of him. He wears that sort of coat' (p.59). The man so identified by Naoise denies he is the priest, but the tinkers half-jokingly threaten him with violence and he eventually consents to bless them in Latin.

One of the running jokes in George Borrow's *Wild Wales* is that the Irish tinkers keep mistaking Borrow for the elusive Father Toban. These incidents were not included in Borrow's original text, but when he submitted the manuscript of the book to his publisher, John Murray, the latter thought there was 'a want of stirring incident in it',[68] so Borrow added some material, including the Toban incident to which Ní Dhuibhne's story refers, which became one of Murray's favourite passages. The 'back story' to the blessing at Holyhead in 'Summer Pudding' therefore enhances the mythical quality of the incident: not only was Father Toban not who the tinkers thought he was, but the humorous string of incidents in *Wild Wales* in which Borrow is mistaken for the priest may well have been invented by the author to please his publisher.

The Ladies of Llangollen, briefly mentioned by Borrow in *Wild Wales*, function for the narrator's sister Mary in much the same way as Father Toban does for Naoise. The historical Ladies, Eleanor Butler and Sarah Ponsonby, were members of the Anglo-Irish Ascendancy who formed a 'Romantic friendship' against the wishes of their well-connected families. In 1778 they eluded the restrictions placed upon them by their relatives and eloped to Wales, where they settled in

Llangollen and lived for over half a century. In 'Summer Pudding', Mary recognizes one of the Ladies in much the same way Naoise 'recognizes' Father Toban: 'How did she know who it was? She knew because the lady ... was wearing trousers. ... Everyone knew that that's what the Ladies wore as soon as they got away from their families' (p.51). Even during their lifetime, the historical Ladies were subject to being mythologized. In 1789, the *General Evening Post* published a sensationalist article about the couple, in which the author provided a fictitious but suggestive description of Eleanor: 'Miss Butler is tall and masculine, she always wears a riding habit, hangs her hat with the air of a sportsman in the hall, and appears in all respects as a young man, if we except the petticoats which she still retains.'[69] By 1898, visitors to Llangollen who enquired why the Ladies had been so famous generally received the reply, 'Oh, they went about dressed like men'.[70]

The historical Ladies died decades before the Famine, but in 'Summer Pudding', both Mary and the narrator refuse to believe rumours that the women who took them in are actually English imitators of their Irish predecessors. However, the sisters have different reactions to the sexual relationship of the Ladies. The narrator admits that, '[t]he thought of what the Ladies did confused me completely' (p.57). Her sister, grateful for the food and shelter provided by their employers, and dreaming of one day becoming a ladies' maid, is less disturbed: 'They are kind. They love one another. What's wrong with that?' (p.57). Forced out of Ireland by famine and fever, Mary needs to believe that she can be saved by the Irish ladies, just as Naoise needs to believe that he can be saved by an Irish priest, though neither the Ladies nor Father Toban may be the genuine article. For Mary and Naoise, myth is where reality meets desire.

For the narrator, it is Naoise and the Irish tinkers who represent the freedom and energy she craves: they were like 'the wind, or a band of mischievous fairies' (p.47). She clings to the idea of Naoise in the same way he clings to Father Toban, and Mary to the Ladies of Llangollen. But Naoise's name also suggests the Irish legend of Deirdre and the Sons of Usnach. Different from the private 'saviour myths' created by each of the characters in 'Summer Pudding', the overarching Deirdre myth, of which the characters themselves are unaware, is used by Ní Dhuibhne to highlight for the reader the pitfalls and ironies created by the attempt to live within the magic circle of other people's mythical plots.

Ní Dhuibhne's version of the Deirdre story is in many ways a reversal of the original, in which Deirdre is betrothed to old king

Conchobhor (the equivalent of Finn), but forces the young hero Naoise to elope with her. The original legend depicts the old king as a jealous begrudger and the young lovers' passion as noble and justified. In 'Summer Pudding', it is Naoise who has an 'old-looking' wife, whom he leaves for the narrator. The latter enchants him by touching his face – an echo of the magical *geis* put on Naoise by Deirdre – but it should also be noted that the tinker in 'Summer Pudding' has a birthmark on his face, which is reminiscent of the 'love spot' on the face of Diarmuid, Naoise's counterpart in the tale of Diarmuid and Grania, which magically makes women fall in love with him. The combination of the woman's face-touching magic and the man's love spot in Ní Dhuibhne's story suggests that both characters are under an involuntary mythical 'love spell' that blinds them to reality.

The form of 'Summer Pudding' is circular, as both the opening and closing scenes show Naoise and the narrator waiting on Holyhead Pier for the boat to Ireland. What awaits the lovers there upon their return is a matter for speculation. The narrator will be on the road with Naoise as his wife, and she herself had earlier noted the fate of her predecessor: 'His wife was pregnant again, yellow-skinned and dirty, with her clothes hanging off her, and smelly and old-looking. She was the way the tinker women are as soon as they are married any length of time at all. Scrap.' A dim awareness of her own future reverberates in her pitying assessment: 'Poor thing, poor thing, poor scrap' (p.53). The scene on the pier evokes other textual echoes, most specifically of Brian Friel's 1993 play *Wonderful Tennessee*, suggesting characters whose lives are perpetually unfulfilled, who can only wait for someone else to arrive, make them happy, and take them 'home'. 'We sailed that afternoon for home' (p.60), the narrator tells us in the final sentence of 'Summer Pudding'; but what is the meaning of 'home'?

Ní Dhuibhne uses the interaction between her story and the texts she references to highlight the contingent nature of all forms of identity, and the extent to which individual lives are shaped by desire and need, and by the myths the characters live by. The slippery nature of the material contained in all these interwoven stories is mirrored by the chiasmic relationship between Mary and her sister, and their respective Irish 'saviours'. Mary defends the Ladies and the work they provide, while her sister is confused by their sexuality and exhausted by the domestic tasks. The narrator takes to the tinkers' way of life while Mary hates their 'loose' ways with a passion and refuses to adopt their unlawful practices. Yet both the tinkers and the Ladies are transgressive characters: they are 'queer' in the sense of being 'at odds with the normal, the legitimate, the dominant'.[71] The Ladies resist the norm by setting up 'home' together in exile, while the tinkers resist the norm by refusing to settle down even when they are 'at home' in Ireland. Their lives point away from each other, but also in the same direction. For Mary and her sister, the tinkers and the Ladies represent the two opposing tugs of the heart's desire, the need to be satisfied on the one hand and the impossibility of satisfaction on the other. As Others, the Ladies and the tinkers function as metaphoric abstractions, but the point of 'Summer Pudding' is, at least in part, to expose the problematic nature of that device. Paul Ricoeur suggests that borrowed plots have to be conquered: 'We are caught in the stories of others, so we are protagonists in the stories we are told by others, and we have to assume for ourselves the stories that the others tell about us, which have their own founding events, their own strategies, their own plots'.[72]

In his play *The Tinker's Curse*, which toured Irish theatres in the spring of 2007, Michael Harding also attempted to depict the way in which Travellers often find themselves trapped in a narrative not of their own making. The play was billed, somewhat problematically, as 'a simple story of loss and remorse that speaks through the rich mythical language of Ireland's Travellers, a world rooted in myth and superstition'. Its protagonist, Delia Rattigan, finds herself 'haunted by a series of accidental events that have led to the tragic death of a loved one. Through superstition and crippling beliefs Delia has been locked into a condition of endless pain.'[73] Reviewing the play for the *Irish Times*, Peter Crawley criticized 'the doomed story of a family of Travellers, persecuted both by settled society and ... by the darkest phantasms of the supernatural', for being repetitive and derivative, and found what Harding was trying to say about the lot of the Travellers in contemporary Ireland 'rather compromised by the stoking of superstition'.[74] Harding defended himself against Crawley's charge that 'the play has nowhere to go' in a letter to the *Irish Times*, in which he argued that he used visual and structural references to Brian Friel, Samuel Beckett and W.B. Yeats 'in order to create the enclosed template within which the Traveller characters of the play are contained in the telling of their story. ... In *The Tinker's Curse*, Travellers have nowhere to go. They are confined in a space not their own. They can do nothing but try to tell their unique story in the cage of another culture's aesthetic.' The fact that *The Tinker's Curse*, as a vehicle for this message, was created, performed and consumed by non-Travellers, may partly account for Harding's failure 'to get that point across'.[75]

Any existing mythic pattern that is superimposed on a particular cultural or ethnic group inevitably functions to fix that group's identity. When, in a literary text, a specific myth is associated with a minority group within the hegemonic culture, especially when the writer of the text is a member of that dominant culture, the myth always serves to stress difference from the norm and to turn the minority culture into an abstraction, an archetype, or a metaphor, setting up a one-on-one equation between that group – in this case the travellers – and its perceived dominant characteristic (be it 'impermanence', 'unnaturalness' or 'pre-lapsarian collectivity'). The mythic abstraction derives from the stereotype, which insists on departure from some idealized norm, and reinforces it; it is also, however, more insidious than the straightforward stereotype in that it can masquerade as its opposite. Serious fictional, dramatic and cinematic art tends to frown on stereotypes, but often embraces mythology. Paul Ricoeur cautions that only those myths are genuine 'which have as their horizon the liberation of humanity *as a whole*'.[76] It appears, however, that most mythic narratives portraying Travellers or 'tinkers' do not perceive them as genuine human beings.

NOTES

1. Amanda Ripley, 'Unwelcome Exposure', *Time*, 7 October 2002, p.10.
2. Richard Kearney, *States of Mind: Dialogues with Contemporary Thinkers* (New York: New York University Press, 1995), p.230.
3. Ibid., p.34.
4. Ibid., p.239.
5. Trumpener, 'The Time of the Gypsies', p.869.
6. John Faa of Dunbar was a famous leader of the 'Egyptians' (Gypsies) in Scotland in the mid-sixteenth century.
7. Philip Pullman, *The Golden Compass* (New York: Ballantine, 1995), p.109.
8. Ibid., p.100.
9. Sean Maher, *The Road to God Knows Where: A Memoir of a Travelling Boyhood* (1972; Dublin: Veritas, 1998), p.9. All subsequent page references in the text are to this edition.
10. Nan Joyce, *My Life on the Road*, ed. Anna Farmar (1985; Dublin: A. and A. Farmar, 2000), p.118. All subsequent page references in the text are to this edition.
11. Information about Robert Jordan's *Wheel of Time* novels taken from the Encyclopaedia WoT. Accessed 2 August 2007: http://www.encyclopaedia-wot.org
12. Charles de Lint, *The Harp of the Grey Rose* (Harmondsworth: Puffin, 2004), p.1.
13. Ibid., p.87.
14. Shariann Lewitt, *Rebel Sutra* (New York: Tor, 2000), p.14.
15. Ibid.
16. Ibid., p.17.
17. Ibid., p.16.
18. Ibid., p.137.
19. Maeve Connolly, '"A Bit of a Traveller in Everybody": Traveller Identities in Irish and American Culture', in Diane Negra (ed.), *The Irish in Us: Irishness, Performativity, and Popular Culture* (Durham, NC, and London: Duke University Press, 2006), p.295.
20. Ibid., p.300.

21. Richard Kearney, *Myth and Motherland*, Field Day Pamphlet 5 (Derry: Field Day, 1984), p.23.
22. Kearney, *States of Mind*, p.239.
23. Ibid., p.243.
24. Quoted in Mary Burke, 'Situating the Emergent Field of Irish Traveller Studies', *Foilsiú*, 4, 1 (2004), pp.13-14.
25. 'Toogood's Husband Has Long Rap Sheet', Fox News Channel website, 27 September 2002. Accessed 30 March 2002: http://www.foxnews.com/story/0,2933,64194,00.htm
26. David Keys, 'Academics Suggest Irish Travellers Are Remnant of Pre-Celtic Culture', *Independent*, 27 March 2005. Accessed 30 November 2006: http://www.independent.co.uk/uk/this_britain/article8105.ece
27. Grattan Puxon, 'We Demand Justice', *La Voix Mondiale Tzigane/The Gypsy Voice/O Glasoromano* (c. 1966), p.1/9.
28. Michael McDonagh, 'Origins of the Travelling People', in Sheehan, *Travellers: Citizens of Ireland*, pp.24–5.
29. Burke, 'Situating the Emergent Field', p.18.
30. McDonagh, 'Origins of the Travelling People', p.23.
31. For a discussion of the use of Irish mythology by satirists of the period, see José Lanters, *Unauthorized Versions: Irish Menippean Satire, 1919–1952* (Washington, DC: Catholic University of America Press, 2000).
32. Burke, 'Situating the Emergent Field', p.16.
33. Ibid., p.17.
34. Olivia Robertson, *Field of the Stranger* (London: Peter Davies, 1948), p.194. All subsequent page references in the text are to this edition.
35. For a more extensive discussion of the novels in light of the ideas held by the Fellowship of Isis, see José Lanters, 'The Mythicizing of Napper Tandy Street: The Novels of Olivia Robertson', *Journal of Irish Literature*, 22, 3 (1993), pp.17–24.
36. Olivia Robertson, *Miranda Speaks* (London: Peter Davies, 1950), p.4. All subsequent page references in the text are to this edition.
37. Olivia Robertson, *Dublin Phoenix* (London: Jonathan Cape, 1957), p.36.
38. Ibid., p.78.
39. Olivia Robertson, *The Golden Eye* (London: Peter Davies, 1949), p.90. All subsequent page references in the text are to this edition.
40. Olivia Robertson, *Dea. Rites and Mysteries of the Goddess. Liturgy of the Fellowship of Isis* (Enniscorthy: Cesara, 1977), pp.6–7.
41. Fellowship of Isis official website. Accessed 12 December 2006: http://www.fellowshipofisis.com
42. Ibid.
43. Joe Cleary, 'Into Which West? Irish Modernity and the Maternal Supernatural', in Brian Cosgrove (ed.), *Literature and the Supernatural: Essays for the Maynooth Bicentenary* (Blackrock: Columba Press, 1995), p.164.
44. Michael McDonagh, 'The Traveller Economy', in Sheehan, *Travellers: Citizens of Ireland*, p.50.
45. Cleary, 'Into Which West?', p.159.
46. Ibid., pp.160–1.
47. Ibid., pp.161–2.
48. Connolly, '"A Bit of a Traveller"', p.285.
49. Ibid., p.282.
50. Ibid., p.312.
51. Marina Carr, 'Afterword', in Frank McGuinness (ed.), *The Dazzling Dark: New Irish Plays* (London: Faber and Faber, 1996), pp.310–11.
52. Mary King, 'The Body Out of Place: Strangers, Intimates and Destabilized Identities in Synge's *When the Moon Has Set* and Marina Carr's *The Bog of Cats ...*', *Critical Survey*, 15, 1 (2003), pp.54–5.
53. Ibid., p.55.
54. Clare Wallace, 'Tragic Destiny and Abjection in Marina Carr's *The Mai*, *Portia Coughlan* and *By the Bog of Cats ...*', *Irish University Review*, 31, 2 (2001), p.438.
55. Marina Carr, *By the Bog of Cats* (Oldcastle, Co. Meath: Gallery Press, 1998), p.23. All subsequent page references in the text are to this edition.

56. King, 'The Body Out of Place', p.58.
57. Wallace, 'Tragic Destiny', p.443.
58. Marina Carr, *Portia Coughlan* (Oldcastle, Co. Meath: Gallery Press, 1998), p.60. All subsequent page references in the text are to this edition.
59. Eileen Battersby, 'Marina of the Midlands', interview with Marina Carr, *Irish Times*, 4 May 2000. Accessed 4 May 2000: http://www.ireland.com/newspaper/features/ 2000/0504/ fea1.htm
60. King, 'The Body Out of Place', p.58.
61. Vic Merriman, 'Decolonisation Postponed: The Theatre of Tiger Trash', *Irish University Review*, 29, 2 (1999), p.315.
62. Regina McBride, *The Nature of Water and Air* (New York: Simon and Schuster, 2001), p.126. All subsequent page references in the text are to this edition.
63. Billy Roche, 'Introduction', *Trojan Eddie* (London: Methuen, 1997), p.v. All subsequent page references in the text are to this edition.
64. Luke Gibbons and Kevin Whelan, 'In Conversation with Stephen Rea', *Yale Journal of Criticism*, 15, 1 (2002), p.14.
65. Gillies MacKinnon, 'Director's Comments.' Accessed 4 April 2005: http://www.gillies-mackinnon.co.uk/bio.html
66. Eilís Ní Dhuibhne, 'Summer Pudding', in *The Inland Ice* (Belfast: Blackstaff Press, 1997), p.59. All subsequent page references in the text are to this edition.
67. Ian Duncan, 'Wild England: George Borrow's Nomadology', *Victorian Studies*, 4, 3 (1998), p.382.
68. Herbert George Jenkins, *The Life of George Borrow* (London: John Murray, 1912), p.452.
69. Elizabeth Mavor, *The Ladies of Llangollen: A Study in Romantic Friendship* (London: Michael Joseph, 1971), p.82.
70. Ibid., p.196.
71. David Halperin, *Saint Foucault: Towards a Gay Hagiography* (New York: Oxford University Press, 1995), p.62.
72. Kearney, *States of Mind*, p.38.
73. Linen Hall Theatre, announcement of Livin' Dred Theatre Company's production of *The Tinker's Curse* by Michael Harding. Accessed 17 May 2007: http://www.thelinenhall.com/ current/index.html#Anchor-DRAMA-14210
74. Peter Crawley, review of *The Tinker's Curse* by Michael Harding, *Irish Times*, 17 May 2007. Accessed 17 May 2007: http://www.ireland.com/newspaper/features/2007/0517/ 1179315433733.html
75. Michael Harding, 'Telling the Traveller Story in the Theatre', letter to the *Irish Times*, 21 May 2007. Accessed 21 May 2007: http://www.ireland.com/newspaper/letters/2007/0521/ index.html
76. Kearney, *States of Mind*, p.239.

CHAPTER 6

Getting Away With Murder: Crime and Detective Fiction

And if you find a pony grazing in your garden plot
Don't blame the noble gypsy but that awful tinker lot.
Ewan MacColl, 'The Gypsy Is a Gentleman'
From *The Travelling People*, a Radio Ballad (1964)

And few remember, when they pray,
The murder'd travelling lad.
Sean Maher, 'The Murder of a Travelling Lad'

With origins in the latter part of the modern period, crime fiction is a formulaic genre whose different manifestations – clue-puzzle, classic police mystery, hard-boiled 'noir' – depend heavily on codes and conventions, which 'are intertwined with the codes and conventions of the society in which the literary texts are produced'.[1] A product of the era of rising capitalism and the development of the scientific method, detective fiction is, by and large, a conservative genre, whose investigative protagonists have the task of restoring order by identifying, capturing and eliminating the disruptive element in society, thereby re-establishing the status quo. According to Maureen Reddy, whiteness, heterosexuality and masculinity are almost always the norms encoded in texts of the detective genre, while the codes governing the representation of ethnicity are among the elements of genre fiction 'most resistant to change'.[2] The reliance of detective fiction on representations of Otherness has led Michael Cohen to wonder 'whether racism [in the sense of fear and hatred of the Other] is a necessary element in mystery and detective stories'.[3] He speculates that this is so, since what readers of such fiction desire 'is that evil should be patent and other when it is often hidden and just like us. ... Mysteries frequently reassure us that the other guys are bad guys and that bad guys are other guys.'[4] When the investigating detective is part of the hegemonic culture, and the victim or the perpetrator of a crime belongs to an ethnic minority, the question of racism becomes especially pertinent.

The late twentieth century witnessed the publication of a spate of crime novels set in Ireland and featuring one or more Traveller characters in the role of suspect, victim, perpetrator or a combination of these – though never in that of the investigator. Some of these fictional narratives are by North American writers, and all are aimed, at least to some degree, at the mass market of the United States, and at readers for whom the Irish setting may have a certain romantic appeal. The investigator in *Unholy Ground* (1989), a literary mystery novel by Dublin-born John Brady, now resident in Canada, is Detective Sergeant Matt Minogue, a native of County Clare but stationed in the area of Dublin. *The Death of an Irish Tinker* (1997), a classic police mystery by Irish-American writer Bartholomew Gill (pseudonym of Mark McGarrity), is also set in and around Dublin, the home of Chief Superintendent Peter McGarr. Dicey Deere's *The Irish Manor House Murder* (2000) represents the genre of the clue-puzzle. According to information on the book's inside cover, the author lives in Sag Harbor, New York, and 'can usually be found at a bed-and-breakfast in Ireland' in May or October.[5] Her character Torrey Tunet, an American by birth and a translator by profession, is a contemporary version of the female amateur sleuth in the Miss Marple tradition, who has settled in a cottage in the rural Irish village of Ballynagh. Ken Bruen's *The Killing of the Tinkers* (2002) falls into the category of the hard-boiled 'noir' detective story. His detective, Jack Taylor, resides in Galway City, Bruen's birthplace; an ex-guard with a drink problem and a cocaine habit, Taylor reluctantly dabbles in private investigation.

Within the romanticized Irish context of some of these works – the cover of Deere's novel cites *Booklist*'s reference to 'the green and silvered gray of Ireland', while *The Death of an Irish Tinker* quotes *Publisher's Weekly*'s touting of 'the rugged vibrancy and anachronisms of Ireland and its citizens' – the 'tinkers' provide additional local colour, and give readers the *frisson* of catching a glimpse of what the *New York Times* reviewer of Bartholomew Gill's *The Death of an Irish*

Tinker called 'the secretive world of Ireland's tinkers, or, as these itinerant bands of social outcasts prefer to be called, "travelers"'.[6] 'Untouchable' by the laws of settled society, the 'tinkers' are often the victims about whom few people care, or the perpetrators who get away with murder.

The short story 'The Tinker's Revenge' by D.M. O'Reilly, anthologized in a collection entitled *Murder Most Irish* (1996) also aimed at the American market, presents in a nutshell the typical position of the tinker figure in crime fiction: victim, suspect and perpetrator of a crime. O'Reilly's tale is a blatant reworking of Liam O'Flaherty's story 'The Pedlar's Revenge', in which the protagonist rids himself of an enemy by tricking him into eating a fatal meal cooked in candle grease. O'Flaherty's pedlar is given the last word of the story when the police sergeant, unable to pin a murder charge on him, resorts to threatening the man with the horrors that will await him on Judgment Day. The pedlar responds, 'Isn't it great to see the law of the land crying out to God for help against the weak and the persecuted. ... I'm laughing out loud, because I fear neither God nor man. This is the hour of my delight.'[7] D.M. O'Reilly not only substitutes a tinker for the pedlar, but also alters the story's ending: like the pedlar in O'Flaherty's story, the tinker escapes a murder charge, but, unlike his counterpart, he does not get away scot-free. The tinker is always guilty of something, even when he is a victim.

The nameless 'tinker' of O'Reilly's story is a trickster figure, 'a clever creature',[8] while his nemesis, Mikey Lawlor, 'wasn't all there' (p.254). Before falling off the pier and drowning, Mikey had accused the tinker of poisoning him. The fishermen who witness the accident, the priest and the junior policeman all assume the tinker is guilty of murder: to the priest, the tinker is 'no good', an 'unbeliever' (p.255), while it is enough for the fishermen that he is 'only a bloody tinker' (p.258). The police sergeant, however, prides himself on his impartiality and proceeds to question the tinker in his caravan, the neatness of which defies the tinker stereotype; its occupant explains that the slovenly Mikey had been a disruptive force in his life, constantly demanding food, and even ransacking his caravan when he himself was away 'doin' an honest bit o' work' (p.261). On the most recent occasion, Mikey had been attracted by the smell of frying bacon fat, but the tinker had spun him a tale that potatoes taste just as good when fried in candle grease, and the hungry fool had ended up poisoning himself by taking the tinker at his word. While the sergeant admires the tinker's ingenuity and clears him of murder charges, he nevertheless arrests him for having an illegal poteen still on his property. The tinker, however, is unperturbed by the prospect of a spell in prison, and has the last laugh when the authorities pour away the alcohol intended for the village *feis*, for which he had been paid in advance.

In the story's formula, the negative tinker stereotype is advanced by bigots, while the upright policeman is only interested in investigating the truth. The tinker is allowed to defy parts of the stereotype – he is neat and clean, and has an honest trade, unlike the man who bullied him – but in the end he is found guilty all the same of breaking the law, thereby conforming to type after all. As a trickster figure, beyond the social pale but also impervious to social conventions, the tinker fears 'neither God nor man' (p.263), and uses his own mischief not to create but to expose the bullying, bigotry and hypocrisy of those around him. The message is reassuring: the law is straightforward, prejudice is frowned upon and tinkers are mischievous characters who add colour to society without posing a real threat to its institutions.

Detective Sergeant Matt Minogue in John Brady's *Unholy Ground* muses that '[t]inkers are like untouchables among us',[9] but Michael Joseph Joyce, the Traveller character who serves as a red herring in the mystery of the murder of the reclusive Englishman Arthur Combs, is only 'untouchable' in the sense of being an outcast. Joyce is arrested for 'snooping around' Combs' house at night in a drunken state, and 'fiddling with' the dead man's horse (p.81). Minogue has Joyce released, however, because he knows it is 'a fright to God to traveling people to be confined' (p.81), and interviews the tinker when he has sobered up the next day. Joyce is able to convince Minogue of his innocence: in fact, being unable to read, newspaper reports of the murder have passed him by completely. Illiterate, drunk and living by the side of the road, Joyce answers to the stereotype of the dispossessed drop-out, and as far as Minogue is concerned, that is all he is guilty of: 'Joyce had adopted the wheedling way of the powerless peasant without a thought that he, no more than his forbears, could ever be any other person dealing with peelers. His whorls of self-pity and whining were the Trojan horses that carried an ancient and enduring hostility within. But that did not mean Joyce was lying' (p.102). Joyce himself suspects a conspiracy against a perpetual victim behind his arrest: 'The whole world is up against the traveler' (p.103).

Having it both ways, Brady's novel presents Joyce both as a victim of sedentary prejudice and of his own unbridled 'tinker' nature. Some time after Joyce has been let go, Minogue learns that he is in custody again, this time for applying a broken bottle to the face of a man in a pub who had made derogatory remarks about the Travellers in general and Joyce's wife in particular. In the meantime, Joyce has recalled more information about Combs, and leads Minogue to the horse's bridle he claims he was given by the Englishman as a present, a story Minogue receives with some scepticism. Sown between its leather straps, Minogue discovers a sachet of negatives relating to the Second World War secrets for which Combs had paid with his life. Despite this helpful revelation, the detective tells the tinker that nothing can be done about the assault charge against him, and that his help with the murder case should in any event have been forthcoming sooner: 'So don't be acting the maggot with me now' (p.160). The tinker has changed: 'Where was the timid and wheedling Joyce of yesterday?' Minogue wonders. Instead, 'Something had given way in him, struck out. Bitterness, a lifetime' (p.160). Earlier, Minogue had reflected on the way in which 'the motorized Irish looked down their passing noses' at the tinkers, '[l]andless but horse-mad' (pp.110–11), and had felt a rush of anger: 'If he were Joyce, he'd steal Jags and Mercedes and money and anything, all day and all night until someone stopped him' (p.111). From his bourgeois perspective, Minogue can understand Joyce's coveting of material possessions, but not his unbridled violence; at the same time, the 'someone' who would have stopped Minogue stealing from the rich 'if he were Joyce' is, of course, detective Minogue himself, who may be sympathetic to a servile victimized tinker, but not to an angry and resentful one. Once Minogue has recovered the negatives from Joyce's caravan, the tinker, now in prison for assault, plays no further part in the story.

Dicey Deere's *The Irish Manor House Murder* follows the classic clue-puzzle pattern as summarized by Stephen Knight:

> The victim has some wealth and authority, [and is] a person against whom malicious hostility and envy can credibly be raised, and also, it would seem, a person whose wealth and status bring danger, in a complex message of identification and anxiety for the wide audience, few of whom are owners of lavish country houses. Most of the real suspects will be relatives or close associates of the important dead person, and they will almost all have something to hide that makes them become ... a series of suspects. But finally they will be reduced to one, or sometimes two working together; they will be revealed by the detective, possibly forced to confess; but they will not be punished.[10]

In this case, the victim is Dr Gerald Ashenden of Ashenden Manor, a famous but unlikeable surgeon, who is killed in a riding accident when his horse is fatally shot with what turns out to be the tip of a knitting needle. Possible suspects include his granddaughter Rowena, who had been involved in an earlier riding incident, and whose secret pregnancy is causing her unexplained terror; her brother Scott, who is resentful about his 'deformed leg' (p.12), and spends much time in Dublin partying with 'gay young men' (p.33); and Dr Padraic Collins of Collins Court, Ashenden's close friend for many years.

Hovering around the edges of the Ashenden estate is a Gypsy woman, whose wagon Torrey Tunet notices in the woods: 'Or maybe it was a tinkers' wagon; they moved about, "travelers" they were sometime called' (p.67). The stranger is identified by the police sergeant as a Romanian Gypsy: 'Not one of the tinkers, but same as them' (p.82). When Torrey takes an interest in the woman because of her own Romanian ancestry, she learns that the Gypsy (who never has a name) had seen 'something evil' (p.105), which the amateur sleuth takes to mean that '*she knows who killed Gerald Ashenden*' (p.107). When the Gypsy herself is subsequently found dead, Torrey's investigations eventually lead her to Dr Collins, who confesses that he had murdered the woman because she was blackmailing him. After further probings by Torrey, he also confesses to killing Dr Ashenden, after discovering that his friend had, during their student days, criminally and ultimately unsuccessfully tried to end his future wife's pregnancy with the use of X-rays (the reason why Rowena fears that her own baby will be genetically damaged). In this revised version of events, Collins claims to have killed the Gypsy for having witnessed the murder of Dr Ashenden. Or so he says, until Torrey unravels the real truth, but only after the doctor has, literally, run away with the Gypsies.

In Bartholomew Gill's *The Death of an Irish Tinker*, Chief Superintendent Peter McGarr of Ireland's Special Crimes unit investigates the drugs-related murder of a man whom the book's cover summary calls a 'tinker', 'one of the mysterious class of itinerant travelers who have roamed Ireland for generations'.[11] Drug-dealing Dublin gangsters and an elusive Irish cultural minority provide Gill with an irresistible combination of urban grit and exoticism for his plot, which begins when, one night in 1984, as she is putting the finishing touches to her pavement art at the top of Dublin's Grafton Street, a Travelling woman named Biddy Nevins witnesses the brutal murder of a drug dealer at the hands of one of Dublin's most notorious criminals. As a recovering heroin addict, Biddy realizes that Des Bacon, also known as 'the Toddler', will want to eliminate any witnesses, so without hesitation she packs her bags and departs for England. The body of her husband, Mickalou Maugham, also well-known to the Toddler, is later found chained to the top of a giant sequoia tree in Powerscourt Gardens. When Biddy, under the assumed identity of her late friend Beth Waters, returns from England twelve years later, having completely remade herself as a successful artist, the Toddler catches up with her again, but this time Biddy tries to take the law into her own hands, even as McGarr is also on the case, and ends up paying for her actions with her life. A group of young Travellers, including Biddy and Mickalou's daughter Oney, are allowed by McGarr to impose their own form of poetic justice on the Toddler, whose mutilated body is subsequently found chained to the top of the sequoia tree in Powerscourt Gardens.

Ken Bruen's *The Killing of the Tinkers* has virtually all the characteristics of the 'a-heroic noir' variety of the hard-boiled detective described by Katharine and Lee Horsley, in which

> murderer and person murdered alike are victims, and ... the protagonist is in fact the perpetrator; the normal world is shown to be vulnerable and easily disrupted; there are no clear distinctions between guilt and innocence; love ends in crime and death; the resolution is ambiguous and irony is pervasive; there is no heroic detective figure in the ascendancy; instead, obsessed, alienated, schizoid characters struggle to make sense of chaotic reality, haunted by dark secrets, their lives possessed by the past, their identities destabilized.[12]

Upon his return from London to his native Galway, Jack Taylor is approached by a Traveller he only comes to know by his nickname, 'Sweeper', to investigate the murders of five young Traveller men. The gardaí have done nothing, Sweeper claims, since 'only tinkers' are involved, and 'everybody knows they're always killing each other'.[13] Taylor receives help from a local former guard named Brendan Flood, and London-based Detective Sergeant Keegan, a Hibernofile described by Taylor as 'a loud, vulgar bigot' (p.43). In true hard-boiled fashion, the first-person narrative of *The Killing of the Tinkers* is in many ways more about the detective and his demons than about the case, which is half-heartedly dealt with by Jack when he is not reeling with drink, being beaten up for consorting with tinkers, or failing in his relationships with women. His suspicions soon fall on an offensive and sarcastic English social worker, 'a sanctimonious prick' named Ronald Bryson (p.113), who has worked with Travellers addicted to alcohol, and who moves without leaving a forwarding address after being unsuccessfully challenged by Taylor. In spite of Keegan's warning that Bryson is just an attention-getter who was himself abused by his alcoholic father, and who has nevertheless provided real help to the alcoholics he despises, and notwithstanding a forensic profile of the likely murderer provided by Flood, which Bryson does not fit, Taylor jumps to conclusions and tips off Sweeper, who arranges for Bryson to be tortured and killed by his men. In the end, Taylor realizes that, in his drugged and drunken state, he has missed several clues that point to the real murderer: Mikey, one of the Travellers who had also helped kill Bryson, is the real killer of the tinkers. Taylor does not inform Sweeper of his error, but uses the reward money he receives from him for solving the case to hire a hit-man to rectify his mistake.

TRAVELLERS, TINKERS AND THE ISSUE OF NAMING

During the period in which the crime novels by Bruen, Deere and Gill were published, 'Traveller' was the internationally accepted neutral term, also favoured by Travellers themselves, for people with a (semi-) nomadic life style, but the titles of two of the books discussed here consciously adopt the term 'tinker', which is regarded as having derogatory overtones. 'Tinker' was perhaps favoured because the use of 'Traveller' might lead an audience, especially a non-Irish one, to expect the murder of a tourist, but the word 'tinker' also, and no doubt intentionally, evokes all the connotations associated with the stereotype, and when it comes to crime fiction, a certain degree of sensationalism can be a selling point. Richard Dyer points out that the matter of designations in identity politics is a thorny issue: 'having a word for oneself and one's group, making a politics out of what that word should be, draws attention to and also reproduces one's marginality, confirms one's place outside of power and thus outside of the mechanisms of change. Having a word also contains and fixes identity.'[14] In crime fiction of the type considered here, the marginal status of Travellers is reinforced by discussions among settled characters concerning the 'correct' word to describe the minority. For example, in a recent British mystery by Janet Neel, *Ticket to Ride* (2005), one character refers to Travellers as 'Gypsies' but qualifies the term by adding, 'or tinkers, as cousin Anne called them',[15] while another character calls them 'tinkers', only to correct herself, 'sorry, that's what Scots call them. Gypsies'.[16] Gill, Deere and Bruen are clearly aware of the issues involved in identity labelling, because all make a point of having their characters bring up the question of designations; the result is invariably a half-hearted mixture of apology and self-justification for the use of what the characters and their creators know is politically incorrect terminology.

Dicey Deere's narrative makes little or no distinction between tinkers and Gypsies, apart from the fact that the latter are Romanians 'who'd arrived in Ireland in the last few years' (p.96), and suggests that all designations are by and large identical. In *The Irish Manor House Murder*, the (anachronistic) 'gypsy wagon' Torrey glimpses in the woods could also be a 'tinkers' wagon', and all these people who 'move about' are also called 'travelers' (p.67). To Inspector O'Hare, 'those itinerants – gypsies, tinkers, and "travelers" as those folks in their caravans were called' (p.153) are also indistinguishable from each other. Deere's choice of a 'Gypsy' rather than a 'tinker' as a minor character in the story may relate to the book's cliché-ridden world of country mansions, thatched cottages and family melodrama. Clue-puzzle mysteries are traditionally set in 'comfortable upper-middle-class (only rarely aristocratic) country settings', which are seen by some critics as a 'modern evolution of the English country-house tradition, now in a capitalist rather than landed gentry form'.[17] Indeed, as far as its setting and plot are concerned, *The Irish Manor House Murder* might as well take place in Agatha Christie's England as in contemporary Ireland.

In Bartholomew Gill's *The Death of an Irish Tinker*, the investigating detective refers to Travellers as tinkers, 'which was the term McGarr thought more traditional and apt but was now used mainly by people of his own generation and older. "Traveler" was a more recent term that the Traveling people now used to describe themselves. "Itinerant" was used by the media, and "Knacker" by bigots' (p.37). This convenient guide allows the reader to identify the Toddler as a bigot, given his fondness of the latter term, but the criminal's use of the phrase 'tinker bitch' also indicates that 'tinker' is a more problematic word than McGarr's explanation suggests. The old-fashioned Superintendent's struggle with politically correct terminology is reflected in his acknowledgement of the changes that are taking place in society in that regard: 'A few years before, he had chaired a Garda commission to establish police guidelines for dealing with the over three thousand families that constituted the "Traveling community", was the current phrase in Ireland, and he was acquainted with their history' (p.42). The issue of naming is also highlighted from Biddy Nevins's perspective, who assumes that, to settled people, she and her husband were '[j]ust two poor Tinkers, who did not [matter]. To the lot of them, Tinkers were scarcely human. "Itinerants" was the word that they used on the telly. At first Biddy, like most of her people, had not known what the word meant, although it sounded bad. And was' (p.30). Although the Traveller character is here allowed her own voice, it is significant that any concrete information about Traveller culture and history is provided by the Chief Superintendent, while Biddy's perspective does not represent her own opinion but projects the negative views of the sedentary world onto herself and her husband – 'just two poor Tinkers'. The narrative voice depicts her as ignorant, 'like most of her people', and at the mercy of outsiders. Biddy's perspective internalizes the Travellers' lack of agency and the victim status they are assigned in the imaginary of the settled population.

In the dark world of *The Killing of the Tinkers*, Ken Bruen's characters have a habit of explicitly going against the grain of the expected cliché, thereby nevertheless invoking it. Travellers in this book never refer to themselves by that name: Sweeper always uses the word 'tinker'. When he introduces himself to Taylor he says, 'You know me? ... I'm Sweeper. ... The tinkers?' (p.23), and when Taylor asks him who would want to kill his people, he answers: 'Watch the news. Everybody hates the tinkers' (p.55). Taylor asks Sweeper about the issue of naming:

> 'Sweeper, don't take this the wrong way, but I need to know what to call ye. ... Travellers, tinkers, gypos ... what? I'm very uncomfortable with tinkers.'
> 'It's what they call us.'
> 'I didn't ask you that, did I? What do I term you?
> 'The clans'. (p.64)

However, Sweeper himself never uses the term 'clans' again, and when Keegan, towards the end of the book, claims to have a solution 'for the gypsy thing', Taylor corrects him, 'Tinker, not gypsy' (p.188).

In her discussion of race in crime fiction, Maureen Reddy points out that, even in police procedurals written by black authors for black readers, 'there are direct commentaries on race matters that only make complete sense if read as directed at white readers, as "scenes of instruction" on race'.[18] The crime novels that feature 'tinker' characters are written by non-Traveller writers for a sedentary, in some instances non-Irish readership, and it is therefore not surprising that they sometimes feature lengthy treatises on Traveller history and culture for the sole benefit of the audience. During a quiet moment in a pub, Superintendent McGarr sits back and recalls 'what he knew of Tinkers', which is a great deal:

> As early as A.D. 400 smiths were traveling throughout the country, and in later times, when famine, poverty, and evictions swelled their ranks, Tinkers offered other services to the resident population. ...
>
> Contrary to current opinion, they were not shiftless vagabonds. ...
>
> The pattern of Tinker life, however, changed drastically after the Second World War with the appearance of cheap metal and plastic goods and mechanized farming that replaced seasonal labor. ... The men went on the dole; the women begged in the streets.
>
> But the greatest tragedy – to McGarr's way of thinking – was the effect city life had on Tinker children. ... Vandalism led to more serious crime, drink, and drugs.
>
> Government efforts to improve the Travelers' lot had largely failed. Only half of Dublin's seven hundred Traveling families were housed, usually in squalid, ghettolike neighborhoods, and the percentage and conditions of life for them countrywide were little better. (pp.42–3)

McGarr is able to give the reader so much information because he has conveniently chaired a commission dealing with relations between the travellers and the Garda Síochána – which also implies that Travellers are often to be found on the wrong side of the law.

The spare, edgy style of Jack Taylor's first-person narrative in Bruen's *The Killing of the Tinkers* does not provide much scope for lengthy reflection, and information about the Travellers deemed necessary for an understanding of the situation is generally conveyed in dialogues between Jack and Sweeper, as when the latter explains the origin of the Travellers: 'After the Great Hunger, if the clans fell out, they'd set fire to each other's abodes, so we got fired' (pp.64–5). The remark suggests that the Travellers were once settled, but were driven to a nomadic existence by an internal dispute in which they were on the losing side. Some comments can only be for the reader's benefit; at the reception after the funeral of one of the murdered Travellers, Taylor silently praises the hotel 'for letting the tinkers in', and explains: 'Recently the tinkers had hit back after years of discrimination, successfully suing pubs that denied access. The publicans had to regroup' (p.63). Such information highlights conflict situations involving Travellers, of the kind that are often highlighted by the contemporary Irish news media.

Newspapers and magazines are the cited source of Torrey Tunet's information about Travellers in Dicey Deere's *The Irish Manor House Murder*:

> Now, any mention of things Romanian in the news caught Torrey's eye. The Romanian gypsies lately escaping into Ireland had joined the itinerant population of tinkers, those 'travelers' who crisscrossed the countryside in painted wagons and caravans, sharpening knives, selling kitchenware, and occasionally stealing. They were largely illiterate. Most pubs barred them from entering, and they were unwelcome in villages; hospitals admitted them only grudgingly. Their caravan camps hung on the fringes of villages, of towns, of cities like Dublin. Torrey read that the Irish government was trying to better the tinkers' situation, even to building housing. But tinkers and gypsies were footloose. Torrey thought of her explorer father and wondered if the Tunets had once been gypsies. (pp.250–1)

The levels of inaccuracy in summaries of this kind may vary, but they all emphasize the Travellers' marginal social position (making much of poverty, crime, drugs and alcohol) and their problematic relationship with institutions and authorities in the sedentary world. In the context of a crime novel, such information cannot but mark Travellers as likely suspects.

ETHNICITY AND PREJUDICE

As Maureen Reddy has pointed out in her study of race in crime fiction, when the genre includes minority characters, its formula requires racism or prejudice to be acknowledged in a general way, even if the investigator is 'almost always exonerated of any taint of racism'.[19] Other characters, however, are allowed to express bigoted opinions. In *The Irish Manor House Murder*, Inspector O'Hare muses that it was 'to the shame of Ireland ... that those itinerants ... were scorned as lesser citizens' (p.153). Apart from suggesting that 'those itinerants' are not included in 'Ireland', the passive construction leaves it undetermined exactly who does the scorning in 'Ireland'. The inspector himself, for all his indignation, refers on several occasions to the 'thievery' of 'tinkers and gypsies', as well as 'their other unfortunate habits' (p.196). A local shopkeeper calls the Gypsies 'sneaky, dangerous' (p.124), but Dr Collins assures his housekeeper that, while Gypsies are 'known to be full of lies, as well as thievery', they are 'not dangerous' (p.84). That does not mean he likes to see the Gypsy woman anywhere near his property: 'Mass of dark hair to her shoulders, half a dozen rings on her dirty fingers, teeth flashing. "Go away!" He called out, trying to sound fierce, "Go away!"' (p.85). Although the Gypsy steals Torrey's tomatoes, the amateur sleuth invites the Romanian into her kitchen for tea, but even she admits that the Gypsy is 'not an appealing lady. Something grasping about her, the greedy way her glance slid about the cottage as she commented, "Pretty things"' (p.96). 'Ireland's' scornful attitude to the Travellers may be to its shame, but the individuals in Deere's mystery are quite shameless in their opinions, even if these are expressed under the guise of tolerance or liberalism.

In John Brady's *Unholy Ground* it is Detective Sergeant Minogue's colleagues who think little of the Travellers, not Minogue himself, but the latter's mental summary of the other guards' prejudices about the many negative characteristics of Travellers allows for those biased opinions to be spun out over the length of a full page: 'Garda Freely would hardly have called Joyce a Mister any more than he would have listened to the man's protestations last night. Joyce was, after all, a tinker. Tinkers were shifty, dishonest, cunning. They drank themselves into a stupor, they stole things. Tinkers left mounds of rubbish behind them when they moved their caravans to a new site' (pp.90–1). And so on. By the time Minogue concludes his reverie with the observation that '[w]ary householders generally held that tinkers a-begging at their door were really sizing up the houses for burglarizing later' (p.91), the reader could be forgiven for failing to remember that these are not the opinions of the Detective Sergeant himself, but of his less enlightened, lower-ranked colleagues and the population at large.

In *The Death of an Irish Tinker*, Peter McGarr's attitude towards Travellers is benign, although he regards them mostly as victims – of modernity, poverty, illiteracy and drugs. The negative attitude of society as a whole is expressed mostly through Biddy Nevins's views of the settled world: 'To the lot of them, Tinkers were scarcely human' (p.30), although '[t]here had to be somebody out there in "Buffer Land", as Mickalou called the settled society, who was good' (p.22). McGarr's junior colleague Ruth Bresnahan has her doubts about the 'illiterate Itinerant girl and heroin addict' and her husband: 'Could they ever have been formally married before a priest in a church?' (p.75). The ban-garda later notices that the van driven by a group of teenage Travellers belches illegal diesel fumes and has dubious tags and no tax stamp, but she 'could imagine some *shadog* [Traveller Cant for policeman] at a road check simply waving the wreck on' rather than dealing with the loud explanations and complaints of the youngsters. 'The assumption being, of course, that Travelers were incapable of obeying the law and didn't know any better' (p.182). The statement manages to imply the injustice of the assumption at the same time that the Travellers' actions shown in the book only serve to confirm its veracity.

In Bruen's *The Killing of the Tinkers*, Taylor is approached by the Travellers to investigate the murders because the guards consider them the outcome of internal Traveller feuding and hence unworthy of their attention. As if on cue, Superintendent Clancy, with whom Taylor has 'history, none of it good' (p.36), warns his ex-colleague off the case: 'Fecking tinkers, they're always killing each other' (p.37). For Sweeper, the motive behind the killings is not hard to surmise: 'Watch the news. Everybody hates the tinkers' (p.55). And so it appears, for even the chain-smoking priest Fr Malachy, another of Taylor's nemeses, claims that 'Tinkers are nobody's children' (p.62). Jack flatters himself that his pariah status makes him welcome in the Travelling community: 'Word was out that I was OK. Neither settled community nor tinker, I was outlaw enough to be accepted' (p.60). Indeed, typical of investigators in 'noir' detective fiction, Taylor actively assumes characteristics of a figure, in this case the stereotypical 'tinker', who is in need of 'control and mastery', in order to 'signify his liminal isolation and difference'.[20] Later, Sweeper explodes Taylor's psychological fantasy by reminding him that he belongs to the settled world: 'No matter how outlaw you think you are, you're part of them' (p.149). The correction tacitly accepts, even reinforces, the notion that tinkers are the outlaws settled people claim they are, and essentializes that quality in terms exclusive to the Traveller community.

According to Richard Dyer, 'the role of stereotypes is to make visible the invisible, so that there is no danger of it creeping up on us unawares', and also to 'make fast, firm and separate what is in reality fluid and much closer to the norm than the dominant value system cares to admit'.[21] Although both Gill's and Bruen's characters and narrators explicitly refer to stereotypical 'tinker' traits, such characteristics are more often indirectly implied by the suggestion that particular Traveller characters differ in some way from an assumed Traveller norm. When Biddy in *The Death of an Irish Tinker* realizes that the Toddler is determined to kill her, she immediately decides never again to return to her inner city flat, to the disbelief of her neighbour, since 'settled people just did not leave like this' (p.31). Biddy does not think twice about leaving everything behind: 'It was what it meant to be a Traveler – even a straight, honest, law-abiding, working, bill-paying Traveler who was Queen of the Buskers. Nothing was permanent' (p.32). Biddy's husband is equally atypical as Travellers go: 'In Mickalou she had found a man who was different from the common run of Travelers and muckers she had known – not selfish and brutal and demanding but kind and considerate and fun to be with' (p.30). The underlying assumption that most Traveller husbands are abusive is confirmed in a more straightforward manner from McGarr's perspective, when he notes to himself that '[b]attering was an all-too-common feature of many Traveler marriages' (p.41). When the narrative depicts Travellers behaving 'atypically' (where the 'typical' traveller behaviour is negative), the 'tinker' stereotype is reinforced rather than denied; at the same time, the atypical behaviour is never allowed to persist. There is no positive representation of Traveller culture in *The Death of an Irish Tinker*, and only praise when the characters are not behaving as negatively as is expected of them.

However atypical Biddy may be in some respects, her 'tinker' nature is nevertheless inscribed on her face: 'Like some Travelers whose clan had "married close", she had one blue eye, the other brown. But her high cheekbones and fine, even features were those of her mother's prominent Traveling family, the Maughams, and she looked all of what she was: an exotic creature in every regard' (p.21). Cursory references to what is, in actuality, a complex issue of consanguineous marriages within the Traveller community, are used in this novel to suggest that being a traveller is 'bred in the bone', and that the shared gene pool produces similar looks and behaviours in all members of the community. Consequently, Biddy and her daughter Oney cannot help but revert to type in the second half of the book. After twelve years in England, Biddy returns to Dublin a well-known and well-off artist. The new Traveller in her life, Tag Barry, is a 'handsome young man, who was often mistaken for her brother or ... [her father's] son, the three of them looked so much alike' (p.109). Tag's resemblance to herself tinges Biddy's disapproval of his drinking and general fecklessness with a hint of self-disgust, as does her dismissal of his personality as 'all piss and wind, like the proverbial Tinker's mule' (p.110). Biddy also disapproves of her daughter, who 'had chosen mots and bowsies as friends when at school she had the daughters of the country's elite' (p.113). When the Toddler tries to get Oney hooked on heroin, he uses a young Traveller as a lure, a drug addict (like all of his peers in this novel), who 'looked enough like Oney Maugham to be her brother – or Mickalou Maugham's son – apart from his two-colored eyes. They, of course, were like Oney's mother' (p.185). Travellers in Gill's novel thus all act and look alike, something also confirmed by the Chief Superintendent at the end of the book: 'Strike one Tinker, and you strike ... the whole clan' (p.237).

In the world of the 'noir' crime novel, distinctions between guilt and innocence, and between hero, criminal and victim tend to be blurred. Bruen's *The Killing of the Tinkers* presents an ambiguous picture of the tinkers as well as the detective that both defies and confirms stereotypical expectations about each class of character, sometimes in a knowingly ironical manner. Sweeper consciously defies preconceptions about Travellers by always dressing impeccably in a suit and tie: 'I have to stay respectable. They expect us to be tinkerish, but I give the lie to their assumptions' (p.76). Unlike Taylor, he is not a 'bookish' man, but that does not mean he is 'unlearnt' (p.28), and his handwriting is 'superb' (p.170). Although he sometimes drives a battered, untaxed van, he also owns a spotless white vehicle. The down-and-out Taylor is allowed to stay in a house owned by some Travellers who 'didn't settle' (p.29), while Sweeper lives in 'a large three-story affair with adjoining garage' (p.244), stuffed with antiques and leather furniture. But there is also another side to Sweeper, when he goes off to defend 'his position as leader of the clan. Literally. Every so often, a young buck would challenge and they'd settle it bare knuckled. Venues were usually held round Mullingar and attracted huge crowds. The betting aspect was the magnet, and fortunes were wagered' (p.129). By making his main Traveller character a respectable, wealthy man who lives in a fancy house, whereas his detective has no home of his own to go to, Bruen manages to convey that much of the otherness of the Travellers is in the eye of the beholder, even if they also have their own customs of which the settled world is largely unaware. Yet Sweeper creates the impression that he merely performs the part of the respectable citizen in public, while his 'true' identity as a tinker comes out in a parallel universe that is hidden from the settled world.

The message that Travellers are closer to the norm of respectability than the stereotype allows is counterbalanced by the dissoluteness of the investigating detective – a quality that in Taylor's case is associated with 'tinkerishness', however, so that the immediate stereotype that is dispatched by Sweeper's suavity is nevertheless returned through the back door of association. An alcoholic, Taylor suffers from an 'affliction' Sweeper diagnoses as common among Travellers: 'My people suffer similarly' (p.31). After Taylor has had his nose and teeth broken by local hooligans for consorting with 'tinkers', and has thrown up all over himself, an elderly couple passing by in the street are scandalized, and Jack feels like shouting, 'What do you expect? I'm a tinker' (p.67). On another occasion, he drives a battered, untaxed van belonging to Sweeper, and is asked by some children if he is a tinker; later, he finds they have scratched the word on the side of the vehicle. Ken Bruen plays with perceptions: Sweeper is smartly dressed and wealthy, but still dismissed by sedentary society as a 'tinker'. Jack Taylor resembles the 'tinker' stereotype and is labelled accordingly, including by himself. The Travellers portrayed in the book, however – the generic crowd Sweeper refers to as 'my people' – do drive untaxed, battered vans, are alcoholics, and take the law, often violently, into their own hands. But so does Jack Taylor. Rather than dismiss the tinker stereotype, the dark, alienated vision of the 'noir' hard-boiled detective suggests that, in the destabilized and fragmented post-modern world, everybody is a tinker: the Tinker is Everyman.

SEXUAL DEVIANCE AND PROMISCUITY

What Artelia Court calls 'the venerable Irish and British popular tradition of the sexual promiscuity of Gypsies and Tinkers'[22] was given a veneer of scholarly respectability when the Gypsy Lore Society published an article in 1887 that highlighted the 'widely suspected practice of adultery, promiscuity, and wife-swapping' supposedly prevalent among the Travellers.[23] That perception is still widespread and persistent, and particularly evident in the crime novels discussed here. Regarded as lawless and out of control by the majority population, the Travellers are often considered to be without boundaries and taboos of any kind, including those concerning family and sexuality. In crime fiction, accepted norms and values and the transgression thereof are central to the genre, even if the transgressions only serve to create suspense and suspicion around a character whose deviancy ultimately turns out to be a red herring in the plot. Often behaviour that deviates from the norm is introduced almost gratuitously, and appears to function as a reminder to readers that the value system they depend on is forever in danger of being destabilized, mostly by outsiders.

In *The Death of an Irish Tinker*, Biddy Nevins's mismatched eyes represent, in a way, her two identities as the marginalized Traveller she was and the respected artist she becomes. At the same time, their signification of 'incestuous' marriage customs also foregrounds the Travellers' perceived transgression of, and disregard for, the norms and values relating to marriage, family and sexuality prevalent in the sedentary world. Biddy's father, we are told, 'had dropped her off in Dublin during the winter she turned nine – to "harden" her, he said' (p.19).[24] Living with other Travellers on a rubbish dump in Ringsend, she had 'begged and stolen and run in a wilding pack with other abandoned children. They had terrorized tourists, stolen cars and anything that wasn't nailed down, and booted drugs' (p.21). Free initial doses of heroin soon turned them all into addicts, after which the descent was rapid: 'gang-raped by some friends of the gearmen when she was nodding off after her first injection, then living for years on heroin, sweets, and whatever money she could make turning tricks for old men in a quayside walk-up that the Toddler owned' (p.161). From a care shelter (where she was further abused by the nun in charge), Biddy went into 'rehab', where she met her future husband. Mickalou had been an extremely accomplished musician and international folk music collector before he, too, succumbed to drug addiction, depicted in this novel as a disease to which Travellers are particularly 'susceptible' (p.189).[25] Gill's emphasis on the universal nature of Traveller drug addiction, and the often unsuccessful attempts at 'rehab', serves as a contemporary variation on the theme of traveller 'rehabilitation' that has been reiterated in Irish society and literature since the beginning of the twentieth century.

The exaggerated horrors of Biddy's early years contrast starkly with the life of the woman she becomes after her flight to England, where her artistic talent and photographic eye, which allows her to draw anything from memory, including pages from the Book of Kells, quickly land her a job in an advertising firm, despite her illiteracy. The assistance during this process of Cheri Cooke, an art photographer, comes with a sexual price tag: 'Cheri's house, Cheri's tutoring, even Cheri's money that she gave Biddy as "pay" she called it while Biddy was learning did not come without strings. But as a lover Cheri Cooke was not demanding and seemed to need sharing and companionship most' (p.98). Soon successful as a photographic artist who exhibits her work in London, Paris and New York, Biddy transforms herself into Beth Waters, using contact lenses to straighten out her mismatched eyes. Her return to Dublin, however, where she shares a house with her parents, daughter, and male and female lovers, is also a partial return to her Traveller origins. As a lesbian, Cheri Cooke is also a 'transgressive' character, who for a time 'had been good for – no *essential* to – Biddy, who wouldn't be where she was today without her', but who is now regarded by her as 'a carping, crippled old shrew' (pp.111–12). Tag Barry, too, has fallen out of favour: 'Biddy wondered if she could ever have loved Tag Barry. Or had it simply been narcissism, since they looked so much alike?' (p.112). As for Tag, he intends to use the substantial sum of money he has stolen from Biddy to 'run through half the easy young women in Dublin' (p.115). 'Marrying close' is only one of the many types of transgressive sexual behaviour ascribed to the Traveller characters in this narrative: rape, prostitution, gratuitous gender-bending, and general promiscuity are all in evidence and presented as if they are as self-evident as the child abandonment, drug use and thieving that seem to come so naturally to the Travellers in *The Death of an Irish Tinker*.

Transgression of the assumed heterosexual norm is also focused on as part of the generally deviant behaviour ascribed to 'tinkers' in John Brady's *Unholy Ground*. Looking for a motive in the murder case of 73-year-old Arthur Combs, Detective Sergeant Minogue asks the Englishman's neighbour if Combs had been homosexual, something for which there is otherwise no evidence. Puzzled as to why Combs would have befriended Michael Joseph Joyce and given him money for drink, the detectives pursue a similar line of inquiry with the tinker in question, even though the man is a married father of seven: 'Any idea in your mind that Mr. Combs was a homosexual? ... Didn't he want a little something for his troubles?' (p.104). That Joyce is scandalized does not diminish the fact that he is asked the question in the first place, which speaks volumes about what is commonly assumed about the sexual proclivities and morals of Travellers. A pseudoscientific twist is given to the theme in Janet Neel's *Ticket to Ride*. Wondering how Travellers would have felt about a gay man in their midst, one of the characters remembers being told by a social worker 'that in all societies that repress their women male homosexuality is an acceptable norm. Well, that fitted gypsy society all right, so perhaps nobody had minded.'[26]

In *The Irish Manor House Murder*, detectives puzzle over the possible connection between two murders (only one of which is acknowledged in the book's title): 'An eminent surgeon and a gypsy! What's going on there?' (p.135). The answer seems obvious to Inspector O'Hare once Dr Collins has confessed to killing the woman for trying to blackmail him: the respected physician, 'secret frequenter of hookers in Cork and God knew where else', had killed the Gypsy for fear of having his 'unbridled sexual need' exposed. Inspector O'Hare 'wondered on which stormy night, with the roads deluged, had Dr Collins found his way in the woods to the gypsy's wagon' (p.206). Here, too, the fact that Collins had in actuality killed the Gypsy to prevent her from revealing that his own loyal housekeeper had murdered Ashenden, who would otherwise have killed Collins for finding out about the X-ray affair, is less significant than the unquestioned assumption by the authorities of the gypsy woman's promiscuity. The fact that Collins later finds sanctuary within the Gypsy community further suggests that his lack of sexual restraint is not regarded as a problem there.

DOUBLE TROUBLE: VICTIMS AND PERPETRATORS

Crime authors make a point of including overt statements about society's discriminatory behaviour against Travellers into their narratives, while themselves exploiting Travellers as colourful, exotic creatures who are impervious to the rules and regulations of the society that spurns them. This doubleness translates itself into the ambiguous roles Travellers play in several of these novels: they are victims, but, like the perpetrators of crime, they exist on the fringes of society and therefore inevitably find themselves on a par with criminals and outlaws. Indeed, as murderers themselves, or harbourers of killers, Traveller characters, victimized though they may be in some way, are often no different than, and sometimes even identical to, the 'killers of the tinkers' they abhor. Caught in this criminal bind, Traveller characters in crime fiction are not seldom depicted as hating both themselves and their fellow 'tinkers'.

The numerous deliberate and accidental role reversals in *The Death of an Irish Tinker*, as well as the novel's circular plot, reflect the equivocal position of the Traveller characters within the context of law and order. In a climactic shoot-out in Biddy Nevins's house in Raglan Road towards the end of the book, the police mistake the Toddler for Biddy, while Biddy is shot dead by a Garda sergeant who assumes that she is the Toddler. The drug lord manages to get away, and without hard evidence to prosecute him, McGarr instead allows a group of young Travellers, including Biddy's daughter Oney, to assault the Toddler in his own mansion. As the teenagers, armed with iron pipes, hurling sticks and knives, surround him in his Jacuzzi, the criminal manages to grab and kill one of the girls before McGarr hits him over the head with a chair. The inspector then allows the Travellers to do their worst: 'hacking, swinging, punching, stomping. His face, his neck, the groin, the wound' (p.231). Once the Toddler has been castrated with a pair of garden shears, Oney arranges for him to be left to die at the top of the same tree where her father Mickalou had met his demise many years before. McGarr's only action is to make sure that the police will return the next day to '"straighten things up", so there'd be no evidence of who might have murdered him, he meant. Not even the dead girl, whose corpse would be taken back to her own people and not left there for the police, if McGarr knew anything about Travelers' (p.231). Oney and her friends get away with killing the Toddler because, as in the case of Dr Collins, poetic justice has been served. The untouchable criminal is eliminated by the Travellers, who are themselves equally beyond the pale, while the law turns a blind eye. Mickalou's corpse from the beginning of the book is indistinguishable from the Toddler's at the end: murderer and victim reflect each other as in a mirror image.

Early on in Ken Bruen's *The Killing of the Tinkers*, Sweeper echoes the popular wisdom that 'the tinkers are always killing each other' (p.24), and asks Jack Taylor to identify the murderer of five Traveller men. Taylor too quickly points the finger at Bryson, and his accusation leads the Travellers to torture and eventually kill the disturbed and sarcastic social worker. Only afterwards does Taylor realize that he has made a mistake, and that the real killer is not an outsider to the Travelling community, but Mikey, a member of Sweeper's entourage. Like Biddy/Beth with the mismatched eyes in *The Death of an Irish Tinker*, Mikey is a character with a double life and a split personality. The van he owns 'looked battered till you got in and saw it had been custom fit' (p.242), and the person who drives it is also not who he appears to be on the outside. 'I'm not a tinker', Mikey tells Jack, and explains: 'My mother, when I was four, had me out walking at midnight. ... A van hit her, killed her instantly. Not that she felt anything, she was too drunk for that. The tinkers adopted me. ... Their van' (pp.243–4). Typically in male 'noir', the 'sins' of the guilty mother in the background 'constitute an explanation of their psychologically damaged offspring',[27] but in the case of Mikey the mother's guilt is shared by the tinkers who killed her. Schizoid, alienated and full of self-hate, Mikey veers between deep contempt for the settled community and denial that he is a 'tinker'; dismissive of where he lived as a child with his mother – 'a flat in Rahoon. ... You wouldn't put a dog in them. A Galway ghetto' – he also sneers at the opulent 'three-storey affair' where Sweeper resides (p.244). To the extent that Mikey is a 'tinker', they are indeed killing each other: once again, the enemy is to be found within. The Travellers, meanwhile, have murdered an innocent man, an error that Jack will rectify by making sure that a sixth and final tinker will be eliminated. The detective, who is in many respects a mirror image of Mikey and, like him, has his own issues with a mother he hates, ends up committing the crime he was hired to solve. Irony is pervasive in the resolution of this narrative without heroes, in which everyone, victim, perpetrator or investigator, settled or Traveller, lives up to the worst image of the stereotypical 'tinker'.

In Dicey Deere's mystery, the murderers of Dr Ashenden go into exile from the settled world, and install themselves in the community of the Gypsy who was also killed by them. Some time after the disappearance of Dr Collins and his housekeeper shortly before their arrest for murder, Torrey Tunet comes across a newspaper story about an injured Gypsy child who had been saved by 'one of the Romanian gypsies, an old fellow who surprisingly had some medical knowledge. The gypsy was even said to help with gypsy women in childbirth, generally a woman's job' (p.251). Putting two and two together, Torrey eventually discovers Dr Collins in a horse-drawn wagon on the edge of Clonakilty, where he reveals the true circumstances of the murders, and confesses that he now lives with '[g]uilt. And expiation. ... It's mostly the children that need medical care. Hospitals aren't friendly to gypsies and travelers – "tinkers", they're called. Ireland is changing, the government is trying, but still' (pp.255–6). Torrey also discovers that the doctor is suffering from Lupus, a disease whose symptoms he tries to mask with make-up around his eyes: 'some of it had rubbed off, showing darkness' (p.252), so that his features mimic 'the gypsy's dark face' Torrey had recalled to memory earlier on (p.247). Having killed a Gypsy, the doctor escapes punishment by 'becoming' a Gypsy and tending to the medical needs of the victimized community. Travellers 'roved about, footloose' (p.67); the laws of the land do not touch them, and they apparently do not object to harbouring an outlawed stranger and killer of one of their own. The villain has put himself beyond the pale, and Torrey has no intention of turning in the doctor for masquerading as a Gypsy; rather, she proclaims, 'I love him for it' (p.257).

The underlying assumption in crime fiction is that minorities like the Travellers are 'the read, not the readers; the looked-at, not the lookers'.[28] Recent crime novels set in Ireland and featuring Traveller characters perpetuate the received opinion that, in Paul Delaney's words, 'the Travellers exist at the borders of respectable society, and beyond the pale of permissible behaviour'.[29] That perception is reinforced by 'true crime' publications like *Scam!* (1996) by Don Wright, and *The Outsiders: Exposing the Secret World of Ireland's Travellers* (2006) by *Sunday World* journalist Eamon Dillon, both of which focus exclusively or almost exclusively on fraudulent practices allegedly committed by Travellers in Ireland and/or the United States. While Dillon begins his book's introduction by stating that there is 'no such thing as a typical traveller',[30] he concludes it with the assumption that there is, at the same time, a typical 'experience' of Travellers among non-Travellers, which is, in his view, overwhelmingly negative, and which his book seeks to document: 'a book detailing traveller success stories, where travellers have shattered perceived stereotypes by becoming lawyers, academics, Olympians, successful entertainers and actors, would have done nothing to address the real experience the vast majority of people have of travellers'.[31]

In crime fiction, Traveller characters, because they are dispensable outsiders, and all but invisible to the authorities, are easily victimized, but their marginal status also allows them to kill without consequences. In the popular imagination reflected in Irish crime fiction, members of the Traveller community are considered suspect, even guilty from the outset, until they are eventually proven to be ... guilty, of something, even if not the crime originally under investigation. Essentially, the Travellers in such crime fiction inhabit a parallel universe where they operate almost entirely outside the official system of justice. In the end, they simply vanish back into their own world of losers, caught as they are in a self-perpetuating, self-destructive loop that inexorably determines their preconceived roles as victims and perpetrators.

NOTES

1. Maureen T. Reddy, *Traces, Codes, and Clues: Reading Race in Crime Fiction* (New Brunswick, NJ, and London: Rutgers University Press, 2003), p.1.
2. Ibid., p.2
3. Michael Cohen, 'The Detective as Other: The Detective *Versus* the Other', in Kathleen Gregory Klein (ed.), *Diversity and Detective Fiction* (Bowling Green, OH: Bowling Green State University Popular Press, 1999), p.144.
4. Ibid., p.153.
5. Dicey Deere, *The Irish Manor House Murder* (New York: St Martin's, 2000). All subsequent page references in the text are to this edition.
6. Marilyn Stasio, 'Crime', review of *The Death of an Irish Tinker* by Bartholomew Gill, *New York Times*, 21 September 1997. Accessed 16 November 2006: http://www.nytimes.com archive.
7. Liam O'Flaherty, 'The Pedlar's Revenge', in *The Pedlar's Revenge and Other Stories* (Dublin: Wolfhound Press, 1976), pp.32–3.
8. D.M. O'Reilly, 'The Tinker's Revenge', in Ed Gorman, Larry Segriff and Martin H. Greenberg (eds), *Murder Most Irish* (New York: Barnes and Noble, 1996), p.257. All subsequent page references in the text are to this edition.
9. John Brady, *Unholy Ground* (1989; South Royalton, VT: Steerforth Press, 2002), p.92. All subsequent page references in the text are to this edition.
10. Stephen Knight, *Crime Fiction, 1800–2000: Detection, Death, Diversity* (Basingstoke: Palgrave Macmillan, 2004), pp.87–8.
11. Bartholomew Gill, *The Death of an Irish Tinker* (1997; New York: Avon Books, 2001). All subsequent page references in the text are to this edition.
12. Katharine Horsley and Lee Horsley, '*Meres Fatales*: Maternal Guilt in the Noir Crime Novel', *Modern Fiction Studies*, 45, 2 (1999), p.371.
13. Ken Bruen, *The Killing of the Tinkers* (Dingle, Co. Kerry: Brandon, 2002), p.24. All subsequent page references in the text are to this edition.
14. Dyer, *The Matter of Images*, p.9.
15. Janet Neel, *Ticket to Ride* (New York: St. Martin's Minotaur, 2005), p.78.
16. Ibid., p.86.
17. Knight, *Crime Fiction*, p.87.
18. Reddy, *Traces, Codes, and Clues*, p.66.
19. Ibid., p.119.
20. Liam Kennedy, 'Black *Noir*: Race and Urban Space in Walter Mosley's Detective Fiction', in Katharine Gregory Klein, *Diversity and Detective Fiction*, p.226.
21. Dyer, *The Matter of Images*, p.16.
22. Artelia Court, *Puck of the Droms: The Lives and Literature of the Irish Tinkers* (Berkeley, CA: University of California Press, 1985), p.35.
23. Delaney, 'Representations of the Travellers', p.54.
24. Bartholomew Gill may have derived Biddy's story in part from details in Sharon Gmelch's *Nan: the Life of an Irish Travelling Woman*, but if so, he made them more grisly and lurid. Nan relates how her father put her on the train to Dublin at the age of 14 to take up a position in a draper's shop, having decided that it was time for her to 'get out' and 'do' for herself (p.57). Nan remembered feeling scared and lost. Later in life, Nan spent a winter near the city rubbish tip in Ringsend, where a number of Traveller families found the materials to build huts and shacks to see them through the cold season. She describes hers as beautiful: 'We painted it blue, and I was happy, meself and the kids' (p.149).
25. A 2005 report on the extent of illegal drug use among Travellers by the National Advisory Committee on Drugs, entitled *An Overview of the Nature and Extent of Illicit Drugs Use Amongst the Traveller Community: an Exploratory Study*, suggested that, while substance abuse was on the rise within the community, levels at the time of writing were 'perceived to be lower than those in the general population'. Cited in Sinead Smith, 'Racism, Social Exclusion and Drug Use: Why Are Travellers an "at Risk" Group for Problematic Drug Use?' *Pavee Point Newsletter*, 2, 5–6 (2006), p.16.

26. Neel, *Ticket to Ride*, pp.104–5.
27. Horsley and Horsley, '*Meres Fatales*', p.371.
28. Reddy, *Traces, Codes, and Clues*, p.171.
29. Delaney, 'Representations of the Travellers', p.55.
30. Eamon Dillon, *The Outsiders: Exposing the Secretive World of Ireland's Travellers* (Dublin: Merlin, 2006), p.ix.
31. Ibid., pp.xv–xvi.

CHAPTER 7

A Different People: Traveller Life Writing

Oh, the road isn't easy, but it's what I choose,
I'm not always a winner, but I'll never lose,
I'm the pride of me race and the last of the few
And I live like my father taught me.
Pecker Dunne, 'The Last of the Travelling People'

In mainstream literature and media, Irish Travellers are never represented as just themselves, but always as Other to the norm of the settled population. This persistent Othering has prompted Paul Delaney to ask 'whether it is possible to recognize and depict another culture as also Irish'.[1] Some scholars argue that the problem resides in the very notion of representation itself: that representation per se has become, as Sidonie Smith puts it, complicitous with 'the imperialistic designs of a speaking subject intent on "naming [and] controlling"'.[2] For Richard Dyer, even the study of representations of marginal or subordinate groups has the effect of 'reproducing the sense of the oddness, differentness, exceptionality of these groups, the feeling that they are departures from the norm'.[3] The image that exists among the sedentary population of the nature of Travellers as exotic and threatening may in part be the result of the virtual absence of Traveller self-representations in the Irish written and broadcast media. As schooling was often erratic, either because of the semi-nomadic lifestyle of the Travellers, or because they were shifted from site to site by the authorities, or in some cases because they did not value formal education, which contributed little to the practical skills by which they made their living, Traveller culture has traditionally been oral rather than written. However, since the 1960s Travellers have begun to speak for and represent themselves, on video tape and in writing, for example through organizations like the Irish Traveller Movement, the Dublin-based Pavee Point Travellers Centre, and the Cork Traveller Visibility Group. Like the empire in Salman Rushdie's much-quoted phrase, the Travelling community has started writing back, albeit on a still modest scale.

While Traveller organizations focus on disseminating factual information related to issues like health, employment and housing, and on creating awareness of the rights and needs of Travellers as an ethnic minority group, most texts produced by individual Travellers take the form of life stories. Even though Travellers have been a part of Irish life for centuries, Traveller writing, because it is such a recent phenomenon, shares many characteristics with immigrant writing, which is also frequently autobiographical in nature. Like many recent immigrant groups, Travellers use life writing predominantly to address the majority population – in their case, a settled audience – as a 'countermeasure, as a disclosure of self that seeks to correct the negative stereotypes encountered in the public realm'.[4] Because this is a defensive strategy, and because Travellers, in their quest for greater understanding, also emphasize their difference from the settled community, it is questionable whether such an approach can ever entirely achieve the desired effect.

The published life stories of Travellers fall into a number of different categories. Some academic accounts of individuals' lives portray their subjects as entities to be studied from an anthropological perspective; the researcher recorded the Traveller's life story on tape and subsequently presented it in written form, edited and with comments. Examples of such studies, which blend biographical and autobiographical writing, are *Nan: The Life of an Irish Travelling Woman* (1986), presented by anthropologist Sharon Gmelch, and *The Book of Sandy Stewart* (1988), the life story of a Scottish Traveller related by folklorist Roger Leitch. The very assumptions behind these studies, which isolate their subjects as ethnic minorities or as manifestations of 'folk life', exoticize Travellers and set them apart from the majority population. There are also more straightforward autobiographies. In *The Road to God Knows Where* (1972), Sean Maher presents a slightly fictionalized account of his life, with his name changed to Sean Devine. In the case of *My Life on the Road* by Nan Joyce (1985), and the life stories of William Cauley and Pecker Dunne (both 2004), the author's words were recorded on tape and transcribed without commentary by an editor. Nan Joyce remarks in an 'Author's Note' preceding the main text of her book that '[i]t's an awful sad thing to have no education. If I knew how to write properly and had good spelling I wouldn't have done this book on tape.' Scottish Traveller Betsy Whyte wrote her own life story in two volumes, *The Yellow on the Broom* (1979) and *Red Rowans and Wild Honey* (1990).[5] Other life stories take the form of brief personal accounts or memoirs of life on the road and had their genesis in Traveller community writing or heritage projects. These include the narratives collected by the Southwark Traveller Women's Group under the title *Moving Stories* (1992), or by the Clondalkin Travellers Development Group, entitled *Travellers: A Way of Life* (1993), or the accounts in the Pavee Point publication *Traveller Ways Traveller Words*, which emerged from a Travellers' Cultural Heritage Centre project. Many life stories are by women, who seem on the whole more interested in writing than men, perhaps because they have fewer opportunities for expression outside the domestic realm, or because women are more often the target of development projects aimed at Travellers. According to Sinéad Ní Shuinéar, 'the supposedly gender-neutral local Traveller support groups are essentially female' and do not offer men the training and facilities they offer women and children.[6]

In many instances, the oral qualities of the narrative are much in evidence, even in the cases where the narrator was able to write his or her own story. Betsy Whyte claimed that she resisted writing down the final part of her story before she had composed the entire narrative in her head: 'I have not been writing. It is just a traveller superstition, not to count chickens ... If a publisher is found then I will write night and day. It is all in my mind. I will only have to set it down.'[7] Often embedded within the life story are other stories (ghost stories heard around the campfire, tales about the origin of Traveller beliefs) and songs about the Travelling life. For Travellers, songs, stories and other lore are an integral part of their life story, not separate from it; they are 'an expression of their reality'.[8] In the absence of formal education, songs and stories contain life lessons, communicate values and beliefs, and instil a sense of identity and belonging. Scottish folk singer and Traveller Belle Stewart emphasized the importance of the songs she sang and wrote as follows: 'Dinna mak a fool o the sangs. Love them as if you yerself was living through them, and if ye love singing them, for God's sake dae it wi aa yer hert'.[9] It is therefore important for Traveller life stories to preserve this oral form of expression even when the words appear in print. As Paul

Delaney points out, however, the collision between oral tradition and print history can lead to pressures which 'are exaggerated in cases where there is an imbalance of power between the oral and the written traditions', particularly when the oral tradition is imperilled.[10]

HISTORICAL SELF-EXPLANATION

William Spengemann identifies the formal strategies of self-representation as 'historical self-explanation, philosophical self-scrutiny, poetic self- expression, and poetic self-invention'.[11] Since the Traveller community 'is very much present-time oriented' and, unlike other nomadic peoples, has not maintained a strong sense of its own history,[12] historical self-explanation often takes the form of poetic self-invention. Dubious historical theories are not solely the prerogative of the Travellers themselves. In the early twentieth century, Eóin MacNeill, drawing on the questionable eighteenth-century scholarship of Charles Vallancey, who had linked the earliest settlers of Ireland to the Phoenicians, argued that the Travellers were descended from pre-Celtic tribes, which were subsequently conquered by the Gaels, the ancestors of the Irish people of today. A similar scenario of aboriginal roots was put forward by Grattan Puxon in a pamphlet from the mid-1960s, in which he argues that '[t]housands of years ago a free travelling people lived on the island today called Ireland. They roamed as they wished, seeking the best grazing land for their animals. ... and lived in the same kind of tents that many families on the road still use, covering their wattle frames with skins instead of canvas.'[13] Sean Maher's protagonist in *The Road to God Knows Where* is told by an old Travelling man that written history is less reliable than the Travellers' oral tales: 'Make no mistake, son, we on the road are descended not from the famine era or the Cromwellian era but from the days of the kings of Ireland and their clans' (p.105).

Travellers sometimes endow themselves with respectable ancestors by casting important cultural and historical figures into the role of Travellers. Lily McDonagh ends her poem 'Traveller's Feelings' (included in the anthology *Black Stones Around the Green Shamrock*) with the verse, 'Jesus was a Traveller, / He roamed the world around, / I read it in the Bible, / And that's just what I found'.[14] Sean Maher's protagonist argues that 'our Blessed Lord himself was a traveller' (p. 64), that 'the Irish monks of long ago ... were travelling people' (p.82), that 'Shakespeare was a traveller for most of his early years', that 'Chaucer travelled in pilgrimage', and that Bunyan was the son of a tinsmith (p.100). The same old man who informed him about his ancient roots also tells him that 'St Patrick himself was a great pavvy' (p.106). Such stretching of the parameters of what a Traveller is conflicts with the narrower ethnic definition put forward today by Traveller organizations, but it fits the specific agenda of Sean Maher's protagonist, which is to receive an education and to become a priest or a writer. The old man tells Sean:

> You know, son, I would like if a lad like you or someone else off the road, could one day become famous. It would be good to get back to the beauty of learning like in the days of long ago. It was then, my lad, that the people of the road were an example and a heritage to be proud of. Today, alas, we are treated and looked upon as ignorant savages. (p.112)

Often Travellers emphasize their historical survival skills in a settled culture as a way of expressing pride in their culture. In Paddy McDonagh's words: 'Travellers are proud that we can survive and do well against the odds. We run successful businesses without any support from governments, without having had an education and in the face of discrimination. Older Travellers are highly respected because they are the real survivors.'[15] Nan Joyce relates how, in Cromwellian times and during the Famine, settled people took to the roads and mixed with the Travellers: 'The travellers were used to coping with cold and hardship and hunger, they could survive anywhere because they had their own way of working and their own culture. But the settled people weren't used to managing on their own, they slept in old sheds and barns and did a sort of slave work on the farms' (p.2). In *Red Rowans*, Betsy Whyte also suggests that poor settled people went hungry more often than Travelling people, because they lacked the survival skills of the latter (p.26). In Sharon Gmelch's *Nan*, one of Nan Donohoe's sons defines a tinker as 'a man who thought of a hundred ways of surviving. ... He was a better survivor than the rest' (p.15), and William Cauley expresses a similar sentiment when he says, 'Travellers can survive anywhere, be it country or city. We are great survivors! We've had to be, I suppose!'[16]

SELF-SCRUTINY AND SELF-CONSCIOUSNESS

Life writing calls for self-scrutiny, which in its most basic form involves a critical look at physical appearance and material culture. Because Travellers are often discriminated against purely on the basis of how they look and sound, there is a self-consciousness in their stories about ways in which they differ from settled people. A study of Traveller children in Limerick suggests that they are aware very early on 'of the fact that as Travellers they ... [are] different from other children', including in terms of physical appearance;[17] likewise, in his life story, Pecker Dunne claims to have been aware of 'a distinction between us and the rest of the Irish people' from the moment he was able to walk.[18] Arguably, in the rural parts of Ireland in the early twentieth century, where all women wore big skirts and shawls, the differences in appearance were minimal; according to Nan Donohoe, '[y]ou wouldn't know a tinker woman from a farmer's wife, except that the country woman kept herself cleaner because she had water to wash herself' (p.129). However, many older Travellers talk about wearing the cast-off clothes they were given by settled people, which did set them apart. Nan Joyce remembers that her younger brother was given a coat which 'was miles too big, dragging on the ground but still he wore it because he was frozen and soaking wet' (p.44). Nellie Joyce (born in 1942) points out that Travellers are better off than they used to be: 'They can pick what they want. In my day they didn't have a choice. They had to take what they got. But they can wear anything now. They wear all the stylish stuff now.'[19] All the same, Martina Joyce (born in 1972) says that Travellers often consciously try not to look like Travellers when they go out for fear of not being admitted to a pub or club: 'We'll say to try an' brighten yourself up a small bit better an' try for ta see would they think that you're not a Traveller. ... To try an' make yourself look like a country girdle or a country biy.'[20]

VULNERABLE SUBJECTS

Sharon Gmelch and Roger Leitch observed the Travellers as part of their academic research. Although verbatim transcriptions of the recorded voice of the Traveller are included in their studies, these are presented within a framework in which the Traveller is subject to the researcher's observation, which means that she or he ultimately only speaks on the mediator's terms, whose voice is dominant and who holds the power to structure and edit the narrative. Thomas Couser points out that anthropological ethics 'reminds us that harm can be done to communities as well as to individuals' by such studies, and that anthropological practices have been changed by 'self-assertion on the part of historically marginalized subjects and groups'.[21] In the studies discussed here, the endnotes and researchers' comments at times reinforce the notion that Travellers are quaint and exotic if not actually in need of correction.

Descriptions by these observers of the Traveller's physical appearance are not neutral, but foreground difference from the settled norm. Sharon Gmelch describes her first encounter with Nan Donohoe, when she used a kitten as a means of introduction:

> A cluster of religious medals hung from a safety pin on her chest; a pierced earring dangled from one ear – the other ear had been ripped. Her eyes were a calm blue-gray, the right one flecked with brown. She must have been attractive once; beneath the web of wrinkles and small white scars was a faded beauty. She looked at the kitten.
>
> 'Ah, he's beautiful', she said. Her voice was deep and raspy. 'Is he a Persian?'
>
> I wondered a second at the question, alert for signs of ridicule. But she only looked at the kitten, an ordinary tabby, and stroked it.
>
> 'What's his name?'
>
> 'Hillary.'
>
> 'Hillary.' She repeated the name with difficulty, then looked up and smiled through three thin decaying teeth. 'He's going to be big. He looks like a very clever cat.'
>
> I smiled involuntarily at the absurd, yet sincere flattery. (p.27)

This observation selectively highlights elements that imply religious superstition, violence, hardship and naive ignorance.

Roger Leitch introduces Sandy Stewart as follows:

> In appearance, Sandy is a small man, his wiry frame tending to be lagged with an extra layer of clothing irrespective of the weather, the fit, or the frills of fashion. Sandy Stewart cuts his own dash and wears his cloth as he finds it. The bonnet on his head may be tatty, bitten, or singed, but it is the way that bonnet is worn which best sums up the man. His is a face of character: wrinkled, weatherbeaten, pleasing features. His eyes are shrewdly perceptive with a hint of mischief, his demeanour sometimes elfish. But beneath whatever exterior Sandy cares to present to the outside world, there is an inner man with a warm heart and a far from bitter acceptance of his lot in the world.
>
> Beyond his toothless roars of laughter there lurks a true survivor.[22]

The description is heavy with presuppositions (such as the expectation that Sandy's 'lot in the world' – being a Traveller? – should make him 'bitter'), as well as references to departures from the unspoken norm (like the implication that a 'tatty' bonnet should be discarded, not worn), in spite of which deviations, or so the commentator seems to imply, Sandy has managed to survive and remain cheerful to boot. Elsewhere, Sandy is described as wearing a 'pinstriped jacket with large lapels, suede shoes and a long navy-coloured greatcoat: better dressed than a banker and more interesting' (p.94). The outfit is predominantly interesting because Sandy is not a banker, and because the idea of a Traveller banker is itself presented as incongruous. To borrow a phrase from Edward Said, the Travellers here emerge as 'dislocations' in the dominant discourse, which takes itself for granted and does not speak its own name.[23]

Anthropological studies often include information that is not volunteered by their subjects because it is potentially embarrassing or damaging. Sharon Gmelch comments: 'Nan never mentioned drinking herself during our many conversations, and for long stretches of time she probably didn't. But Galway Travellers who knew them remember both Mick and Nan as "fond of the drink"' (p.138). Roger Leitch mentions in his introduction to *The Book of Sandy Stewart* that, 'Yes, he may enjoy a bottle of wine but he is not alone in that respect' (p.xii); several of the entries in Leitch's notebook (attached to the volume as an appendix) mention Sandy being 'half-cut' or having 'partaken' of 'sherry' or '*peeve*' (pp.94; 95) in no small measure. My argument here is not that such observations are untrue or irrelevant, but rather that the details included in the life narrative are controlled by the mediator rather than the Traveller, who is what Thomas Couser calls a 'vulnerable subject' – 'vulnerable to the writer's domination, in part because ... [she is] among "those who do not write"'.[24]

Nan Joyce, Sean Maher, Pecker Dunne, William Cauley and the writers in the collections published by various community projects, have more control over their own life stories, in that they can decide what information to include and what to omit. At the same time, each of these writers, too, faces the problem of how to represent her- or himself as both an individual and a member of a marginalized and often stereotyped community. In relation to Nan Donohoe, Sharon Gmelch points out that '[w]hile no individual can fully represent an entire culture, Nan's life is not atypical. Most of what happened to Nan – the many births and marital disputes, the alternating periods of travel and settlement, her emigration to England and experiences with settled people – is typical of Travellers' (p.18). By comparison, the *Moving Stories* written by the Southwark Traveller Women's Group are emphatically introduced as not 'typical':

> In our search as readers to understand minorities within our society we sometimes read accounts where the subjects of the book have become the objects of research which also isolates the subjects [*sic*] being in relation to others. Accounts like these then become more a reflection of the author's social theories than a revelation of the lives we are trying to understand. This book does not treat Travellers as material for research. ... The Traveller Women's Group have written a collection of subjective, individual accounts about experiences they have had in relation to their past and present. They do not represent their culture, they write in relation to it and have given us ... 'the chance to stop being strangers to each other'.[25]

At the same time, however, according to the same introduction, the book provides 'an important insight into the experience of being on the margins of a very hostile society', allowing 'us' to see that society 'through Travellers' eyes',[26] thereby drawing a line between the book's subjects and the book's target audience. The titles of these collections – *Moving Stories: Traveller Women Write*, and *Travellers: A Way of Life* – reinforce the suggestion that these stories are representative of how the Travellers as a group experience life. The very strategies that are meant to reduce the marginal status of a minority group often have the opposite effect, merely by drawing attention to the otherness of that group.

DEFENSIVENESS AND DIALOGISM

For most Travellers, then, '[h]olding their ethnic identity without experiencing discrimination is extremely difficult'.[27] It may be the realization of this conundrum that makes some Travellers reluctant or hesitant to resort to any kind of generalized definition of what it means to be a Traveller. In September 2002, some weeks after Irish-American Traveller Madelyne Gorman Toogood made the national headlines, she was interviewed on CNN by Gary Tuchman, who asked her the following question: 'Now you were alluding to the fact that you are an Irish Traveller. ... Can you explain, first of all: What is an Irish Traveller? This is an important point to tell our viewers.'[28] Toogood's ethnicity had been made much of in the media – 'a self-contained, anachronistic universe', *Time* magazine had called the world of the Travellers[29] – and her response is revealing: 'I said before it's hard to explain – it's hard to explain what you are. To me, an Irish

Traveller is me ... but that's just a small part of me.'[30] In other words, Toogood is anxious to stress that she is an individual rather than a stereotype, and to translate the general back into the particular. The Travellers' resistance to metaphor, and to being represented as anything other than themselves, is perhaps best conveyed by a poem written by Bernard Power, published in an anthology of verse by and about Travellers. The poem is entitled 'Travellers', and both the first and the last stanza proclaim:

> Travellers are Travellers for all eternity.
> Travellers were Travellers in ancient history.
> Travellers, I would say it world wide.
> Travellers are Travellers I will say it with pride.[31]

In their life stories, Travellers often comment defensively on the way in which they are unfairly typecast by the settled community. Kit Gaffey, one of the contributors to *Moving Stories*, writes in one of her poems (which, she emphasizes, are not just about Travellers): 'People think we're stupid / And thick in the head – / But can't we make a living / And keep us all well fed?'[32] Traveller life stories are often dialogic in that they contain an awareness of, and a response to, the reputation of Travellers in the settled community, for example, the widely held opinion that they are dishonest, sexually promiscuous or given to excessive drinking. When Nan Donohoe talks about her father, a chimney sweep, she volunteers the information that the farmers 'trusted him; they'd leave the whole house under him' (p.32). Nan Joyce also mentions that, in the past, 'we were trusted', but that 'today people are told to be afeared of the travellers' (p.3). Often the denial of a stereotype is cast in the form of a generalized abstraction similar to the stereotype that is being denied ('Travellers always ...', 'Travellers never ...'). Betsy Whyte, angered by the stereotype that all Travellers are thieves, explains that honesty was essential when working on a farm, and 'any traveller who broke this code was not allowed to stay on the encampment'.[33] Chrissie Ward expresses the generalization that, in the past, Travellers 'never bored theirself with drinkin'', that there was 'wan night's drink out of a year' and that was Christmas eve.[34] Johnny Collins maintains that life in the old days in a tent was healthier, and that 'ya had no sickness or ailments or anythin' like that'.[35] Such bold statements are subsequently often contradicted or modified by examples from actual lived reality.[36]

Many Travellers are self-consciously aware of being perceived by settled people as dirty, and devise strategies of dealing with the issue that carefully negotiate between acknowledging varying standards of cleanliness and emphasizing that Travellers are no less aware of the importance of hygiene than settled people. Nan Joyce remarks early on in her narrative that

> Mother and Father had this thing for cleanness. Even though we only had an old wagon or tents in the summer everything had to be shining. The mugs might be washed perfectly clean but still a kettle of water would be boiled and thrown over them before Father would drink the tea. Mother was always bathing us and washing our hair. (p.4)

Brigid Ward writes: 'Traveller children are the same as settled children. They might not be as clean as settled children, because they don't have bathrooms, if they are living on sites. Their clothes might not be as clean as settled children's but their skin is completely clean.'[37] The Traveller child who claims that he 'wouldn't like to be a buffer, they think they're cleaner',[38] simultaneously expresses awareness, criticism and denial of the negative stereotype in his statement. Such explicit or implicit denials in themselves often inadvertently perpetuate the prejudice by invoking it. In *The Yellow on the Broom*, Betsy Whyte deals with the stereotype by explaining a philosophical difference between Travellers' and settled people's perceptions of dirt: 'The earth to us was not dirt. How could it be dirt? Everyone, everywhere, kings and queens as well, depended on the earth for almost everything that they ate. If the earth is dirty, then everyone must have dirty insides. It will not harm anyone's outside either' (p.166). Mud is not dirt, she argues in *Red Rowans*: to Travelling people, 'dirt was anything that issued from the human body. A really dirty man or woman was an unchaste one' (p.67).

Nan Joyce eventually drops her defensiveness, and rather than denying the presence of dirt, she points to the degrading conditions that are the cause of it.

> I used to sit down and cry when I couldn't keep the children clean. All the Travelling women were the same. I wasn't special. When it rained the mud would come in like a river and when you'd wash the children they'd fall into it. There was no way of keeping a dry blanket or a clean towel, no matter how hard you tried you couldn't keep them clean. (p.69)

The admission of defeat is more painful because of her awareness of how Travellers are perceived in the settled world. However, the recognition of the underlying causes of those conditions is also the beginning of her activism to better those conditions. The camp site at

Tallaght where she lived for a while 'was a lovely place and we used to try and keep it tidy but when you have no bin collection the dirt piles up' (p.99). In this scenario it is not the Travellers who are responsible for the dirt, but the city Corporation. The activist response to the stereotypical, 'look at how the dirty tinkers live' is, 'look at how they make us live'. In the 1991 television documentary *Travelling People*, Nan Joyce says: 'The conditions here are really awful because the things you would find in the third world you would find in here, like children with chest infections, gastro-enteritis, diarrhoea and kidney infections. ... And it's just because they're Traveller children they're allowed to live like that.'[39]

Artelia Court writes that '[t]he venerable Irish and British popular tradition of the sexual promiscuity of Gypsies and Tinkers flies in the face of all reliable accounts of their actual practices'.[40] Many Traveller narratives mention the importance of modesty in dress and behaviour for women, and point out that Travellers are 'shy' and keep their children in the dark about the facts of life. In a scene described by Betsy Whyte in *Red Rowans*, all the men walk away, 'some of the young ones with red faces', when a visiting non-Traveller woman sits by the fire with her legs apart and her dress above her knees (p.67). Pecker Dunne also concedes that pregnancy and childbirth were conversational 'no-go areas',[41] and Ellie Carr (born in 1912) maintains that her husband did not know about a new baby until a fortnight before it was born, and 'divil a man doctor ever seen my belly!'[42] However, because of their reluctance to discuss such matters, it is not always clear from their stories to what extent Travellers are aware of their general reputation for promiscuity.[43] An incident from her youth related by Betsy Whyte in *Red Rowans*, when she mischievously (and jokingly) told her mother in front of some non-Traveller farm workers that she was raped by the young man (her future husband) with whom she had been working in a field, suggests an awareness of the stereotype. Her mother, not fooled, invited the blushing young man to have a cup of tea, at which point Betsy's mischief paid off:

> I did hear murmurings from the non-travellers and one woman say, 'Ee, isn't that awful? Fancy giving him tea and him after raping her lassie'.
>
> They thought so little of us that I felt a strange delight in making myself even worse than they thought. (p.33)

Most Travellers do not have Betsy Whyte's self-confidence or sense of humour about the issue and avoid referring to it altogether.

SELF-INVENTION AND ACTIVISM

Many Travellers mention that they were fond of watching movies (particularly before the widespread introduction of television), and in their narratives they often borrow the imagery of American Westerns, which were particular favourites,[44] to position themselves historically and imagine themselves as victors and survivors, partly because these movies feature a familiar infrastructure of horses, wagons and tents, but also because they provide a conflict model with which Travellers can identify. John Ward recalls his grandfather's days at the time of the First World War, before Travellers lived in wagons: 'They could build tents – probably seen some Indian at it in a film, a silent film, that's how they learned it.'[45] Nan Joyce remembers a man who came to take care of her and the other children every evening when her mother was in prison: 'He'd get back on his horse then and ride into Portadown, it was like a cowboy movie with him riding into the sunset!' (p.49). When she travelled in Northern Ireland during the worst time of the Troubles, she says she got used to the bullets and riots because it was 'like seeing a cowboy picture' (p.76).

Cowboy imagery is also part of the language of activism against being 'shifted' or evicted from unofficial sites and the fight for better living conditions, which demanded rhetorical forms of self-invention that turned Travellers from downtrodden victims into activist heroes. In Dublin, conflicts between Travellers and the settled population came to a head in 1963, as the Dublin Corporation attempted to clamp down on the 'itinerant problem'. Nan Joyce recalls a scene at Tallaght when a crowd of settled people decided they wanted to get the Travellers out of their neighbourhood: 'Some of them came up – ordinary people not guards – and gave us forty-eight hours to get out. It was like something from a cowboy movie, and yet this was Ireland, a Catholic country, a great Christian country for years and years' (p.100). Travellers were aided in their resistance by Grattan Puxon, a young English journalist, who organized the Itinerant Action Group and helped Irish Travellers formulate their objectives. At the time, both Nan Donohoe and Nan Joyce camped at Cherry Orchard, in the Ballyfermot area of greater Dublin. Nan Joyce describes the conditions in the makeshift huts on the muddy, rat-infested field as awful. Nan Donohoe outlines what happened: 'Me brother Joe, Grattan Puxon and his wife, the students from Trinity College, and the Travellers – we all stood up against the Corporation and the guards. There were some bad fights out in Cherry Orchard; the students and

Travellers held on to the wagons and wouldn't let the Corporation in' (p.157). Grattan Puxon describes the Traveller resistance to the evictions in his pamphlet 'We Demand Justice':

> The high up officials looked from one to another as the travellers put forward their demands. They had never heard of travellers speak up for themselves before. The head man grew red in the face and banged the desk with his fist. 'You have no right to come into our land. We will give you nothing' he shouted. The men matched his anger and shouted back, 'We have a right to live'. Then they left the hall and galloped their horses furiously back to the camp to spread the news of how they had been received.[46]

Puxon's cowboy movie rhetoric ties in with his historical take on the origin of Travellers as the aboriginal occupants of the land, which 'had once belonged to us, the free wanderers of thousands of years ago'.[47] In this scenario, the Travellers are tacitly equated with the Native Americans, displaced from their natural habitat by settlers who claimed the land as property for themselves.

AMBIGUITY AND SELF-REFLECTION

Like Native Americans, and like recently arrived immigrants in a new country, Travellers form a minority culture within a dominant culture, struggling to hold on to their own ethnicity while experiencing pressure to adapt to, and blend in with, the majority culture. Characterizing the tone of recent immigrant writing as 'dialogic and self-reflexive', Azade Seyhan argues that such writing 'registers its distance from social and cultural norms by questioning the logic of the traditions it has inherited as well as those it is subjected to in the new world'. The dialogic nature of these texts manifests itself as 'a conversation between opposing voices or as conflicting self-perceptions of ethnic groups. ... Thus, the narrator is caught in an ambiguous, self-ironic discourse of guilt, doubt, conflicting loyalties or preferences.'[48]

The self-scrutinizing aspect of many Traveller life stories reflects these characteristics, a symptom of which is a slippage within the narrative between insider and outsider perspectives, between 'them' and 'us'. In the kind of life writing that serves as a corrective to stereotypes, the writer develops a sense of self 'by taking the perspective of important others'.[49] Sean Maher's narrator, for example, rhetorically positions himself somewhere in between the world of Travellers and that of settled people: 'We were strange people, with strange customs, but always loyal to each other. No outsider ever meant anything to us' (p.17). Sean is fascinated – some might say obsessed – with Traveller culture, and ready to defend its difference: 'We are different, not by creed or colour but by an indefinable something with which settled people have not come to terms' (p.122). At the same time, he asks a friend, 'What is ever any good on the road? ... Nothing. ... This is not life; this is not a fit existence for even a dog, let alone a human being' (p.156). Betsy Whyte begins *The Yellow on the Broom* with a conversation in which her mother explains Traveller customs to a young woman named Mary, who is not a Traveller by origin: 'She had been cooped in the mill for five years and the fresh air and outside life since she married Johnnie had agreed with her. But she was a bit befuddled with some of our strange customs' (p.1). Traveller narratives display an intense awareness of difference, which manifests itself in this need to explain, justify, defend or sometimes denounce the Travelling life.

When describing the degrading conditions in which they were forced to live, and the attendant psychological pressures, some Travellers deal with the shame and humiliation by denying their own abjection and projecting their self-loathing onto their non-Traveller neighbours. Nan and Mick Donohoe shared a house in Birmingham with a number of other immigrant families. Nan lived in a state of fear – of Mick, but also of the other families in the house: 'I'd heard that the Indians would put a knife into you' (p.168). But it was not the Indians who wielded knives. On one occasion, Mick stabbed Nan during a domestic dispute, while an Indian neighbour tried to intervene; on another, Nan stabbed an Indian matriarch who tried to force her out of the communal kitchen: 'I never meant it. ... I'd never attack anyone with a knife' (p.169). In *My Life on the Road*, Nan Joyce describes the similar living conditions in what she calls the 'slummy place' in Glasgow where she moved with her husband shortly after her marriage, by initially adopting the exclusive third person plural: 'each landing had about five rooms off it, with a poor family in each one. Some of them were Irish, not travellers, and some were poor Scotch people. The way they were living was disgraceful.' In the next sentence, 'they' slips into general 'you': 'There was no bath and you had to wait in a queue for the toilet, there was only one little cooker in the kitchen and you'd wait in line for one woman to boil her dinner before you'd have your turn.' When she continues, 'you' becomes 'I', but only in denial: 'I used to sit at the open door, I couldn't bear to look at this place we were living in' (p.63).

Many Traveller life stories are characterized by different types of ambiguity and doubleness, as the narrator is split between conflicting preferences and emotions. The strain of negotiating between a minority culture and a dominant culture is doubtless one of the causes of this, as it is in immigrant writing. But traditionally, Traveller existence was a life of uncertainty. Travellers often lived from hand to mouth, generally making only enough money to have a meal at the end of the day. Long-term planning was rare, and money was almost never saved. The travelling lifestyle meant that children's schooling was frequently erratic. Often the uncertainty was not of the Travellers' own choosing, as they were shifted from place to place by the local authorities against their will, making long-term planning an impossibility. The combination of these factors makes many Travellers profoundly split within themselves, proud of their heritage and of what they have learned to call their ethnicity, but never entirely satisfied with the life they are leading.

Many Travellers are torn between the freedoms of life on the road and the relative stability of a settled existence.[50] For most of her travelling life, Nan Donohoe wanted a house because life on the road, in a bad caravan or a tent, was very hard. However, once she had her council house she felt that '[y]ou're never free in a house, you're in prison. You're always trying to keep everyone happy' (p.203). Sean Maher was troubled throughout his early life by ambiguous feelings: 'As a very young lad I had a dislike for the road and yet again a liking for it' (p.9). Distressed by his father's drinking, all he wanted was to go to school and become a priest. When the family moved into a house, they found it hard to adjust to living indoors, and found the house 'very depressing' (p.13). Back on the road, however, Sean tells his mother, 'I wish we could live in a house again, like other people do; I bet we would be happy then' (p.66). In the end he confesses to a friend, 'I don't like the road, and yet I feel chained to it in a mysterious kind of way' (p.141). A Traveller child interviewed for the Limerick research project also seems ambivalent:

> I: Do you like living in a caravan?
>
> C: No, not really, getting a house soon, in December.
>
> I: Are you looking forward to that?
>
> C: No, not really.[51]

Many of the accounts in *Moving Stories* mention conflicts about accommodation. Margaret McDonagh grew up in a house at her mother's instigation, although her father hated it: 'He was fed up with having nobody to chat to. He said you'd go mad in this house.'[52] McDonagh describes similar arguments in her own marriage: 'When we got a house I was all delighted[,] I couldn't wait to move in but my husband wasn't sure. We got the furniture and everything so on the day we were to move in my husband changed his mind. He said he couldn't do it. We had a big row over this.'[53]

REFLECTION AND EVALUATION

Like most autobiographies, Traveller life stories end with statements of reflection and evaluation. Betsy Whyte claims to have had caring parents and a gentle husband, and she was a strong-willed and intelligent woman who went her own way. Happily settled in Montrose, she ends the second volume of her autobiography with an expression of contentment: 'Of course the old restless itch to wander returns almost every year when the yellow appears on the broom, but it does not really distress me any more. I now have many friends amongst non-travellers and I am pleased that we settled in this part of Scotland' (p.211). Mixed feelings are a more common sentiment, however. Nan Donohoe, at the end of her story, says she would choose the travelling life again, but 'I'd go a different way. I'd like to be a bit better off and more happier. I wasn't so happy. And I wouldn't go with the cruelty I went through' (pp.221–2). Like Nan, what Sean Maher hates about the road is the 'hardship, misery, drunkenness, brawling and sheer cruelty' (p.141). What Nan Donohoe describes, however, is ultimately more a metaphysical condition than a matter of physical circumstances – a condition of having no agency and being constantly at the mercy of forces beyond one's control, be they her abusive husband or the state or local authorities: 'I was always coming and going. I never was really settled. No matter what I used to have or what I'd do, I never could say, "Well, I'm here now and I'm settled"' (p.222). Nan Joyce describes the general feeling that is expressed in many Traveller life stories: 'We were always going: it was like following an elusive dream of some kind, as if you were looking for something and you didn't know what it was' (p.68).

One effect of a long history of harassment is that the Travellers in these stories are psychologically unsettled, feel *unheimlich*, and wish for a sense of belonging, regardless of whether they choose to live in a house or on the road. At the same time, Travellers may have a culturally distinctive way of experiencing subjectivity. Writing about the culture of mobility in early modern England, Patricia Fumerton suggests 'a new notion of "low" subjectivity – economic, social, psychological, and metonymic – that escaped the "bound" and made a home of homelessness'.[54] She argues that 'unsettledness' as a condition of physical displacement results in a distinctive perception of the self: 'the most extreme form of unsettledness (extensive physical displacement) can ... be seen as being composed of dispersed, serial "selves" – variously defined occupationally, relationally, or spatially'.[55] Máirín Kenny also argues that Irish Travellers may have a 'nomadic mindset, indicating an ever-present sense of being on the move'.[56]

Writing one's life story – taking control of one's own narrative, inventing oneself poetically, and imagining oneself into the future – is a step towards psychological homecoming. While life writing is ostensibly aimed at influencing the attitude of a settled audience, it may therefore effect greater changes in the writers themselves. Marianne Gullestad argues that life writing by immigrants that challenges an imposed self-image aims at creating 'a *sustainable self-image*, a concept that implies the possession of self-respect and dignity over time, in spite of challenges and attacks'.[57] Nan Joyce ends her life story in a similar vein: 'We are a different people but what we want most of all is a better understanding with the settled people: that we should understand them and that they should understand us – the Travelling people' (p.118). Irish Travellers want to be acknowledged as being both Irish and different. The discussion in the preceding chapters, of their representation in narratives produced by and for the settled world, serves as an indication of why attaining that goal remains such an uphill struggle.

NOTES

1. Delaney, 'Representations of the Travellers', p.65.
2. Sidonie Smith, *A Poetics of Women's Autobiography: Marginality and the Fictions of Self-Representation* (Bloomington and Indianapolis: Indiana University Press, 1987), p.8.
3. Dyer, *The Matter of Images*, p.141.
4. Marianne Gullestad, 'Tales of Consent and Descent: Life Writing as a Fight against an Imposed Self-Image', in Paul John Eakin (ed.), *The Ethics of Life Writing* (Ithaca, NY: Cornell University Press, 2004), p.216.
5. Whyte sent the material for her first book piecemeal, over a period of months, to her publisher, Ian Gould of W. and R. Chambers, who edited and reorganized the episodes. She had great difficulty in finishing the second volume, however, and according to ballad singer and traveller Sheila Stewart (author of *Queen Amang the Heather*), some of the material was recorded on tape, and subsequently transcribed. Stewart also suggests that Whyte was discouraged from including distressing details about her personal life and her marriage in the narrative (personal conversation with Sheila Stewart, 3 October 2007).

6. Sinéad Ní Shuinéar, 'Othering the Irish (Travellers)', in Ronit Lentin and Robbie McVeigh (eds), *Racism and Anti-Racism in Ireland* (Belfast: Beyond the Pale, 2002), p.188.
7. Betsy Whyte, *Red Rowans and Wild Honey* (1990; Edinburgh: Birlinn, 2002), p.vi. All subsequent page references in the text are to this edition.
8. John D. Niles, *Homo Narrans: The Poetics and Anthropology of Oral Literature* (Philadelphia, PA: University of Pennsylvania Press, 1999), p.165.
9. Sheila Stewart, *Queen Amang the Heather: The Life of Belle Stewart* (Edinburgh: Birlinn, 2006), p.viii.
10. Paul Delaney, 'Stories from Below: Sean Maher and Nan Joyce', *Studies*, 93, 372 (2004), p.465.
11. William C. Spengemann, *The Forms of Autobiography: Episodes in the History of a Literary Genre* (New Haven, CT and London: Yale University Press, 1980), p.xvi.
12. Paul Noonan, 'Pathologisation and Resistance: Travellers, Nomadism and the State', in Paul Hainsworth (ed.), *Divided Society: Ethnic Minorities and Racism in Northern Ireland* (London: Pluto Press, 1998), p.153.
13. Puxon, 'We Demand Justice', p.1/9.
14. Michael O'Reilly and Máirín Kenny (eds), *Black Stones Around the Green Shamrock: A Poetry Anthology By and About Travellers* (Blackrock: Blackrock Teachers Centre, 1994), p.30.
15. Paddy McDonagh, 'Travellers Will Always Keep Their Distinct Culture', *Irish Times*, 28 February 2001. Accessed 28 February 2001: http://www.ireland.com/newspaper/ireland/2001/0228/ct3.htm
16. Cauley, *The Candlelight Painter*, p.9.
17. Eleanor Gormally, *Whiddin to the Gauras/Talking to Our Own: Traveller Researchers Talk to Limerick Traveller Children* (Dublin: Veritas, 2005), pp.119–20.
18. Dunne, *Parley-Poet and Chanter*, pp.36–7.
19. Gearóid Ó Riain (ed.), *Traveller Ways Traveller Words* (Dublin: Pavee Point Publications, 1992), p.196.
20. Ibid., p.75.
21. Thomas Couser, *Vulnerable Subjects: Ethics and Life Writing* (Ithaca, NY: Cornell University Press, 2004), pp.31–2.
22. Roger Leitch (ed.), *The Book of Sandy Stewart* (Edinburgh: Scottish Academic Press, 1988), pp.xi–xii. All subsequent page references in the text are to this edition.
23. Quoted in Russell Ferguson, 'Introduction', in Russell Ferguson, Martha Gever, Trinh Minha and Cornel West (eds), *Out There: Marginalization and Contemporary Cultures* (Cambridge, MA: MIT Press, 1990), p.11.
24. Couser, *Vulnerable Subjects*, p.37.
25. Southwark Traveller Women's Group, *Moving Stories: Traveller Women Write* (London: Traveller Education Team, 1992), p.7.
26. Ibid., p.6.
27. Gormally, *Whiddin to the Gauras*, p.120.
28. Gary Tuchman, 'Mom: "No Excuse" for Striking Child', *CNN Access*, 23 September 2002. Accessed 30 March 2003: http://www.cnn.com/2002/US/Midwest/09/23/tuchman.toogood.cnna
29. Amanda Ripley, 'Unwelcome Exposure', *Time*, 7 October 2002, p.10.
30. Tuchman, 'Mom'.
31. O'Reilly and Kenny, *Black Stones*, p.27.
32. Southwark Traveller Women's Group, *Moving Stories*, p.86.
33. Betsy Whyte, *The Yellow on the Broom: The Early Days of a Traveller Woman* (Edinburgh: W. and R. Chambers, 1979), p.95. All subsequent page references in the text are to this edition.
34. Gearóid O Riain, *Traveller Ways*, p.54.
35. Ibid., p.34.
36. Delaney, in 'Stories from Below', argues that such internal narrative discrepancies are evidence of the orality of Traveller culture, which places 'a different emphasis on patterns of plausibility and consistency' (p.467).
37. Clondalkin Travellers Development Group, *Travellers: A Way of Life* (Dublin: Community Arts, 1993), p.38.
38. Gormally, *Whiddin to the Gauras*, p.113.

39. Michael Quinn (dir.), *Travelling People*, prod. Simon Wood (Belfast: Northern Visions, 1991).
40. Court, *Puck of the Droms*, p.35.
41. Dunne, *Parley-Poet and Chanter*, p.46.
42. Ó Riain, *Traveller Ways*, p.85.
43. Examples of the prejudice abound. Delaney, in 'Representations of the Travellers', mentions the widespread late-Victorian suspicion that Travellers indulged in 'adultery, promiscuity, and wife-swapping' (p.54). The stereotype persists in many contemporary works of fiction which feature Travellers as characters.
44. In *Nan*, Gmelch records that, when she was living among Travellers, '[y]oung adults and teenagers often departed to see a film, usually a Western, which they later told in meticulous detail' (p.186). Speaking from personal experience, William Cauley states in *The Candlelight Painter* that, 'like many Travellers I've always been fond of Westerns. ... The kids love them too because of the horses and all the action' (p.104).
45. Clondalkin Travellers Development Group, *Travellers*, p.42.
46. Puxon, 'We Demand Justice', p.3/9.
47. Ibid.
48. Azade Seyhan, 'Ethnic Selves/Ethnic Signs: Invention of Self, Space, and Genealogy in Immigrant Writing', in E. Valentine Daniel and Jeffrey M. Peck (eds), *Culture/Contexture: Explorations in Anthropology and Literary Studies* (Berkeley, CA: University of California Press, 1996), p.186.
49. Gullestad, 'Tales of Consent', p.218.
50. Some Travellers regard the expression 'settled Traveller' as an oxymoron. A Traveller who lives in a house is still a Traveller and hence not 'settled'.
51. Gormally, *Whiddin to the Gauras*, p.77.
52. Southwark Traveller Women's Group, *Moving Stories*, p.64.
53. Ibid., pp.66–7.
54. Fumerton, *Unsettled*, p.4.
55. Ibid., p.51.
56. Kenny, 'Final Thoughts', p.184.
57. Gullestad, 'Tales of Consent', p.218.

Conclusion

In the century that has passed since Lady Gregory interviewed her local Galway informants about their impressions of the 'Wandering Tribe', remarkably little has changed in the way the Travellers are perceived in the non-Traveller community, despite official and unofficial efforts at consciousness-raising and a growing outspokenness by Travellers themselves. Hostility towards Travellers among the population at large today is higher than it has been in many years, discrimination in the areas of education, employment and housing is still prevalent, and in 2006 the number of Traveller families living without facilities by the side of the road increased for the first time in a decade. Sinéad Ní Shuinéar rightly remarks that 'it remains acceptable ... to say things about Travellers one would not dream of saying in relation to any other group'.[1] Perhaps unsurprisingly, therefore, fictional representations of the Travellers – in literature, film and television shows – have also remained remarkably static. In this regard, Michael Hayes concludes that 'the core intent and spirit of the "Othering" process has remained virtually the same into the present day. It is a process which has constructed an identity for Travelling people, one that situates Travellers within the non-Traveller community's own terms of reference.'[2] Too often, the voices of Travellers are still occluded, but the sedentary writers and film makers who speak for them have exchanged the more blatant language of romanticization and vilification that used to prevail in the past for what at times almost resembles an attempt at ventriloquism.

Such ventriloquizing is evident, for example, in two novels written around the turn of the millennium: *Tribe* (1999) by John F. McDonald, and *Paveewhack* (2001) by Peter Brady. The first-person narratives of both novels are related in stream-of-consciousness fashion by a Traveller character who speaks non-standard English heavily interlaced with Cant words and phrases. The deliberate use of Shelta or Cant also evident in recent Traveller autobiographies may in part have a 'political' motive, in that its unfamiliarity affirms the community's cultural difference from the settled world; alternatively, it may be a defensive move that reflects 'the huge assimilative pressure' felt by the minority culture within Irish society and a sense that the knowledge and use of Cant within the Traveller community is gradually diminishing.[3] As such publications have led to a growing awareness of Cant in the sedentary world, some Travellers have begun to notice outsiders using Cant words when addressing Travellers; many find the experience discomforting, especially when the words are uttered by those perceived as hostile to their community, since Travellers regard the use of their language as an invasion and an appropriation of their culture. Neither McDonald nor Brady is a Traveller, and each author introduces Cant in a context that suggests that both the Travellers and their language are on the road to extinction. John McDonald's varied career, according to information on his novel's dust-jacket, has included 'working with Travelling People', while Peter Brady, a school administrator, was inspired to write his book when he heard a Traveller speaking Cant on the Late Late Show: 'I was mesmerised by it. I thought it was very colourful, it was Chaucerian in its richness and earthiness.'[4] Brady relied heavily on first-person accounts in the Pavee Point publication *Traveller Ways Traveller Words* to construct a credible voice for his narrator, but also claims that *Paveewhack* is not actually written in Cant but in 'my version of a dialect that Travellers might use'.[5]

The narrator of John McDonald's *Tribe*, Owen McBride, is the son of Irish Travellers, a community he describes as 'not really my people any more',[6] who is torn between settling down in a Manchester council flat with his non-Traveller girlfriend, a software programmer, and spending his days and nights with a group of assorted Travelling people of Irish, Romani, Mongolian and Cajun descent living on a halting site by the Manchester Ship Canal, who train horses and go in for bare-knuckle fighting. The air around them is 'full of Shelta and Cant and Gamon [*sic*] and Romany' (p.23), all of which are reflected in Owen's own idiolect. Owen experiences pressure from both outside and inside the Traveller community to become part of mainstream society. When a friend asks him if he is still 'fart-arsing about with them fucking Tinkers', he reminds him, 'I *am* a fucking Tinker, and so are you' (p.10). His girlfriend also thinks it is 'time you got away from those people' (p.15), whom she later identifies as 'those filthy Tinkers' (p.37). Owen keeps going back because, in his words, 'you can take the man out of the Tinker but you can't take the Tinker out of the man' (p.23). At the same time, he often feels slighted in his girlfriend's 'Gorgio' world of fancy restaurants, where 'the cunts can somehow tell I'm a Tinker' (p.38).

Owen is unsure what he wants to do or be in his life, and lacks restraint in his relations with women, his attitude towards violence, his use of obscene language and his intake of alcohol. In the overall context of the book, his prevarication and his ambivalent tinker/gorgio (or 'buffer') status are used by McDonald as an expression of his alienated condition in a post-modern, post-industrial world, more so than his ethnic affiliation:

> Life's such a confusing cunt of a thing altogether. Especially if you can read and write. And it's all shite like the single European currency and shrinking international markets and commodities flying up and down and fucking sideways too. Zillions of digital dollars zooming through the air all around us and everybody shiteing on themselves to be a millennium millionaire.
>
> As well as all that every day some new story showing the total lack of any morals amongst the rich and powerful – and the fucking poor as well. (p.8)

At the end of the novel, Owen apparently has his mind made up for him by the forces of global capitalism, as the Traveller camp is suddenly gone one day, removed by the Greater Manchester Council to make way for 'car-parking facilities as part of an overall development of the area for the information technology industry' (p.264), including his girlfriend's company. He is left to contemplate a potential future that includes marriage and a job with his father-in-law: 'Will good triumph over evil or evil over good? And who knows these days which is fucking which?' (p.272).

In Peter Brady's *Paveewhack*, the vanishing past also runs up against the modern present, as a dying Traveller, Jack 'Whack' Joyce, tells his nephew a story he has kept to himself for forty years. The nephew, 'Pecker' Joyce, is a settled Traveller who has completed a third level degree in education and has married a non-traveller fellow schoolteacher. He is proud of his heritage and makes it his project to record the voice of his uncle as he lies in his hospital bed, 'similar to the way the Irish Folklore Commission had done in the 1930s, when the Travellers' folklore was faithfully recorded'.[7] Jack's story focuses on a period of four months in the early 1960s, when he was a boy of 14. His father had just moved the family into a house in Tullamore, a decision resented by Jack, who felt 'too fond of the road and too set in me ways to want to settle in wuth a crowd a stuck up buffshams' (p.13). The story, designed by Peter Brady to shock and reflect the brutal aspects of Traveller life at the time, relates the particular lows and highs of that period in Jack's life, culminating in his incarceration for the murder of the police sergeant who had been responsible for his father's violent death. The uncle uses non-standard English and Cant throughout his story: 'I get bounced round intiv different places then an before I know it one decade borrow another. There's no way they going to forgive ya for killin a shadog, specially a auld magarlach of a sarghint' (p.208). His settled, educated nephew, on the other hand, writes his frame story in standard English: 'What follows is an unabridged version of Whack's tale related to me over the space of three weeks during that dismal summer of 1998' (p.11).

Both *Tribe* and *Paveewhack* present the use of Cant in a context that suggests Traveller culture is dying, not only as a result of the modernization and development of the nation as a whole, but also as a consequence of Travellers' decisions to abandon 'the old ways' in favour of a sedentary existence and a mainstream education. That premise also underlies the American television series 'The Riches', which premiered on the FX Network in the spring of 2007. Central to the show (originally to be named 'Low Life') is a family of Irish-American Travellers, Wayne and Dahlia Malloy and their three children. The series' creator, Dmitry Lipkin, having himself grown up in Louisiana as a Jewish refugee from Russia, was looking for a context in which to write about a family that pretends to be something it is not, when his wife suggested he consider the Irish Travellers, about whom he knew nothing at the time. What attracted him to the idea was that, as he saw it, Travellers are social and cultural outsiders who are a complete mystery to the average American. In the voice-over at the beginning of the series' first episode, Wayne Malloy says, 'We are Irish Travellers. Some call us Gypsies. Others call us thieves. Most people don't know anything about us at all.' Given this ignorance – and even though Eddie Izzard, the series' lead actor, has argued that the show is not about Travellers but about a family that is 'of the Travellers' – the depiction of the Malloys will lead most Americans to assume, as did the reviewer for the *Boston Globe*, that the Travellers are 'a nomadic society of Irish crooks who survive by conning law-abiding Americans'.[8]

On the run from their Traveller 'clan' after resisting an arranged marriage for their teenage daughter and stealing the patriarch's hoard of cash, the Malloys seek for a way to go under cover, which is when Wayne decides, on the spur of the moment, literally to 'steal the American dream' by appropriating the identities of Doug and Cherien Rich, a well-off couple who are on their way to a new suburban life when they die in a car crash for which the Malloys are partly responsible. Once he has settled his family into the Riches' home in the affluent Eden Falls gated community in Baton Rouge, Louisiana, Wayne cons his way into a position as a lawyer for a real estate developer named Hugh Panetta. Himself no stranger to ruthless and shady business practices, Hugh appreciates what he perceives as his new employee's unorthodox methods: 'You're a sick mother, Doug, and I like that in a liar.' Dahlia, meanwhile, recently released from prison with a newly acquired drug habit, discovers that bored suburban housewives are no strangers to the world of controlled substances.

'The Riches' is all about 'faking it', on multiple levels. As newcomers to the American dream, the Malloys 'are merely the new pretenders in a massive game of social pretend'.[9] Even the fact that both Izzard and Minnie Driver, who plays Dahlia, are British actors pretending to be Irish Americans 'bring[s] a vaguely alien quality to their characters'.[10] While the Malloys argue among themselves about the desirability of sticking with their new life – Wayne, as a 'half buffer' who did not grow up as a Traveller, is more convinced than Dahlia, who is considered 'royalty' in her clan – they also have to contend with Dale Malloy, a dangerously unhinged relative who tracks them down and threatens to expose them, but who, in order to do so, himself has to infiltrate Eden Falls. The show is ironically self-conscious about its many layers of deception; on one occasion, when Dale confronts Wayne in public, he gives his last name as 'Buffer', which makes Wayne roll his eyes in mock outrage. John Leonard sums up what 'The Riches' is really 'about': the show suggests that 'social hierarchies are themselves mimicry, impersonation, and charade; that nothing is as it appears...; that we are surrounded by impostors, subverted by leprechauns, and live in terror that someone will see through the make-believe to who we really are, frauds and fakes'.[11]

At the other end of the spectrum from such metaphorical appropriations are recent attempts to present a more 'authentic' image of the Travellers, often with the intent of raising awareness about their disadvantaged status and of, at least potentially, helping to change their circumstances. Perry Ogden's 2005 film *Pavee Lackeen* (Traveller girl), a low-budget docudrama about a family living in a small caravan on an industrial site in Ringsend, used Travellers as actors to represent characters based to a large extent on themselves. One of the lead roles in Joe Comerford's 1981 film *Traveller* had also been performed by a member of the Travelling community, Judy Donovan, but her character had been 'voiced by, and openly credited to, another actress (Marian Richardson)'.[12] Maeve Connolly argues that the use of dubbing was part of that film's avant-garde concern with issues of performativity, while Kevin Barry has read the strategy as the director's 'exploration of disjunctive cultural identity',[13] but Comerford himself has suggested that the alienating strategies came about precisely as a result of working with performers like Donovan, who themselves were changed by the experience of working as actors in the film.[14] In *Pavee Lackeen*, Winnie Maughan, her sister Rose and her mother Rosie used their own voices, names and living situation in a hyper-realistic, almost narrative-less account of life on the side of a dangerous road, without access to any kind of facilities other than a standpipe – and, eventually, not even that.

Representations of marginal groups always highlight their difference, and calling attention to negative issues associated with Travellers in order to alleviate them may only end up exacerbating them. The film's director – an English photographer who had previously documented Traveller children in a book entitled *Pony Kids* – introduced a number of elements in his film that were meant to be representative of problems within the Traveller community at large, including alcohol abuse, drug use, and petty theft. Using the Maughans as actors provided Ogden with an element of authenticity, but at the same time the director, a non-Traveller, remained in charge of the narrative, at times providing his actors with a script, at other times allowing them to improvise scenes or, essentially, be themselves. Potentially vulnerable subjects, the Maughans were therefore actors in a story of which they themselves were not in full control.

At various times, the family members expressed worries that audiences might think that the film accurately portrayed their own lives. Twelve-year-old Winnie, the 'star' of *Pavee Lackeen*, told interviewers that she wanted people to know that she was not really sniffing petrol in the film, and that the substance in the container was in fact apple juice. Rosie 'mum', too, who is shown in one scene getting drunk with other travellers around a campfire, was at pains to point out later that she was only acting and that she was drinking nothing stronger than water. In the film's improvised scenes, on the other hand, the characters sometimes reveal things about themselves that have implications of which they may not be entirely aware, as when Winnie genuinely worries that stealing might be a sin for which she will go to hell. In an interview in August 2005, shortly after the release of *Pavee Lackeen*, Winnie said that she did not want to get married but was eager to attend college to 'be someone, be something. Like be a teacher or be a dancer.'[15] Reminded of that statement by another interviewer in October of the same year, she claimed, 'I didn't know it was going to be in the paper, I thought it was just messing'.[16] In that conversation, she also maintained she had not known *Pavee Lackeen* would be shown in the cinema: 'I thought it was just a video that he'd give us, not a movie.'[17] In February 2006, Fiachra Gibbons went to see whether anything had improved in the Maughans' lives since the film's release, and concluded that their situation had 'not changed an iota'. The wind was still blowing through a window that had been broken while the Maughans were away at the Venice Film Festival five months earlier, lorries were still rumbling past the caravan, and Winnie was missing a lot of school. Used to being disappointed, Rosie remained philosophical: 'Life's a terrible torture that's sent to try us.'[18]

While Perry Ogden hoped that *Pavee Lackeen* would create 'a bit of a stir' that would lead to an improvement in the Maughans' living conditions,[19] his film does not set out to make any kind of overtly anthropological or political point. A number of recent theatre productions by and/or about Travellers have taken a more activist approach. Charlie O'Neill's play *Rosie and Starwars* was staged in 1997 by Calypso Productions, a company operating from the premise that theatre should be a force for progressive change that challenges injustice and social exclusion, as their main project for the European Year Against Racism. Set in Ennis, the play focuses on the relationship of Seánie 'Starwars' Whelan, whose father is part of a shady consortium of land developers, and Rosie Joyce, a settled Traveller and single mother. It juxtaposes the town's celebration of County Clare's victory in the All Ireland Hurling championship with an attack by a gang related to the developers on an unofficial Traveller halting site. In an article about the work of Calypso Productions, Victor Merriman argues that *Rosie and Starwars* stages a deliberate response to the overwhelmingly negative and pejorative construction of Travellers in texts produced from a bourgeois perspective by asking the question, 'how might ... [the] injurious impact [of such depictions] on travellers' social participation be mitigated or negated?'[20]

A similar sense of political awareness underlies the work for the theatre by Rosaleen McDonagh. A Traveller woman with cerebral palsy who uses a wheelchair, McDonagh holds an M.Phil. in Ethnic and Racial Studies from Trinity College, and ran as a university candidate for the Seanad Eireann in 2000 and 2007 on a platform that included the need for greater Traveller participation and representation in Irish politics. In 2003, she received the Metro Eireann Multimedia award for *The Baby Doll Project*, a one-woman show which she performed based on her own life. Reviewing the show in the *Irish Times*, Stephen Dixon commented, 'McDonagh defies you to see her as a victim. The pitiful details of her early life in and out of institutions and daycare centres are not presented tear-jerkingly but as a necessary prelude to her inevitable politicisation.'[21] Her second play, *John and Josey*, was staged as part of Traveller Focus Week in 2005 and explores the search for acceptance, both in and outside of their own community, of two Traveller characters, one gay, the other a single parent who chooses to live in a council house.

The plays by O'Neill and McDonagh can be seen as what Merriman calls 'cultural intervention[s] within limitations', projects that are overtly pedagogical and political in terms of the points they make, and thereby run the risk of being 'marginalized on similar grounds to those advanced as a rationale for travellers' position on the margins of Irish society'.[22] From an artistic perspective there are drawbacks to productions that are overly emphatic in the way they present their message, as theatre audiences tend to be wary of performances that smack of didacticism or 'agitprop'. While the impact of these plays has been modest, McDonagh's work in particular, despite its defiance that might by some be perceived as defensiveness, is important because it speaks directly from within the Traveller experience, unmediated by outside voices which still, too often, set the agenda for Travellers and presume to speak on their behalf.

The last word of this book should therefore belong to a Traveller. In a letter to the *Irish Times* of 2 March 2007, Patrick Nevin, a Traveller from Dublin, drew attention to the fact that organizations representing Travellers and set up to create leaders within the community have mostly remained in the control of non-Travellers, and are therefore helping to perpetuate a problem they were initially created to solve. For Travellers to speak on their own behalf requires both support and encouragement from the settled community, and the assumption of leadership roles by Travellers themselves. Such an initiative has long-term implications for the representation of Travellers in fiction as well as in reality. Nevin concludes: 'Until this imbalance is addressed settled people will continue to create an imaginary voice for Travellers while the Traveller voice is muffled'.

NOTES

1. Ní Shuinéar, 'History as Dialogue, p.71.
2. Hayes, *Irish Travellers*, p.113.
3. Ibid., pp.246–7.
4. C. McB., 'Peter Brady – Mushes, Helms, and a Bit of Genre-Jumping', interview with Peter Brady, *Galway Advertiser*, 2 May 2002. Accessed 22 June 2007: http://www.galwayadvertiser.ie/dws/story.tpl?inc=2002/05/02/entertainment/25204.html
5. Ibid.
6. John F. McDonald, *Tribe* (Dublin: Wolfhound Press, 1999), p.8. All subsequent page references in the text are to this edition.
7. Peter Brady, *Paveewhack* (Dublin: New Island Books, 2001), p.11. All subsequent page references in the text are to this edition.
8. Matthew Gilbert, 'Stealing the American Dream Is a Family Affair', *Boston Globe*, 12 March 2007. Accessed 22 June 2007: http://www.boston.com/ae/tv/articles/2007/03/12
9. Ibid.
10. Ibid.
11. John Leonard, 'Suburban Warfare', *New York Magazine*, 12 March 2006. Accessed 22 June 2007: http://www.nymag.com/arts/tv/reviews/28875
12. Connolly, '"A Bit of a Traveller"', p.305.
13. Cited in ibid., p.306.
14. Ibid., p.306.
15. Helen Murray, 'Moving On', *Sunday Tribune*, 21 August 2005, p.11.
16. Róisín Ingle, 'Starring Role in a Trailer', *Irish Times*, 19 October 2005. Accessed 25 October 2005: http://www.ireland.com/newspaper archive.
17. Ibid.
18. Fiachra Gibbons, '"Life's a Terrible Torture That's Sent to Try Us"', *Guardian*, 10 February 2006. Accessed 28 February 2007: http://www.guardian.co.uk/filmandmusic/story/01706139,00.html
19. Ingle, 'Starring Role'.
20. Victor Merriman, 'Songs of Possible Worlds: Nation, Representation and Citizenship in the Work of Calypso Productions', in Eamonn Jordan (ed.), *Theatre Stuff: Critical Essays on Contemporary Irish Theatre* (Dublin: Carysfort Press, 2000), p.285.
21. Stephen Dixon, review of *The Baby Doll Project* by Rosaleen McDonagh, *Irish Times*, 15 January 2003. Accessed 5 September 2004: http://www.ireland.com/newspaper archive.
22. Merriman, 'Songs of Possible Worlds', p.287.

Select Bibliography

Bailey, Nathan, *The New Universal English Dictionary ... To which is Added, a Dictionary of Cant Words*, corrected by Mr Buchanan (London: James Rivington and James Fletcher, 1759).

Baird, Rev. John, *The Scottish Gipsy's Advocate: Being a Short Account of the Gipsies of Kirk-Yetholm, etc.* (Edinburgh: John Lindsay and Co., 1839).

Baker, Margaret, *The Black Cats and the Tinker's Wife* (1923; New York: Dodd, Mead and Co., 1938).

Bancroft, Angus, *Roma and Gypsy-Travellers in Europe: Modernity, Race, Space and Exclusion* (Aldershot and Burlington, VT: Ashgate, 2005).

Barlow, Jane, *Strangers at Lisconnel: A Second Series of Irish Idylls* (1895; Freeport, NY: Books for Libraries Press, 1971).

Beier, A.L., *Masterless Men: The Vagrancy Problem in England 1560–1640* (London and New York: Methuen, 1985).

Borrow, George, *Wild Wales: Its People, Language and Scenery* (1862; London: John Murray, 1923).

Botheroyd, Paul, 'The Years of the Travellers: Tinkers, Tramps and Travellers in Early Twentieth-Century Irish Drama and Society', in Heinz Kosok (ed.), *Studies in Anglo-Irish Literature* (Bonn: Bouvier, 1982), pp.167–75.

Brady, John, *Unholy Ground* (1989; South Royalton, VT: Steerforth, 2002).

Brady, Peter, *Paveewhack* (Dublin: New Island, 2001).

Breathnach, Ciara and Aoife Bhreatnach (eds), *Portraying Irish*

Travellers: Histories and Representations (Newcastle: Cambridge Scholars Press, 2006).
Brittaine, George, *Irishmen and Irishwomen* (1830; Dublin: Richard Moore Tims, 1831).
Brown, Terence, *The Life of W.B. Yeats* (Dublin: Gill and Macmillan, 1999).
Bruen, Ken, *The Killing of the Tinkers* (Dingle, Co. Kerry: Brandon, 2002).
Bulfin, William, *Rambles in Eirinn* (1907; Dublin: Roberts Wholesale Books, n.d.).
Burke, Mary, 'Situating the Emergent Field of Irish Traveller Studies', *Foilsiú*, 4, 1 (2004), pp.5–27.
——, 'Eighteenth-Century European Scholarship and Nineteenth-Century Irish Literature: Synge's *Tinker's Wedding* and the Orientalizing of "Irish Gypsies"', in Betsey Taylor FitzSimon and James H. Murphy (eds), *The Irish Revival Reappraised* (Dublin: Four Courts Press, 2004), pp.205–16.
Cahalan, James M., *The Irish Novel: A Critical History* (Boston, MA: Twayne, 1988).
Carleton, William, *The Works of William Carleton,* vol. 2 (1881; Freeport, NY: Books for Libraries Press, 1970).
Carr, Marina, *Portia Coughlan* (Oldcastle, Co. Meath: Gallery, 1998).
——, *By the Bog of Cats* (Oldcastle, Co. Meath: Gallery, 1998).
Cauley, William, *The Candlelight Painter: The Life and Work of William Cauley, Traveller, Painter and Poet*, transcr. and ed. Mícheál Ó hAodha (Dublin: A. and A. Farmar, 2004).
Chambers, William, *Exploits, Curious Anecdotes, and Sketches of the Most Remarkable Scottish Gypsies or Tinklers. Together with Traits of Their Origin, Character, and Manners* (Edinburgh: William Chambers, 1823).
Cleary, Joe, 'Into Which West? Irish Modernity and the Maternal Supernatural', in Brian Cosgrove (ed.), *Literature and the Supernatural: Essays for the Maynooth Bicentenary* (Blackrock: Columba Press, 1995), pp.147–73.
Clifford, Sigerson, *Travelling Tinkers* (Dublin: Dolmen Press, 1951).
Clondalkin Travellers Development Group, *Travellers: A Way of Life* (Dublin: Community Arts, 1993).
Cohen, Michael, 'The Detective as Other: The Detective *Versus* the Other', in Kathleen Gregory Klein (ed.), *Diversity and Detective Fiction* (Bowling Green, OH: Bowling Green State University Popular Press, 1999), pp.144–57.

Committee for the Reformation of Gipsies in Scotland, *First Report of the Committee for the Reformation of the Gipsies in Scotland* (Edinburgh: Thomas Constable, 1840).

Connolly, Maeve, '"A Bit of a Traveller in Everybody": Traveller Identities in Irish and American Culture', in Diane Negra (ed.), *The Irish in Us: Irishness, Performativity, and Popular Culture* (Durham, NC, and London: Duke University Press, 2006), pp.282–317.

Cottaar, Annemarie, Leo Lucassen and Wim Willems, *Mensen van de reis: woonwagenbewoners en zigeuners in Nederland (1868–1995)* (Zwolle: Waanders, 1995).

Court, Artelia, *Puck of the Droms: The Lives and Literature of the Irish Tinkers* (Berkeley, CA: University of California Press, 1985).

Couser, Thomas, *Vulnerable Subjects: Ethics and Life Writing* (Ithaca, NY: Cornell University Press, 2004).

Crawford, Michael H., 'Genetic Affinities and Origin of the Irish Tinkers', in Elizabeth S. Watts, Francis E. Johnston and Gabriel W. Lasker (eds), *Biosocial Interrelations in Popular Adaptation* (The Hague and Paris: Mouton, 1975), pp.93–103.

Cross, Tom Peete and Clark Harris Slover (eds), *Ancient Irish Tales* (1936; New York: Barnes and Noble, 1969).

De Lint, Charles, *The Harp of the Grey Rose* (Harmondsworth: Puffin, 2004).

Deere, Dicey, *The Irish Manor House Murder* (New York: St Martin's, 2000).

Dekker, Thomas, 'The Wonderfull Yeare. 1603', ed. R.S. Bear. Renascence Editions. Accessed 10 October 2005: http://darkwing.uoregon.edu/~rbear/yeare.html

Delaney, Paul, 'Migrancy and Cultural Disappearance', in P.J. Mathews (ed.), *New Voices in Irish Criticism* (Dublin: Four Courts Press, 2000), pp.170–9.

——, 'Representations of the Travellers in the 1880s and 1900s', *Irish Studies Review*, 9, 1 (2001), pp.53–68.

——, '"A Marginal Footnote": O'Faolain, the Subaltern, and the Travellers', *Irish Studies Review*, 11, 2 (2003), pp.155–64.

——, 'Stories from Below: Sean Maher and Nan Joyce', *Studies*, 93, 372 (2004), pp.461–72.

Dillon, Eamon, *The Outsiders: Exposing the Secretive World of Ireland's Travellers* (Dublin: Merlin, 2006).

Duncan, Ian, 'Wild England: George Borrow's Nomadology', *Victorian Studies*, 4, 3 (1998), pp.381–403.

Dunleavy, Gareth W., and Janet Egleson Dunleavy, 'Editor Moore to Playwright Hyde: On the Making of *The Tinker and the Fairy*', *Irish University Review*, 3, 1 (1973), pp.17–30.

Dunleavy, Janet Egleson and Gareth W. Dunleavy, *Douglas Hyde: A Maker of Modern Ireland* (Berkeley, CA: University of California Press, 1991).

Dunne, Pecker, *Parley-Poet and Chanter: Pecker Dunne*, transcr. and ed. Mícheál Ó hAodha (Dublin: A. and A. Farmar, 2004).

Dyer, Richard, *The Matter of Images: Essays on Representation* (London and New York: Routledge, 1993).

Edgeworth, Maria, *Belinda* (1810; Oxford: Oxford University Press, 1999).

——, *Popular Tales* (Paris: Baudry, A. and W. Galignani, Bobée and Hingray, 1827).

Eliot, George, *The Mill on the Floss* (1860; Edinburgh and London: William Blackwood and Sons, n.d.).

Ferguson, Russell, 'Introduction', in Russell Ferguson, Martha Gever, Trinh T. Min-ha and Cornel West (eds), *Out There: Marginalization and Contemporary Cultures* (Cambridge, MA: MIT Press, 1990), pp.9–14.

Foster, R.F., *The Apprentice Mage*, vol.1 of *W.B. Yeats: A Life* (Oxford: Oxford University Press, 1997).

Fumerton, Patricia, *Unsettled: The Culture of Mobility and the Working Poor in Early Modern England* (Chicago and London: University of Chicago Press, 2006).

Gainsford, Thomas, *The Glory of England* (London: Edward Griffin, 1619).

Gibbons, Luke and Kevin Whelan, 'In Conversation with Stephen Rea', *The Yale Journal of Criticism*, 15, 1 (2002), pp.5–19.

Gill, Bartholomew, *The Death of an Irish Tinker* (1997; New York: Avon Books, 2001).

Gmelch, Sharon, *Tinkers and Travellers* (Dublin: O'Brien Press, 1975).

——, *Nan: The Life of an Irish Travelling Woman* (New York and London: W.W. Norton, 1986).

Gormally, Eleanor, *Whiddin to the Gauras / Talking to Our Own: Traveller Researchers Talk to Limerick Traveller Children* (Dublin: Veritas, 2005).

Gregory, Lady Augusta, *Poets and Dreamers* (1903; New York: Oxford University Press, 1974).

Gullestad, Marianne, 'Tales of Consent and Descent: Life Writing as a Fight against an Imposed Self-Image', in Paul John Eakin (ed.),

The Ethics of Life Writing (Ithaca, NY: Cornell University Press, 2004), pp.216–43.

Halperin, David, *Saint Foucault: Towards a Gay Hagiography* (New York: Oxford University Press, 1995).

Hamill, Denis, *Fork in the Road* (London: Scribner, 2000).

Harvley-Felder, Zena, 'Author Profile: William H. Hooks', *Library Media Connection*, 21, 5 (2003), pp.48–51.

Hayes, Michael, *Irish Travellers: Representations and Realities* (Dublin: Liffey Press, 2006).

Helleiner, Jane, *Irish Travellers: Racism and the Politics of Culture* (Toronto: University of Toronto Press, 2000).

Hogan, Robert and James Kilroy, *Laying the Foundations, 1902–1904,* vol. 2 of *The Modern Irish Drama: A Documentary History* (Dublin: Dolmen, 1976).

Hooks, William H., *Circle of Fire* (New York: Atheneum, 1982).

Horsley, Katharine and Lee Horsley, '*Meres Fatales*: Maternal Guilt in the Noir Crime Novel', *Modern Fiction Studies*, 45, 2 (1999), pp.369–402.

Hunter, Mollie, *Cat, Herself* (New York: Harper and Row, 1985).

Hyde, Douglas, *The Tinker and the Sheeog*, trans. Lady Gregory, in Lady Augusta Gregory, *Poets and Dreamers* (1903; New York: Oxford University Press, 1974), pp.194–204.

——, *Legends of Saints and Sinners* (London: Gresham, 1915).

Jenkins, Herbert George, *The Life of George Borrow* (London: John Murray, 1912).

Jervis, John, *Transgressing the Modern: Explorations in the Western Experience of Otherness* (Oxford: Blackwell, 1999).

Joyce, Nan, *My Life on the Road*, ed. Anna Farmar (1985; Dublin: A. and A. Farmar, 2000).

Jütte, Robert, *Poverty and Deviance in Early Modern Europe* (Cambridge: Cambridge University Press, 1994).

Keane, John B., *The Field* (1965; Cork: Mercier, 1991).

Kearney, Richard, *Myth and Motherland*, Field Day Pamphlet 5 (Derry: Field Day, 1984).

——, *States of Mind: Dialogues with Contemporary Thinkers* (New York: New York University Press, 1995).

Keenan, Celia and Mary Shine Thompson (eds), *Studies in Children's Literature, 1500–2000* (Dublin: Four Courts Press, 2004).

Kennedy, Liam, 'Black *Noir*: Race and Urban Space in Walter Mosley's Detective Fiction', in Kathleen Gregory Klein (ed.), *Diversity and Detective Fiction* (Bowling Green, OH: Bowling

Green State University Popular Press, 1999), pp.224–39.

Kiberd, Declan, *Synge and the Irish Language* (Totowa, NJ: Rowman and Littlefield, 1979).

King, Mary, 'The Body Out of Place: Strangers, Intimates and Destabilized Identities in Synge's *When the Moon Has Set* and Marina Carr's *The Bog of Cats ...*', *Critical Survey*, 15, 1 (2003), pp.48–59.

King, Mary C. *The Drama of J.M. Synge* (London: Fourth Estate, 1985).

Kirk, John M. and Dónall P. Ó Baoill (eds), *Travellers and their Language* (Belfast: Queen's University Press, 2002).

Knight, Stephen, *Crime Fiction, 1800–2000: Detection, Death, Diversity* (Basingstoke: Palgrave Macmillan, 2004).

Kuhling, Carmen, 'New Age Travellers on *Cool* Mountain', in Michel Peillon and Eamonn Slater (eds), *Encounters with Modern Ireland: A Sociological Chronicle 1995–1996* (Dublin: IPA, 1998), pp.147–53.

Lanters, José, 'The Mythicizing of Napper Tandy Street: The Novels of Olivia Robertson', *Journal of Irish Literature*, 22, 3 (1993), pp.17–24.

——, *Unauthorized Versions: Irish Menippean Satire, 1919-1952* (Washington, DC: Catholic University of America Press, 2000).

Lawrence, D.H., *Seven Novels by D.H. Lawrence* (London: Heinemann/Octopus, 1976).

Leese, P.J., B. Piatek and I. Curyllo-Klag (eds), *The British Migrant Experience, 1700–2000: An Anthology* (London: Palgrave Macmillan, 2003).

Leitch, Roger (ed.), *The Book of Sandy Stewart* (Edinburgh: Scottish Academic Press, 1988).

Lewitt, Shariann, *Rebel Sutra* (New York: Tor, 2000).

Lucassen, Leo, 'Eternal Vagrants? State Formation, Migration and Travelling Groups in Western-Europe, 1350–1914', in Jan Lucassen and Leo Lucassen (eds), *Migration, Migration History, History: Old Paradigms and New Perspectives* (Bern: Peter Lang, 1997), pp.225–51.

Lynch, Patricia, *The Turf-Cutter's Donkey* (London: J.M. Dent, 1934).

——, *King of the Tinkers* (New York: E.P. Dutton, 1938).

——, *A Storyteller's Childhood* (1947; New York: W.W. Norton, 1962).

——, *Tinker Boy* (1955; London: J.M. Dent, 1960).

Macalister, R.A. Stewart, *The Secret Languages of Ireland*

(Cambridge: Cambridge University Press, 1937).
McBride, Regina, *The Nature of Water and Air* (New York: Simon and Schuster, 2001).
McCann, May, Séamas Ó Síocháin and Joseph Ruane (eds), *Irish Travellers: Culture and Ethnicity* (Belfast: Institute of Irish Studies/Queen's University Belfast, 1994).
McClure, Gillian and Paul Coltman, *Tinker Jim* (New York: Farrar Straus Giroux, 1992).
McCormick, Andrew, *The Tinkler-Gypsies* (1906; Darby, PA: Norwood, 1973).
MacDonagh, Donagh, 'God's Gentry', *The Word: A Catholic Pictorial Magazine*, February 1964, no pagination [pp.23–6].
——, *God's Gentry*, no pagination, 60 pp. Accessed 20 November 2004: http://members.tripod.com/IrishBornMan/Gods_Gentry.htm
McDonald, John F., *Tribe* (Dublin: Wolfhound Press, 1999).
McGillis, Roderick (ed.), *Voices of the Other: Children's Literature and the Postcolonial Context* (New York and London: Garland, 2000).
MacGrath, Seán, 'The Tinkers of Ireland', I, *Irish Times*, 15 November 1955, p.5.
——, 'The Tinkers of Ireland', II, *Irish Times*, 16 November 1955, p.5.
McGuinness, Frank (ed.), *The Dazzling Dark: New Irish Plays* (London: Faber and Faber, 1996).
MacLaughlin, Jim, *Travellers and Ireland: Whose Country, Whose History?* (Cork: Cork University Press, 1995).
——, 'The Evolution of Anti-Traveller Racism in Ireland', *Race and Class*, 37, 3 (1996), pp.47–63.
MacMahon, Bryan, 'A Portrait of Tinkers', *Natural History*, 80, 10 (1971), pp.24–35, 104–9.
MacManus, Francis, *Watergate* (1942; Swords, Co. Dublin: Poolbeg Press, 1980).
McVeigh, Robbie, 'The Specificity of Irish Racism', *Race and Class* 33, 4 (1992), pp.31–45.
Macken, Walter, 'The Eyes of the Cat', in *The Coll Doll* (London: Macmillan, 1969), pp.112–18.
——, 'Battle', in *City of the Tribes* (Dingle: Brandon, 2001), pp.11–29.
Maher, Sean, *The Road to God Knows Where: A Memoir of a Travelling Boyhood* (1972; Dublin: Veritas, 1998).

Mahon, Bríd, *The Search for the Tinker Chief* (1968; New York: Scholastic Book Services, 1971).

Mavor, Elizabeth, *The Ladies of Llangollen: A Study in Romantic Friendship* (London: Michael Joseph, 1971).

Mayall, David, *Gypsy-Travellers in Nineteenth-Century Society* (Cambridge: Cambridge University Press, 1988).

Mayhew, Henry, *London Labour and the London Poor*, vol. 1 (1851; New York: Dover Publications, 1968.

Merriman, Victor, 'Decolonisation Postponed: The Theatre of Tiger Trash', *Irish University Review*, 29, 2 (1999), pp.305–17.

——, 'Songs of Possible Worlds: Nation, Representation and Citizenship in the Work of Calypso Productions', in Eamonn Jordan (ed.), *Theatre Stuff: Critical Essays on Contemporary Irish Theatre* (Dublin: Carysfort Press, 2000), pp.280–91.

Moore, Brian, *The Mangan Inheritance* (1979; London: Corgi, 1981).

Morley, Henry (ed.), *Character Writings of the Seventeenth Century* (London: Routledge, 1891).

Mulock, Diana Maria (Mrs Craik), *Two Little Tinkers: A Simple Story,* in *The Laurel Bush* and *The Two Tinkers* [*sic*] (Leipzig: Tauchnitz, 1876), pp.237–88.

Murphy, Paul, 'J.M. Synge and the Pitfalls of National Consciousness', *Theatre Research International*, 28, 2 (2003), pp.125–42.

Neel, Janet, *Ticket to Ride* (New York: St Martin's Minotaur, 2005).

Netzloff, Mark, '"Counterfeit Egyptians" and Imagined Borders: Jonson's *The Gypsies Metamorphosed*', *ELH*, 68, 4 (2001), pp.763–93.

Newell, Mike (dir.), *Into the West* (Miramax, 1993).

Ní Dhuibhne, Eilís, 'Summer Pudding', in *The Inland Ice* (Belfast: Blackstaff Press, 1997), pp.44–60.

Ní Shuinéar, Sinéad, 'Othering the Irish (Travellers)', in Ronit Lentin and Robbie McVeigh (eds), *Racism and Anti-Racism in Ireland* (Belfast: Beyond the Pale, 2002), pp.177–245.

——, 'Apocrypha to Canon: Inventing Irish Traveller History', *History Ireland*, 12, 4 (2004). Accessed 14 July 2005: http://www.historyireland.com/magazine/features/12.4FeatA.html

Niall, Ian, *No Resting Place* (1948; London: Readers Union/Heinemann, 1950).

Niles, John D., *Homo Narrans: The Poetics and Anthropology of Oral Literature* (Philadelphia, PA: University of Pennsylvania Press, 1999).

Noonan, Paul, 'Pathologisation and Resistance: Travellers, Nomadism and the State', in Paul Hainsworth (ed.), *Divided Society: Ethnic Minorities and Racism in Northern Ireland*. (London: Pluto Press, 1998), pp.152–83.

Nord, Deborah Epstein, *Gypsies and the British Imagination, 1807–1930* (New York: Columbia University Press, 2006).

North, Kari E., Lisa J. Martin and Michael H. Crawford, 'The Origins of the Irish Travellers and the Genetic Structure of Ireland', *Annals of Human Biology*, 27, 5 (2000), pp.453–65.

O'Connor, Ulick, *Travels with Ulick* (Cork: Mercier Press, 1967).

O'Donovan, John, *Ordnance Survey Letters: Donegal*, ed. Michael Herity (Dublin: Four Masters Press, 2000).

O'Faolain, Sean, *The Collected Stories of Sean O'Faolain* (London: Constable, 1980).

O'Flaherty, Liam, *The Tent* (London: Jonathan Cape, 1926).

——, *The Pedlar's Revenge and Other Stories* (Dublin: Wolfhound Press, 1976).

O'Reilly, D.M., 'The Tinker's Revenge', in Ed Gorman, Larry Segriff and Martin H. Greenberg (eds), *Murder Most Irish* (New York: Barnes and Noble, 1996), pp.253–63.

O'Reilly, Michael and Máirín Kenny (eds), *Black Stones Around the Green Shamrock: A Poetry Anthology By and About Travellers* (Blackrock: Blackrock Teachers' Centre, 1994).

Ó Riain, Gearóid (ed.), *Traveller Ways Traveller Words* (Dublin: Pavee Point Publications, 1992).

Perkins, Lucy Fitch, *The Irish Twins* (Boston and New York: Houghton Mifflin, 1913).

Pullman, Philip, *The Golden Compass* (New York: Ballantine, 1995).

Puxon, Grattan, 'We Demand Justice', *La Voix Mondiale Tzigane / The Gypsy Voice / O Glasoromano* (c.1966), no pagination (9 pp).

Quinn, Michael (dir.), *Travelling People,* prod. Simon Wood (Belfast: Northern Visions, 1991).

Rafroidi, Patrick, *Irish Literature in English: The Romantic Period (1789–1850),* vol. 1 (Gerrards Cross: Colin Smythe, 1980).

Reddy, Maureen T., *Traces, Codes, and Clues: Reading Race in Crime Fiction* (New Brunswick, NJ, and London: Rutgers University Press, 2003).

Rhodes, Robert E., '"More Matter for a May Morning": J.M. Synge's *The Tinker's Wedding*', in Alexander G. Gonzalez (ed.), *Assessing the Achievement of J.M. Synge* (Westport, CT: Greenwood Press, 1996), pp.97–117.

Rid, Samuel, *The Art of Jugling or Legerdemaine* (London: Samuel Rand, 1612).
Robertson, Olivia, *Field of the Stranger* (London: Peter Davies, 1948).
——, *The Golden Eye* (London: Peter Davies, 1949).
——, *Miranda Speaks* (London: Peter Davies, 1950).
——, *Dublin Phoenix* (London: Jonathan Cape, 1957).
——, *Dea. Rites and Mysteries of the Goddess. Liturgy of the Fellowship of Isis* (Enniscorthy: Cesara, 1977).
Roche, Billy, *Trojan Eddie* (London: Methuen, 1997).
Saddlemyer, Ann (ed.), *Theatre Business: The Correspondence of the First Abbey Theatre Directors: William Butler Yeats, Lady Gregory and J.M. Synge* (Gerrards Cross: Colin Smythe, 1982).
Salgādo, Gāmini (ed.), *Cony-Catchers and Bawdy Baskets: An Anthology of Elizabethan Low Life* (Harmondsworth: Penguin, 1972).
Sawyer, Ruth, *Doctor Danny* (New York and London: Harper, 1918).
Scott, Mike, *Judith and the Traveller* (Dublin: Wolfhound Press, 1991).
——, *Judith and Spider* (Dublin: Wolfhound Press, 1992).
——, *Good Enough for Judith* (Dublin: Wolfhound Press, 1994).
Seyhan, Azade, 'Ethnic Selves/Ethnic Signs: Invention of Self, Space, and Genealogy in Immigrant Writing', in E. Valentine Daniel and Jeffrey M. Peck (eds), *Culture/Contexture: Explorations in Anthropology and Literary Studies* (Berkeley, CA: University of California Press, 1996), pp.175–94.
Sheehan, Erica (ed.), *Travellers: Citizens of Ireland* (Dublin: The Parish of the Travelling People, 2000).
Sherry, Brian, Raymond McHugh and Brian O'Flaitheartaigh (eds), *Along the Black Pig's Dyke: Folklore from Monaghan and South Armagh* (Castleblayney: Castleblayney Community Enterprise, 1993).
Sinclair, A.T., 'The Secret Language of Masons and Tinkers', *Journal of American Folklore*, 22, 86 (1909), pp.353–64.
Smith, Sidonie, *A Poetics of Women's Autobiography: Marginality and the Fictions of Self-Representation* (Bloomington and Indianapolis: Indiana University Press, 1987).
Smith, Sinead, 'Racism, Social Exclusion and Drug Use: Why Are Travellers an "at Risk" Group for Problematic Drug Use?' *Pavee Point Newsletter*, 2, 5–6 (2006), pp.16–17.
Somerville, E.Œ. and Martin Ross, *All on the Irish Shore: Irish Sketches* (New York: Longmans, Green, and Co., 1903).

Southwark Traveller Women's Group, *Moving Stories: Traveller Women Write* (London: Traveller Education Team, 1992).

Spengemann, William C., *The Forms of Autobiography: Episodes in the History of a Literary Genre* (New Haven, CT and London: Yale University Press, 1980).

Stephens, James, *The Demi-Gods* (1914; Dublin: Butler Sims, 1982).

Stephens, John, *Language and Ideology in Children's Fiction* (London and New York: Longman, 1992).

Stewart, Sheila, *Queen Amang the Heather: The Life of Belle Stewart* (Edinburgh: Birlinn, 2006).

Swift, Jonathan, *Collected Poems of Jonathan Swift*, ed. Joseph Horrell (Cambridge, MA: Harvard University Press, 1958), vol.2.

Synge, J.M., 'The Vagrants of Wicklow', *The Shanachie*, 1 (1906), pp.93–8.

——, *Plays*, ed. Ann Saddlemyer (Oxford: Oxford University Press, 1969).

Thomson, William, *Mammuth; or, Human Nature Displayed on a Grand Scale in a Tour with the Tinkers, into the Inland Parts of Africa* (1789), in Jeanne K. Welcher and George E. Bush, Jr. (intro.), *Gulliveriana*, 4 (Delmar, NY: Scholars' Facsimiles and Reprints, 1973), pp.229–384.

Thornton, Duncan. *The Star-Glass* (Regina, SK, Canada: Coteau, 2004).

Tracy, Honor, *The Quiet End of Evening* (New York: Random House, 1972).

Troy, Una, *The Benefactors* (London: Robert Hale, 1969).

Trumpener, Katie, 'The Time of the Gypsies: A "People without History" in the Narratives of the West', *Critical Inquiry*, 18, 4 (1992), pp.843–84.

Wallace, Clare, 'Tragic Destiny and Abjection in Marina Carr's *The Mai*, *Portia Coughlan* and *By the Bog of Cats* ...', *Irish University Review*, 31, 2 (2001), pp.431–49.

Walsh, Maurice, *The Road to Nowhere* (New York: Frederick A. Stokes, 1934).

——, 'Son of a Tinker', in *Son of a Tinker and Other Tales* (London and Edinburgh: W. and R. Chambers, 1951), pp.7–34.

Watson, Nancy, 'A Revealing and Exciting Experience: Three of Patricia Lynch's Children's Novels', *The Lion and the Unicorn*, 21, 3 (1999), pp.341–6.

Whitney, Kim Ablon, *See You Down the Road* (New York: Alfred A. Knopf, 2004).

Whyte, Betsy, *The Yellow on the Broom: The Early Days of a Traveller Woman* (Edinburgh: W. and R. Chambers, 1979).
——, *Red Rowans and Wild Honey* (1990; Edinburgh: Birlinn, 2002).
Woods, James, *Annals of Westmeath, Ancient and Modern* (Dublin: Sealy, Bryers and Walker, 1907).
Wordsworth, Dorothy, *Journals of Dorothy Wordsworth: The Alfoxden Journal 1798; The Grasmere Journals 1800–1803*, ed. Mary Moorman (Oxford: Oxford University Press, 1971).
Yeats, W.B., *The Variorum Edition of the Plays of W.B. Yeats*, ed. Russell K. Alspach (New York: Macmillan, 1966).

Index

Thomas Kinsella

Designing for the Exact Needs

Maurice Harmon

This comprehensive study interprets Thomas Kinsella's extraordinary progress from lyric poems and meditations about fragility and impermanence to complex assessments of individual isolation and helplessness in the modern world. His work, which has been knitted to Dublin city, expresses his engagement with Irish life and culture in 'Nightwalker', *Poems from Centre City, Personal Places,* and *The Pen Shop.* His involvement with Irish history, evident in his absorption with the past and his creative interpretation of the arrival and settling in of prehistoric people, is demonstrated in his extensive translations from Irish literature.

He is also a universal poet who has explored Jungian archetypes in *New Poems*, psychological stress in the 'Wormwood' sequence, and the notion of meaninglessness in *Her Vertical Smile* and of living on the edge in *Marginal Economy.* In his persistent search for understanding he has examined the effects of evil whether expressed in man's proclivity for destruction, the direct concern of *Man of War,* or the reality of death in the elegies for Seán Ó Riada, John F. Kennedy, and his own father. Deprived of a community of shared values and the reassurances of philosophy or religion, he has conducted a systematic investigation of the question of causality and responsibility in the human and divine spheres, whether articulated by artists like Gustav Mahler or Seán Ó Riada or thinkers like St Augustine, Eriugena or Aurelius, and has verified the role of the artist as measured and exact recorder. His poems dramatise issues through narrative, elegy, allegory, and myth and commemorate love, ceremony, natural beauty and creativity itself.

2008 272 pages
978 0 7165 2951 4 cloth €65.00/£30.00/$79.95
978 0 7165 2952 1 paper €24.95/£30.00/$32.95

Oscar Wilde's Plagiarism

The Triumph of Art over Ego

Florina Tufescu

Why did a genius like Oscar Wilde rely on plagiarism from the beginning to the end of his career? Why did Edgar Allan Poe, Charles Baudelaire or Walter Pater do this as well? And how should teachers, critics and editors deal with the evidence of plagiarism at the heart of the canon? This book offers a compact history of the meanings and uses of plagiarism from antiquity to the present, an interpretation of Oscar Wilde's plagiarism and of its impact on Joyce, Borges, Gide et al and the revelation of a plagiaristic, counter-romantic tradition from Poe to Ackroyd.

Oscar Wilde's plagiarism practices across genres are seen as part of a neo-classical tradition. His allegory of plagiarism in *An Ideal Husband* is compared to those created by fellow playwrights, including Ibsen and G. B. Shaw. Wilde's polemical imitation of Shakespeare's cut-and-paste method in *The Portrait* of Mr. W.H. inspires Joyce to experiment with the erasure of quotation marks in *Ulysses*. The blatant collage of Wilde's poetry anticipates T. S. Eliot's *The Waste Land*, just as it recalls Manet's paintings, which provocatively assert artistic status by drawing attention to their flatness. The mosaic-like structure of *The Picture of Dorian Gray* is akin to that of other anti-individualist masterpieces, notably Goethe's Faust and D. M. Thomas's *The White Hotel.*

The extent of sophisticated plagiarism in the canonical works and the impressive list of its apologists from Ackroyd to Zola indicate the need for new models of authorship and intellectual property, models that would benefit scholarly and artistic creativity and solve the paradox of plagiarism as simultaneously one of the most serious and most common of literary crimes.

2007 208 pages

978 0 7165 2904 0 cloth €45.00/£30.00/$55.00

Four Irish Rebel Plays

James Moran

This book collects together for the first time, plays written by the well-known Irish nationalists Patrick Pearse, Thomas MacDonagh, James Connolly and Terence MacSwiney. In the months before 1916 MacDonagh staged *When the Dawn is Come*, and Pearse staged *The Master*, both works were designed to persuade the Dublin populace to support the advanced nationalist cause. At the same time, MacSwiney staged his play *The Revolutionist* in order to win the support of Redmondite nationalists in Cork. At Liberty Hall, only three weeks before taking part in the armed revolt of 1916, Connolly staged *Under Which Flag?* to persuade socialists to join the rebellion. The plays offer important insights into the rebels' political and military thinking. The introduction explains exactly how the plays influenced the Irish revolution between 1916 and 1921 and explores the theatrical influences that affected the rebels. The context of the plays original staging and subsequent influence both inside and outside the playhouse is also covered. The epilogue outlines the varying afterlives that the plays enjoyed once their authors were dead.

2007 272 pages illus

978 0 7165 2852 4 cloth €55.00£45.00/$75.00

978 0 7165 2853 1 paper €19.95£18.50/$30.00

The Radicalization of Irish Theatre, 1600–1900

The Rise and Fall of Ascendancy Theatre

Desmond Slowey

Foreword by **Christopher Murray**

Placed within a rich social, historical and cultural context, this study illuminates the Irish theatre over three hundred years, and uses it as a lens that focuses the dialectic of Irish society as the theatre mutated from aristocratic control to radical dissent and subversion. English colonists created the Irish theatre, reflecting the preoccupations and prejudices of the aristocrats and courtiers clustered around Dublin Castle. This was a political theatre, involved in outlining and defining its own society; the playwrights were engaged in leading opinion, presenting alternative realities, and forging the national conscience. Early Irish theatre was the Anglo-Irish talking to themselves, as the playwrights engaged the ruling class in a dialogue as to how the country should be ordered. As the Ascendancy lost or relinquished control over the theatre, the image presented by the playwrights became more unflattering and dismissive. This work studies how this portrait of Irish society and its rulers was encoded and evolved in the plays of the three centuries from 1600 to the foundation of the Abbey Theatre. It shows how the plays traced the continually mutating Ascendancy, the growing self-consciousness and national self-awareness, and a developing class-consciousness among Irish playwrights.

2008 272 pages

978 0 7165 2957 6 cloth €59.95/£45.00/$74.95

IRISH LITERATURE
THE EIGHTEENTH CENTURY
An Annotated Anthology

Edited and Introduced by

A. Norman Jeffares and Peter van de Kamp

Foreword by Brendan Kennelly

'This anthology frequently feels like an epic exercise in intellectual and emotional freedom, achieved through clear vision and the most subtle and effective stylistic and technical skills...A truly monumental achievement.'

From the Foreword by Professor
Brendan Kennelly, Trinity College, Dublin

Irish Literature: The Eighteenth Century illustrates not only the impressive achievement of the great writers – Swift, Berkeley, Burke, Goldsmith and Sheridan – but also shows the varied accomplishment of others, providing unexpected, entertaining examples from the pens of the less well known. Here are examples of the witty comic dramas so successfully written by Susannah Centlivre, Congreve, Steele, Farquhar and Macklin. There are serious and humorous essayists represented, including Steele, Lord Orrery, Thomas Sheridan and Richard Lovell Edgeworth. Beginning with *Gulliver's Travels*, fiction includes John Amory's strange imaginings, Sterne's stream of consciousness, Frances Sheridan's insights, Henry Brooke's sentimentalities and Goldsmith's charm. Poetry ranges from the classical to the innovative. Graceful lyrics, anonymous *jeux d'esprit*, descriptive pieces, savage satires and personal poems are written by very different poets, among them learned witty women, clergymen and drunken ne'er-do-wells. Politicians, notably Grattan and Curran, produced eloquent speeches; effective essays and pamphlets accompanied political activity. Personal letters and diaries – such as the exuberant Dorothea Herbert's *Recollections* – convey the changing ethos of this century's literature, based on the classics and moving to an increasing interest in the translation of Irish literature. This book conveys its fascinating liveliness and rich variety.

2005 424 pages
978 0 7165 2799 2 cloth €65.00/£49.50/$79.50
978 0 7165 2804 3 paper €29.95/£22.50/$37.50

IRISH LITERATURE THE NINETEENTH CENTURY

VOLUME I

An Annotated Anthology

Edited and introduced by

A. Norman Jeffares and Peter van de Kamp

Foreword by Terence Brown

'This anthology is a superlative achievement and for at least a generation is sure to be the outstanding work in its field. Jeffares and van de Kamp bring to their task a fine blend of scholarship, good judgment and innovation. And they have produced a fascinating collection of Irish writing which scholars, students and general readers will find both inviting and accessible.'

James H. Murphy, *De Paul University*

This, the first of three volumes, spans the first third of the nineteenth century. It documents Ireland's significant literary contribution to an age of invention, with Thomas Moore's romantic *Melodies*, Maria Edgeworth's regional fiction, and Charles Maturin's voyeuristic Gothic stories. It witnesses the rise of a quest for authenticity – mapping and transmuting the Gaelic past (in Hardiman's *Irish Minstrelsy*, Petrie's essay on the round towers, and O'Curry's research into Irish manuscripts) and faithfully depicting the real Ireland (in the first-hand accounts of Mary Leadbeater, William Hamilton Maxwell, Asenath Nicholson, the peasant fiction of William Carleton and the Catholic fiction of the Banim brothers). In Jonah Barrington's *Sketches* it records the demise of the rollicking squirearchy, while in the stories of Lover it portrays the rise of the stage Irishman. But it also offers a selection from political documents and speeches, and from popular writings which were imprinted on the Irish consciousness. These are contextualised by historical documents, and by Irish forays into European Romanticism.

2005 424 pages

978 0 7165 2800 5 cloth €65.00/£49.50/$79.50

978 0 7165 2805 0 paper €29.95/£22.50/$37.50

IRISH LITERATURE
THE NINETEENTH CENTURY
VOLUME II
An Annotated Anthology

Edited and introduced by

Peter van de Kamp and A. Norman Jeffares

Foreword by Conor Cruise O'Brien

This, the second of three volumes, roughly spans the middle decades of the nineteenth century, a period dominated by the enormity of the Great Famine. Its terror is recorded in first-hand accounts and in the powerless yet forceful reactions which this cataclysmic event engendered in such writers as John Mitchel (who in his *Jail Journal* pits the self against the state). This volume documents the rise of cultural nationalism, in the work of the contributors to *The Nation* (Davis, Mangan, Lady Wilde), and the response of Unionist intelligentsia in the *Dublin University Magazine*. It juxtaposes the authentic Gaelic voice in translation (Ferguson and Walsh) against the haunting intensity of Mangan and the non-conformism of his fellow inauthenticator 'Father Prout'. It witnesses the stage Irishman in Lever's fiction being placed on Boucicault's popular podium, in his reworking of Gerald Griffin's account of *The Colleen Bawn*. It records the rise of Fenianism (in such writers as Charles Kickham), and it sees Ireland taking stock (in the work of W.E.H. Lecky). It notes the emergence of a new literary confidence in the works of Sigerson and Todhunter. It extends well beyond examinations of Irish identity, not only in encapsulating popular writing, but also by incorporating writers of Irish descent who investigated different cultures.

2007 560 pages

978 0 7165 3333 7 cloth €75.00/£49.50/$79.50

978 0 7165 3334 4 paper €29.95/£25.00/$37.50

IRISH LITERATURE
THE NINETEENTH CENTURY
VOLUME III
An Annotated Anthology

Edited and introduced by

Peter van de Kamp and A. Norman Jeffares

Foreword by Bruce Arnold

The last of the three volumes, roughly spans the last thirty years of the nineteenth century, a period which saw the emergence of the Land League, the dynamiting campaign of the Fenians, and the rise and fall of Charles Stewart Parnell. It witnessed changes in all literary genres. Standish James O'Grady conveyed a sense of heroic excitement in his affirmation of Gaelic Ireland's literary heritage. Douglas Hyde promoted Irish language and culture through his foundation of the Gaelic League. Writers affiliated with the Irish Literary Society tried to re-energise Young Ireland's ideals of cultural nationalism. Under the aegis of Ireland's literary renaissance a new interest in Celticism became manifest. The year after the publication of Allingham's *Collected Poems* W.B. Yeats's *The Wanderings of Oisin* marked the emergence of Irish mythology and legend in an elegant, sensuous and highly influential manner. With Wilde, Shaw, Martyn and George Moore he expanded Ireland's aesthetic horizons; as Yeats introduced French Symbolisme in *The Secret Rose* and *The Wind Among the Reeds*, Oscar Wilde preached the paradoxes of decadence, Shaw uncovered society's hypocrisies, while Martyn embraced Ibsen's social realism, and Moore combined Zola's naturalism with the synaesthesia of *Totalkunst*. Major writers combined to form Ireland's National Theatre. Pioneers such as Lafcadio Hearn were exploring different cultures, which were to influence European literature and drama. The last decades of the nineteenth century were a powerfully creative period, rich in its literary collaborations, and profoundly impressive in its vitality.

2007 560 pages

978 0 7165 3357 3 cloth **€75.00/£49.50/$79.50**

978 0 7165 3358 0 paper **€29.95/£25.00/$37.50**